MANAGEMENT CHALLENGES OF EMERGING SERVICE ECONOMY OF INDIA:

Issues and Trends

MANAGEMENT CHALLENGES OF EMERGING SERVICE ECONOMY OF INDIA:

Issues and Trends

Edited by

Dr. P. BALAJI PRASAD
M.B.A. Ph.D.
Associate Professor
School of Business Management
Sri Venkateswara University
Tirupati
Andhra Pradesh, **INDIA**

SERIALS PUBLICATIONS
NEW DELHI

First Published-2003

ISBN: 81-86771-12-3

Published by:

Head Office : **SERIALS PUBLICATIONS**
4, B.S.S. Hall, Khyber Pass Market,
Civil Lines, Delhi-110054 (India)
Phone: 0091-11-3811659
Fax: 91-11-3812678
E-mail: serials@satyam.net.in

Branch Office : 4830/24, Prahlad Street,
Ansari Road, Darya Ganj,
New Delhi-11002 (India)
Phone: 3245225

Typeset by : Sharma Graphics, ☎ 2446920

Price Rs. : 750/-

Printed at: : Tarun Offset Printers

CONTENTS

PREFACE

"Management Challenges of Emerging Service Economy of India" is a result of my endeavour to discover the unique Indian experience in very many fields of service sector of Indian Economy presents basically an assemblage of original, revised works of papers received on UGC National Seminar on "Management Challenges of Emerging Indian Service Economy" organised on March 16-17, 2002 at School of Business Management, Sri Venkateswara University. I am grateful to the authors of all these papers for their efforts in making the seminar a great success.

The intent of this book is to offer a framework to help students of MBA, practioners of service management gain an understanding of the nature and scope of services management in a develoing economy like India. The work is expected to provide 1. Concepts 2. Its operation in Indian Enviornment 3. View points. The work is interesting to student of marketing management as well as Indian Economy and Business Environment while most of the articles written by seminar paper presenting participants, neverthless there were certain gaps. These gaps are filled by original materials presented with the help of students of MBA, rewritten materials or introductory comments, also one or two reprinted works with the due permission from the publishers.

My thanks are due to Prof. M. Chandrasekhar who was responsible for shaping my career at the school as well as provided useful comments as I was developing the original concepts for this work. My thanks are due to Prof. Murali, the Vice-Chancellor of S.V. University, Professor C.S.G. Krishnamacharyulu, Professor Murthy, Dr. Reddy, Sudhir for their encouragement and support.

My special thanks are due to Mr. Hemanath, Ravi and Ramu for helping this typed. My thanks are also due to Dr. P. Malyadri, Dr. K.V.G.Rao, Madhavaiah and Co.for their contribution and moral support. My thanks are also due to Prof. S Jayarama Reddy, Principal, S.V. University College of Arts and Sciences, Prof. T. Siddaiah, Registrar, S.V. University, Prof. S. Balarama Reddy, Head School of Business Management, Dr. S. Durga Rao and Dr. D.V. Ramana for their encouragement and support.

My heartfelt appreciation for my wife Shailaja for her sacrifice as I was busy with work, to my young daughter Shilpa who had to wage a lone battle for her tenth exams during my business, to my father-in-law Veeraiah Retd. SE (R& B) who replaced my domestic duties failings. While the assistance of others is acknowledged only I can be held responsible for any lapses.

Dr. P. Balaji Prasad
Associate Professor
School of Business Management
S.V. University, Tirupati

List of Contributors

Prof. M. Chandrasekhar
Prof. BEVVN Murthy
M. Geeta
Uday Shankar
Dr. C.S.G. Krishnamacharyulu
B. Munirathnam
N.V. Ramasastry
Madhava Krishna Reddy
Prof. P. Murali
Dr. Lalitha Ramakrishnan
Dr. Talluru Srenivas
Dr. R. Sivaram Prasad
Dr. K. Venugopala Rao
Dr. P. Malyadri
Dr. P. Niranjan Reddy
H. Krishnaveni
Dr. J. Katyayani
C. Padmanabha Sivakumar
Sandhya R. Anvekar
Mr. C. Madhavaiah
Dr. M.S. Reddy & B.S. Rao
M.P. Saravana Kumar
Dr. P. Balaji Prasad
C.N. Sivanand
G.S. Mohan Krishna
Ms V. Shanthi Latha
Dr. V.V. Satyanarayana
N.Anil Kumar
Ms. T. Amulya
Shaik Karimullah
M.V. Ramprasad
Bhanushree Reddy
Professor G. Prasad
K. Naga Padmini
Prof. C.N. Krishna Naik
V.D. Santosh Kumar
Dr. J. Prakash Reddy
Chandrasekhar Gotlagunta
B. Sudhir
Dr. P.T. Srinivasan
M.S. Subhas
Ms. K. Lavanyalatha
Ch. Sriram
S. Illayaraja

INTRODUCTION

Services are the fastest growing sector of the most of the developed nations than developing countries. Developed nations economies are called Service Economies because of dominating role of services. In Indian economy services account for 49 per cent of GDP compared to Industry sector and Agricultural sector with 27 per cent and 24 per cent respectively. India has` the potential to be emerging service economy must review and prepare for the structural readjustment in a smooth way with a human face. Service sector firms can be categoriesed and understood from personal services, commercial services, public service organisations and non-profit organisations. These include health care, entertainment service, educational service under personal seriçes; trade, banking, legal and accounting service etc. under commercial services; defence, police and local and general public administrration etc. under public services; religious, spiritual hospital, universities and other social organisations etc., under non-profit services.

If true potential of economy has to be tapped, two more crucial organisations services that have a bearing on the very sustenance and prosperity of service economy must be understood and reviewed in their functioning vis-a-vis various service organisations. They are government service which helps to take care of the welfare of the individual citizen as well as the overall well being of the nation. Since goverments of today are at the commanding height of the economy as a major service provider in a developing nation like ours with unlimited democratic power, limited accountability for their performance. Secondly the role of political parties which include among other things major political formations whether they are left off the centre or right off the central political ideologies, because these service organisations are functioning as a watchdog of the performance of the economy directly as well as indirectly through their participation in the government services delivery.

The book is the result of UGC sponsored National Seminar on Management challenges of emerging service economy of India held during March 16th & 17th 2002 at School of Business Management, Sri Venkateswara University, Tirupati. The seminar is an effort in the direction of understanding the unfolding service economy of India at the 21st century or millennium end. Firstly the papers focused on to evaluate the performance of one of the chosen sectors of service organisations. Secondly the papers as a basis of expected and actual performance of chosen organisations and finally the papers as a valuable material for further research and understanding and sharing of researcher experience through the medium of seminar proceedings. Following the success of the seminar an attempt is being made now to bring out the theme in the form of publication with all inclusive effort of the received papers and supplementation efforts by the editor with his team wherever it is necessary to attain a reasonable balance in the edited version of the publication. Keeping the overall theme in mind the following premise has been kept in the book preparation.

Objectives of the Book

India today dominates the service sector. One out of every two Indians from the organized employment opportunity is working in the service sector. Yet India is a laggard in the service sector. Because there is a huge and silent crisis of unemployment in the organized employment from the service economy for a decade now since 1991. India which is striving to break the age old bondage of man to misery, want and destitution must also understand the basic problems of organizing people of diversified and highly advanced skill and judgement together to overcome the challenges of liberalizing economies and meeting the global inequalities in the globalizing Indian economy.

Framework of the Book

The book has been divided into eight sectors, keeping the overall diversity of the papers available at the editor's desk and nurturing the theme of the book to its logical end. **The first section** lays the ground work for understanding the challenges of emerging service economy of India through four papers. The sections opens with the article by Professor Murthy et. al. on the conceptual frame of Service sector and economy follwed by the article on the challenges ahead of 21st century Indian Economy that is being witnessed in India. The section other papers highlight the conceptual frame of service sector and economy, crisis of unemployment in the new economy and problems of women employees in the aviation sector as a special category employee problems in the service sector. **The second section** looks at Indian service economy first: how it is influenced by global environment trends like globalisation, liberalisation, technology management, human welfare managing of conflict within and across the border etc. Secondly the influence of ruling elite on economic policies and compulsions and obligations as democratic nature of the state.

Section three deals with two articles in the area of service economy and influence of socio-cultural environment. At the end, how material progress without spirituality, the individual is suffocating in the changing social reality for worse. Stressing the importance of cultural action. In another article it looks at how Indian cinema subjected to metamorphosis due to pressures of technology such as digitalisation of film making and changing values of the cine, going public mainly youth -- enoying the life as credo. **Section four** examines the service economy and health sector scene. It has three articles to examine the issues and trend in the health sector. One deals with marketing of health services its concepts and practice the other paper deals with challenges and strategies needed for management of health care institutions like today's modern hospitals of the service economy. Third paper is result of earlier work which looks at among many health care challenges, maternity care service marketing due to continuing paradoxical situation of women inside and outside the family stressing the need for women and child care services under prevailing conditions.

Section five focusses on service economy and educational sector. The first paper highlights the crisis of higher education and MBO as a managerial tool to evaluate the various issues for meaningful action interventions. Second paper examines education in an exhaustive manner for facing the challenges. Third paper applies services concept to educational services especially in the context of WTO Agreements. Fourth paper stress the importance of knowledge management as one of the five resources of the organisation. **Section Six** discusses the impact of financial services sector on the service economy. There are three papers: one looks at the entire gamut of financial services and need for marketing orientation. The second papers focusses on banking sector for innovative techniques under the pressure of LPG especially customer relations management as a strategy The third paper examines the role of merchant banks in the economic development of a developing country like India.

Seventh section concentrates on a more emerging critical sector and its pervasive influence in today's economy for the future challenges namely information technology sector. Out of the five papers paper, one highlights the growth and challenges of IT sector. Second paper overviews IT enabled services as a latest trend and opportunity for Indian economy. Third paper deals with Integrated E-education system as a new opportunity for the organisation to be learning organisation under e-revolution. Fourth paper looks at the untapped potential of a vast part of rural economy through IT services especially for farmers for their upliftment. Last but not least paper under this section deals with how service organisations can be benefitted by IT application of their services such as streamlined queing system for pilgrims visiting Lord Venkateswara at TTD Tirupati. **The last section** of the book though no less important section is an assemblage of papers for more critical sector of the service economy with four papers. Paper one deals with a service quality model approach for training manpower in hospitality industry. The second article deals with another important sector namely transport through rail transport in India, whether there is a case of privitasation. Telecom sector under the revolution of technology is the third paper. The challenges of power sector in the emerging service economy and the bottlenecks meeting better attention to bring back the health of this vital sector to bolster the service economy.

Station: **Tirupati**
Date: **20th June 2002**

Dr. P. Balaji Prasad

Section-I

AN INTRODUCTION TO MANAGEMENT CHALLENGES OF SERVICE ECONOMY

Overview

Section are contains introduction to the management challenges of service economy with the introductory paper on Service Sector and economy authored by Professor Murthy et. al. followed by the paper on management challenges ahead of 21st century Indian economy authored jointly by Prof. M. Chandrasekhar and Dr. P. Balaji Prasad. Third and Fourth papers look at the crisis of unemployment and underemployment looming large in the new economy and management challenges of employing women in a premium service sector like Aviation Industry. Thus the first sections sets the tone for the sub themes by describing the conceptual and operational issues of service sector in the economy and specific components of the service economy that need to be analysed. An evaluation of ability of the service economy in creation, offering and sustenance of the job opportunities, also examination of certain key categories of employees like women in the service economy.

SERVICE SECTOR AND ECONOMY

*** Prof. BEVVN Murthy** ** **C.N. Sivanand** & *** **M. Geeta**

Services lie at the very hub of economic activity in any society. Writing about the role of the service sector in world development, Dorothy Riddle formulated the economic model shown in Figure 1.

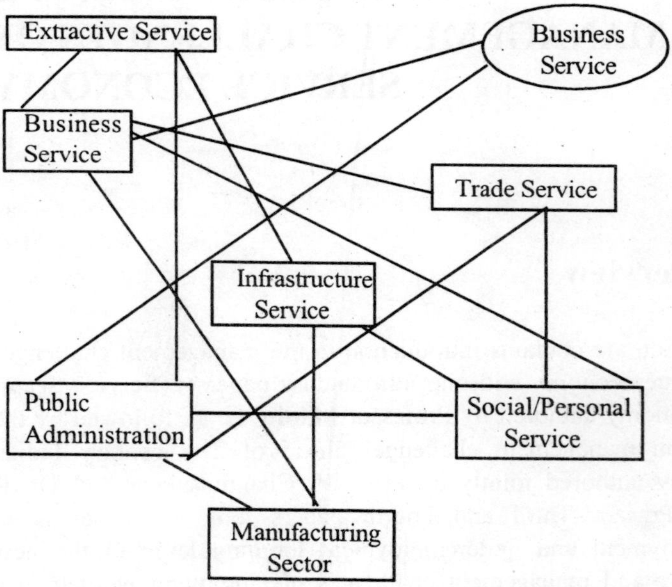

Figure 1: Interactive Model of an Economy.
Source: Dorothy I. Riddle, Service-led Growth, Praeger, New York, 1986, p.27.

---

* Professor & Head, School of Business Management, S.V. University, Tirupati.
** Asst. Professor, Institute of Management Studies, Vellore Institute of Technology, Deemed University Vellore-14.
*** Research Scholar, School of Business Management, S.V. University, Tirupati.

This model shows the flow of activity among the three principal sectors of the economy: extractive (mining and farming), manufacturing and service, which is divided into five subgroups. All activity eventually leads to the consumer.

Examples of Services in Each of Five Subgroups are:

Business Services	:	Consulting, finance, banking
Trading Service	:	Retailing, maintenance, Repair
Infrastructure Services	:	Communications, transportation
Social Personal Service	:	Restaurants, healthcare
Public Administration	:	Education, Government

Infrastructure services, such as transportation and communications, are the essential links between all sectors of the economy. Including the final consumer. In a complex economy, both infrastructure and trade services function as intermediries between the extractive and manufacturing sectors and as the channel of distribution to the final consumer. Infrastructure services are a prerequisite for an economy to become industrialized; therefore, no advanced society can be without these services.

In an industrialized economy, specialized firms can supply business services to manufacturing firms more cheaply and efficiently than manufacturing firms can supply these services for themselves. Thus, more and more often we find advertising, consulting, financing, testing and other business functions being provided for the manufacturing sector by service firms.

Except for basic subsistence living, where individual households are self-sufficient, service activities are absolutely necessary for the economy to function and to enhance the quality of life. Consider, for example, the importance of a banking industry to transfer funds and a transportation industry to move food products to areas that cannot produce them. Moreover, a wide variety of social and personal services, such as restaurants, lodging, cleaning, and child care, have created to move former household functions into economy.

Public administration plays a critical role in providing a stable environment for investment and economic growth. Services such as public education, health care, well-maintained roads. Safe drinking water, clean air, and public safety are necessary for any nation's economy to survive and people to prosper.

Thus, it is imperative to recognize that services are not peripheral activities but rather integral parts of society. They are central to a functioning and healthy economy and lie at the heart of that economy. The service sector not only facilitates but also makes possible the goods-producing activities of the extractive and manufacturing sectors. Services are the crucial force for today's change towards a global economy.

Defining Services

Today clarity on services as a concept, it is appropriate to look at various definitions given by various researchers. Many authors have defined services in different ways, some of them are as follows: one of the first to define services was the American Marketing Association which, as early as in 1960 defined as services as "activities, benefits or satisfaction which are offered for sale, or provided in connection with the sale of goods".

In 1973 Bessom proposed that "for the consumer, services are any activity offered for sale that provide valuation benefits or satisfactions; activities that he cannot perform for himself or that he chooses not to performs for himself."

Stantion in 1974 defined services as "separately identifiable, intangible activities which provide want satisfaction when marked to consumers and/ or industrial users and which are not necessarily tied to the sale of a product or another services."

Lehtinen in 1983 defined services as "an activity or a series of activities which take place in interactions with a contact person or a physical machine and which provides consumers satisfaction."

Kotler and Bloom in 1984 defined services as "any activity or benefit that one party can offer to another that is essentially intangible and does not result in the ownership of anything. Its production may or may be tied to physical product."

Gummesson, highlighting the intangible nature of services, defined "services as something which can be bought and sold but which you cannot drop on your foot."

Taking a lead from the last three definitions proposed by Lehtinen, Kotler and Bloom and Gummesson, in 1990 Gronsoss proposed a working definition. According to him, "A service is an activity or series of activities of more or less intangible nature that normally, not necessarily, takes place in interactions between the customers and service employees and/or physical resources or goods and/or systems of the services provider, which are provided as solution to customers problems."

Unique Characteristics of Services

Services have certain unique characteristics which distinguish them from goods. These unique characteristics are resulting in some implications to the organizations. These characteristics along with associated implications are shown in table 1.

Classification of Services

Ever since marketing researchers started defining services, they also proposed their classification of services. The first one was proposted as early as 1964 and the last, as late as 1989. Summary of the latest classification has been given in Table 2. These classifications not only demonstrate the diversity of

Table 1: **Service Characteristics and Their Implications**

Service Characteristics	Resulting Implications
1. Intangible: Cannot be seen tasted or touched	Cannot be inventoried, Readily displayed or communicated Pricing is difficult.
2. Heterogeneous: No one services are preciously alike.	Service delivery and customer satisfaction depend on employees actions. Service quality depends on many uncontrollable factors. There is no sure knowledge that the service delivered matched what was planned and promoted.
3. Inseparable: Simultaneous production and consumption of service is usual.	Customers participate in and affect the transaction. Customers affect each other. Employees affect the service outcome. Decentralization may be essential. Mass production is difficult.
4. Perishable: Service can not be saved, stored, resold, or returned.	It is difficult to synchronize supply and demand with services. Services cannot be returned or Resold.

services but also suggest how important it is in specific situation to carefully analyze the detailed nature of the service operation.

Table 2: Summary of Proposed Schemes for Classifying Services

Author	Proposed Classification Schemes
Lovelock	1. The nature of the service act. a. Tangible actions to people or things. b. Intangible actions to people or things. 2. Relationship with customers a. Continuous delivery b. Discrete transactions c. "Membership" relationships d. Non formal relationships. 3. Customization and judgement in service delivery

Contd....

	a. Judgement exercised by Customer contact persons.
	b. Customisation of services.
	4. Nature of demand in relation to supply.
	a. Extent to which supply is constrained.
	b. Extent of demand fluctuations.
	5. Methods of service delivery
	a. Single or multi-sit delivery
	b. Service delivered on provider's or cutomer's premises.
Schmenner	1. Degree of interaction and Customization
	a. Low
	b. High
	2. Degree of labour intensity
	a. Low
	b. High
Vandermerwe & Chadwick (1989)	1. Degree of customer/producer interaction.
	a. lower
	b. higher
	2. Relative involvement of goods
	a. "Pure" service
	b. Services with some goods or delivered through goods
	c. Services embodied in goods.

Source: Christian Gronoss, Service Management and Marketing, Lexington Books, Massachusetts, 1990, pp.33-34.

Service Sector and World Economy

The services sector has grown phenomenally over the past decades and acounts for more than 60 percent of gross domestic product (GDP) in the developed economies. The most marked change in the structure of developed economics in the twentieth century, particularly in the later half, has been the transformation from an emphasis on the manufacture of physical goods to the production of intangible services. In the United States, a leader in the transformation to a service economy, the percentage of workers employed in the service sectors has risen from a mere 30% in 1900 to an estimated 80% by 1995. Even this number underestimates the true number of the service employees in the economy, because as many as three-fourths of the workers in manufacturing firms are actually engaged in support services such as maintenance, research, accounting, marketing, personnel management and information processing, rather than direct production of goods. New Technologies, such as information processing and telecommunications, have created enormous new industries and massive restructuring of the economies.

Based on the work activity of their populations many of the so-called advanced industrial nations would be better described as service economies. Table 3 is partial list of industrialized countries ranked in order of the percentage of those employed in service producing jobs. This table contains some surprise, such as finding Canada and Australia (known for their mining industries) high on the list. Several observations can be made global economic development in progressing in unanticipated directions, successful industrial economies are built on a strong service sector, just as it has in manufacturing, competition in services will become global. In fact, many of the largest commercial banks in the world at

Table 3: Percentage Employment in Services Jobs for Selected Industrialization Nations, 1980-1993

Country	1980	1987	1993
Canada	67.2	70.8	74.8
United States	67.1	71.0	74.3
United States	67.1	71.0	74.3
Australia	64.7	69.7	71.8
Belgium	64.3	70.1	70.7
Isreal	63.3	66.0	68.0
France	56.9	63.6	66.4
Finland	52.2	60.1	65.9
Italy	48.7	57.7	60.7
Japan	54.5	58.1	59.9
United Kingdom	60.4	67.7	NA

NA - Not Available

Source: 1993 Statistical Year Book, Department of International Economic and Affairs Statistical Office, United Nations, New York, 1993, pp. 236-242.

present are owned by the Japanese. Trade in services remains as challenges because many countries erect barriers to protect domestic firms. For example, India (till recently) and Mexico, among others, prohibit the sale of insurance by foreign companies.

Service Sector and the Indian Economy

India is no exception to this phenomenon. One of the more special freatures of the evolution of the indian economy in the Nineties has been shift towards the service sector. While a little over a decade ago the three main sectors of economic activity agriculture, industry and services had roughly equal shares in the GDP, the serice sector has now left the other two far behind. According to national income estimates for 1998-99, the service sector accounts for nearly 47 per cent of India's GDP.

Broadly, the agriculture sector comprises crop production, forestry, fishing and livestock. The industrial sector is classified as consisting of mining manufacturing electricity generation and usually construction as well. And the service sector comprises a mixed bag of activities-trade, transport, communication, real estate, finance, personal, community and social service.

It is very clear from the table 4 the service sector contribution to the GDP is increasing year by year steadily and at present it is nearly 50 per cent. Similarly it's contribution towards employment generation is also around 60 per cent, which is confirming the service sector's dominance over the economy; so, it can concluded that the service sector is playing a major role in shaping the economy.

Table 4: Gross Domestic Product (GDP) Sectoral Contributions (Rs. in Crores)

Year	Agriculture Rs.	%	Industrial Rs.	%	Service Rs.	%	Total Rs.	%
Old Series - at 1990-91 Prices								
1990-91	69860	32.9	59493	28.0	82900	39.1	212252	100
1991-92	68480	32.0	58505	27.3	86998	40.7	213983	100
1992-93	724421	32.1	61091	27.2	91728	40.7	225240	100
New Series at 1993-94 Prices								
1993-94	262059	33.5	185070	23.7	334216	42.8	781345	100
1994-95	276012	33.0	202214	24.2	357638	42.8	835863	100
1995-96	275041	30.6	227438	25.4	394511	44.0	896990	100
1996-97	299354	31.0	242352	25.1	422684	43.9	964390	100
1997-98p	296151	29.2	255825	25.3	460840	45.5	1012816	100
1998-99q	315415	29.2	267269	24.7	4991550	46.1	1081834	100

P. Provisional q: quick estimates
Source: Central Statistical Organization

Table 5: Employment in Different Sectors (Lakh Persons as on March 31)

Year	Agriculture Persons	%	Industrial Persons	%	Service Persons	%	Total Persons	%
1991	14.47	5.4	95.99	35.9	156.89	58.7	267.35	100
1992	14.85	5.5	97.06	35.9	158.55	58.6	270.46	100
1993	14.78	5.4	96.85	35.6	160.15	59.0	271.78	100
1994	14.28	5.4	97.26	35.6	162.21	59.2	273.75	100
1995	14.33	5.2	97.73	35.6	163.17	59.2	275.23	100
1996	14.59	5.2	100.87	36.1	163.85	58.7	279.31	100
1997	14.45	5.1	101.51	35.9	166.43	59.0	282.39	100
1998	14.34	5.1	99.56	35.8	166.78	59.1	280.68	100

Source: Ministry of Labour (DGE & T)

References

1. James A Fitzsimmons, Mona J. Fitzsimmons, Service Management: Options, Strategy and Information Technology, McGraw-Hill Singapore, 1998, pp.4-7.
2. Ravi Shankar, "Service Marketing - Some Conceptual Issues" in the Book Services Marketing - The Indian Experience, edited by Ravi Shankar, Manas Publications, Delhi, 1993, pp. 7-8.
3. R.M. Bessom. "Unique Aspects of Marketing McGraw-Hill Tokyo, 1974, p.545.
4. W.J. Stanton, Fundamentals of Marketing McGraw Hill Tokyo, 1974, p.545.
5. J. Lehtinen, Customer - Oriented Service Firm Espoo, Finland, 1983, p.21.
6. Philip Kotler and Paul N. Bloom: Marketing Professional Services, Prentice Hall, New Jersey, 1984, p.174.
7. E. Gummeson, A.Neglected Area in Services marketing", Journal of Services Marketing no.1., 1987, p.22.
8. Christian Gronorss, Service Management and Marketing Lexington Books, Massachusetts, 1990, p.27.
9. Valarie A. Zeithamal, A Parasuraman, and Leonard L. Berry, Problems and Strategies in Services Marketing", Journal of marketing 49 (Spring 1985), pp.33-46.
10. Ravi Sankar (1993), op.cit.
11. Christopher H. Lovelock, "Classifying Services to Gain Strategic Marketing Insights", Journal of Marketing, Vol.47 Summer 1983, pp. 9-20.
12. R.W. Schomenner, "How can Service Business Survive and Prosper", Sloan.
13. S. Vandermerwe and M. Chandwick, "The Internationalization of Service Industries Journal, No. 1, 1989.
14. Round T. Rust, Anthony J. Zahorik, Timothy L. Keiningham, Service Marketing, Eastern Press, Bangalore, 1999, p.3-4.
15. James Brain Quinn, Intelligent Enterprise, The Free Press, New York, 1992 P.4 and Stephen M. Shugan, "Explanations for the Growth of Services", In Service Quality: New Directions in Theory and Practice, Roland T. Rust and Richard L Oliver, eds., Sage Publications, Newburry Park, CA 1993.
16. James A. Fitzsimmons, Mona J. Fitzsimmons, Service Management: Operations Strategy and Information Technology, McGraw Hill Singapore, 1998, pp.4-7.
17. The Hindu News Daily.
18. Ibid.

THE CHALLENGES AHEAD OF 21ST CENTURY SERVICE ECONOMY OF INDIA

Prof. M. Chandrasekhar[1]
Dr. P. Balaji Prasad[2]

ABSTRACT

The paper touches briefly the service sector in its expanding scope, with qualitative dimension. It addresses the unfolding service sector enveloping our economy in the long run. An attempt is made by offering the solutions through understanding the concept of service economy. The discussion calls for a paradigm shift in the meaning and the role of the process of develpment and empowerment, role and relevance of various service organisations, need for professionalized bureaucracy, autonomous and accountable self government institutions and activists enlightened public role in reorienting and strengthening our economy. To face the seemingly diverse challenges of the country means bracing up to the twin task of meeting the demands of poorest of the poor in the country under liberalisation of economy on one hand and facing the challenges from the mightiest of the mighy under globalisation of economy on the other.

Introduction

The paper is though not a blueprint to steer clear the dark clouds hovering around our economy. But it is certainly an attempt to unclutter the challenges being faced by Today's Indian economy. The paper highlights the importance of unfolding dilemmas and challenges of service economy. Examining the relevant issues from the service sector stand point of view implies an attempt to approach the problems of Indian Economy in a perspective.

Service is a paid form of performance from a producer to consumer; unlike physical good it does not result in transfer of any tangible benefit.

---

1. Professor Retired Iran Sri Venkateswara University and presently Director Indian Institute of Advanced Management Visakhapatnam.

2. Associate Professor, School of Business Management, Sri Venkateswara University, Tirupati-517502, A.P. India

While most of the rich economies shifted from Farm to Factories, services are the fastest growing sector of most of the developed nations than developing nations. In fact developed nations economies are called "service economies" because of dominating role of service sector when compared to Agriculture and manufacturing sector in their economies.

India is moving from Agriculture to services without going through and enjoying the fruits of broad based industrialisation. It has got two implications: First in India, however the age of industry never really arrived. There is not much industrialisation in the economy: the business are run by very few large and traditional business houses, often family business whose activities for management professionalisation of needed cadre for the needs of developing economy remain unfulfilled, whose practices are not always in tune with the needs and interests of the large society. Second, its excessive dependence on agriculture leading to low income and low standard of living of the people. Due to low industrilisation large markets are not readily available within the country. A situation prevails that there is a demand for certain products and services exceed supply, however provider remained unresponsive due to various reasons.

Since June 1991 the country has been going through a process of liberalisation, privatisation, and globalisation (LPG) which means replacement of sheltered culture of industry and business by competitive world which should ultimately lead to restructuring of the Indian economy. As a result of the LPG today the service sector dominates Indian economy with one in every two Indians earning their livelhiood by providing service in the organized employment opportunity.

In Indian economy, services account for 49 per cent of GDP compared to Industry sector and Agricultural sector with 27 per cent and 24 per cent respectively. India has leap frogged into services more by default than design. India desiring to be major service economy in the future must attempt to review objectively the performance of various service institutions.

Service industry characterised by many categories of firms/ organisations (see table). Firms offering personal services such as healthcäre, education and entertainment etc., firms producing commercial services such as retailing,accounting, legal and banking services, public service organisations like defence, police, school etc. Not-for-profit organisations such as temples, churches, hosptials and universities.

Table: **Types of Services of Service Sector**

Major service category	*Govern ment service*	*Personal service*	*Commer-cial service*	*Public service organi-sations*	*Non-profit organi-sations*	*Political party organi-sations*
Specific service types	Grievance General Welfare, Develop-ment etc.	Health care, Entertain-ment,Edu-cation etc.	Retailing Banking Legal service Accoun-ting, etc.	Defence Police Postal telegraphs Schools, Local adminis-tration, etc.	Temples and Churches, Hospitals, Univer-sities, etc.	Government forming business
Target groups of concer-ned sub-ject matter	Citizen or Victim etc.	Patient Lover of entertain-ment, knowledge seeker etc.	Conveni-ence seeker Money matters,legal matters, income and expenditure matters etc.	External protection, Law and order Communi-cations, Primary education, Local govern-ment etc.	Faith providers, In patient care, Know-ledge genera-tor and distri-butor etc.	Empower-ment of ordinary individuals and groups

In India the role of two more crucial service organsiations has to be highlighted in order to realise the vast potential of Service Industry in the country's affairs. They are first the role of government at the commanding height of the economy as a major service provider of the developing nation in many areas of service sector. Secondly the role of political parties as a major category of service organisations in the context of government formation efforts from time to time as per the rule of law and as watchdog of government performance leading to its impact on the economy.

While the former category of service organisations offers its service in the form of handling grievances, offering welfare and development services to the needy, the latter help ordinary individuals and groups through the democratic means for their empowerment and demand a due share in the economy and command a just role in the affairs of State.

The nature of service economy of India that is unfolding can be understood by comprehending the state of health of that society, the State and finally the economy.

Indian Society

Indian society is said to be profoundly inegalitarian despite 50 years of political independence--vast disparities of Income and power exists across and among various citizens of the country. A society without transparent nature of mutually benefiting institutions in itself will be a prime candidate for being corrupt because people will compensate for their experience of powerlessness and lack of appreciation of their worth through a competitive exercise of power. This will affect the privileged as well since their status anxieties will be greater in such a society than those of the dispossessed. The state and society, which does not know how to prevent people from feeling humilitated simply because of who they are, will produce individuals who excel in the art of humliating others in turn.

Indian State

Indian State- its functioning even in the best of times - for more ordinary citizens - still distant, inaccessible and arbitrary - State agencies such as courts, police, bureaucracy and even Universities exemplify this intransigence than any achievement towards it citizens and nations.

In the globalising world the quest for generation of wealth than promotion of human welfare is a dangerous game let loose on the poor by the State.

The State may boast of achievement in many spheres of material gains and wealth maximisation. In the words of French philosopher Bergson that "we would be crushed under not by our failures but by our success". The perils of running the state and its economy into an unprecedented direction will be an unmitigated disaster in a socity like ours.

The twin threats posting problems to service economy are the threat to individuals in the form of deteriorating law and order, loss of confidence of the citizen in the ability of state, war of ganglords, increased criminalisation of politics. The other threat looming large is to the integrity of state due to unhealthy linkage between corrupt politics and corrupt business. If allowed, it results in a steady weakening of the financial sector in the form of damage to capital markets and financial institutions triggered by globalisation and liberalisation of capital inflow. If neglected, there will be a point when government find that they cannot afford to pick up the pieces yet again. If unchecked, the deluge when it comes will unfortunately consume the citizen.

It is in this context we shall examine some of the relevant issues though it may not be exhausitive in the scope of analysis and discussion. First the role of services marketing in the new economy. Second the needed paradigm shift in the meaning and role of the following. The process of development and empowerment, role and relevance of various service organisations, professionalised bureaucracy, independent yet accountable self governing units and activist enlightened public.

The Good Governance

The concept of good governance in the new service economy can be understood in two ways: one is as the public policy versus business policy perspective, the other one from services marketing and human resource perspective. However for our discussion we can assume the services marketing and business policy as one dimension and public policy and human resource management as another dimension of discussion and analysis of good governance. The following paragraphs will provide scope and direction of facing the challenges of service economy in two dimensions. First dimension of discussion will be in the form of approach to services management, the central assumptions, guiding principles and blueprint for action. The second dimension of discussion leads us to know the process of development, empowerment, role, relevance of various service organisations, need for professionalised bureaucracy and independent yet accountable self governing units and activist enlightened public.

Services Marketing Perspective: The Emerging View of Services Marketing in the New Economy

Central Assumptions

Every organisation is a service, be it private or public, whether it produces a physical product or not; it produces a service meant either for commercial purpose or for non-profit purpose.

The primary purpose of the organisation is to satisfy customers because we know that markets are increasingly becoming global, as information transfer becomes more efficient and as intangible goods become a larger percentage of the economy; and markets are becoming increasingly competitive satisfying the customer who will become more and more important.

Customers' requirements which are constantly changing. The only constant is change, premium is placed on continuously monitoring and adopting to the changes in the market place. The causes of change are the acceleration of technological change, profound social changes. People who make up those cultures and subcultures have dramatically different needs and wants than their previous generations.

Guiding Principles

Improve service continually. No matter how good a job the organisation is doing of supplying service it must continously improve with an emphasis on customers and their changing needs rather than the efficiency of internal processes.

Concentrate on the areas most important to customer retention, make sure service improvements efforts are financially accountable. Reject the idea of improving everything all at once. Resources are instead focused on the areas that will have the greatest impact. Emphasis on customer retention than customer attraction.

Third principle is to user customer satisfaction to expand revenues. Revenue expansion results from customer satisfaction through the mechanism of customer retention and word of mouth.

Fourth principle is to make sure that service improvement efforts are financially accountable - thus expenditure must all be made with consideration of the rate of return and service improvements are no exception. Delight -- don't just satisfy -- the customer, mere satisfaction is generally thought of as resulting from problem avoidance but any competitive advantage from customer satisfaction will often have to be based on a higher order of customer satisfaction which is commonly called, "customer delight" and arises from surprising and exceptional service.

The first task is to focus the organisation. This involves figuring out the purposes of the organisation: how the organisation should be positioned against competition and which customer groups will be targeted. Second task is to attract customers. The third task is to listen to the customer which is inherently informal i.e. let the customers determine the areas that the organisation should come about the most. The fourth task is to measure the customers' satisfaction on the areas which customers have identified as being important. Fifth task is to determine the return on quality. Sixth task is that of improving service to which many issues are relevant such as relationship management, employee empowerment, close links to customers. Finally, the organisation that desires to be successful in the long run must always look to the future and especially the trends in technology adopting a market positioning that will not make organisations obsolete.

A Blueprint for Action

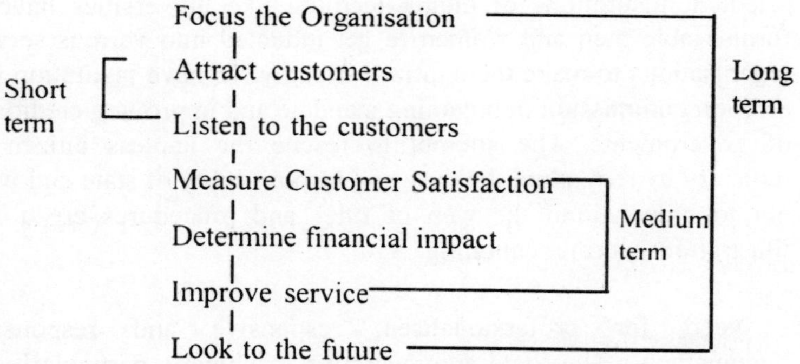

Fig. An Approach to Services Marketing

The Human Resource View point:

The Paradigm Shift

The first issue will be the very concept of development in the context of our economy and society. Development does not mean extending doles and sops in the form of schemes as a knee jerk reaction. The development starts with people - who are they?

> the poor, the illiterate, the hungry, the sick, the ignorant villages and the victims of social injustice -- those who are the backbone of the nation -- the industrial worker -- the soldier. Where is the man who sysrnpathises with them, who shares in their joy and sorrows?

The development starts with people and their empowerment through education, organisation, discipline. Without all these three all our concern does not produce any tangible gains nor inspire the confidence of citizens especially the underprivileged about the ability of the state to be their benefator.

Second issue is the desirable role across the spectrum of various service organisations occupying the space of service economy interfacing between the citizens and the state. For eg., the role of media in such a society to their audience would be to offer news and views that will be interesting, action and satisfaction oriented. Institutions of higher learning like universities have to furnish able men and women to get inducted into various service organisations to make them citizen friendly. To have institution like election commission in obtaining mandate and improving credibility of governments. The attempt to rescue the hapless citizen by judiciary by reminding the duty and responsibility of state and warn not to hide behind the web of rules and procedures are a few illustrations worth mentioning.

Need for professionalised, responsive and responsible bureaucracy : The State administrative machinery, particularly the civil servants who are considered to be the steel frame, does not create any awe in the minds of citizens. In fact there is diminishing respect due to entry of doubtful characters that could be probably one of the causes even when in their distress they fail to attract any sympathy among the public. The people who were trained and worked under control oriented regime may lack in liberal sentiments and social sensitivity. As such it is difficult to expect delivery of consistently high quality of service regardless of organisation, situation involved. One alternative to strengthen the bureaucracy could be to recruit more specialists and experts from specialised agencies rather than a generalist.

Encourage autonomous and accountable units of self governing institutions: Instead of allowing to bureaucratic control over service organisation, they can customize the service by providing autonomy, freedom to the organisation structure, and allowing the service provider organisation to customize the service to the needs and preferences of individual customers. For eg. the demand for more powers, funds and freedom to state governments, local self governments therefore might appear genuine and one approach is to concede to the demands of these units. Eg formation of smaller States like Jharkhand, Uttaranchal and Chattisgadh recently earlier in W.B. and automates district for goorkhas. Such an approach reduces the leadership turn over and their irresponsibility in case of political leadership. Employee turnover in case of an employee and increases citizen satisfaction and loyalty thereby producing greater lasting peace over the long run.

Last but not the least, encourage the role of activists enlightened citizen or public: It is of great importance today - Because it is they who can influence the people's mind directly or indirectly to build support for a movement for restoration of semblance of equality. An enlightened person who stands up to the test of truths of life.

The "test of the truth" in the words of Swamy Vivekananda,

> "Anything that makes you weak physically, intellectually and spiritually 'reject as poison, there is no life in it. It cannot be true. Truth is strengthening. Truth is purity, truth is all knowledge. The greatest truths are the simplest things in the world. Simplest as your own existence".

The enlighted public who have to show their concern through the use of their intellectual ability, irrespective of their social, physical conditions and their age considerations for the plight of the underprivileged by breaking the mental barrierrs of many other indifferent publics who are in large number above those hapless citizens. These are the very publics who needs to be awakened who are refusing to grasp the reality of the situation. The task of the enlightened person is to set free the captives of exclusionist mental prison and to enable them to reach out in love and service to a world in need.

In the words of Swamy Vivekananda what it mean reaching out in love and service to a world in need.

"See how simple - hearted these poor, illiterate people are ! will you be able to relieve their miseries to some extent at least? .... Let us go from village to village devoting ourselves to the service of the poor. Let us, through the force of our character and spirituality and our austere living, convince the rich about their duties to the masses, and get money and the means wherewith to serve the poor and distressed..."

Conclusion

The emerging view results from great changes taking place in the economy -- especially reflect the pervasive influence of the Information revolution. Profound shift in the perspectives leading to greatly increased attention to satisfying the customer. Service economy in India is very complex and vital for vibrancy. To face the seemingly diverse challenges of the country means bracing upto the twin taks of meeting the demands of the poorest of poor in the country under liberalisation of economy on one hand and facing the challenges from the mightiest of mighty under globslisation of economy on the other.

References

Harish Khare, "Obligations of a Lameduck", May 16 The Hindu p.12.

Krishna Iyer, "A tryst betrayed", The Hindu, 11th November 1999.

Michael, J. Etzel, Walker and Stanton, Marketing, International edn., Mc Grawhill Inc. 1997 Edn. pp. 513.

Pavan K Verma, "Perception versus Reality-- The Challenge before the Indian Middle class".

Peter F Drucker, Marketing and Economic Development, Reprint from Marketing Management and Indian Economy edited by S. Neelameghum 2nd edn., Vikas Publishing Pvt. Ltd.

Philip Kotler, Marketing Management Analysis, Planning and Control, Prentice Hall India Millennium edition.

Pratap Bhanu Mehta, "Corruption as Empowerment", The Hindu, August 11th 2001.

Rama Mohan Reddy C., "Capitalism Indian Style", The Hindu, August 12th 2001 p.15.

Ronald T. Rust, Anthony, J. Zahorik and Timothy, L Keiningham, Services

Marketing 1999 edition Addison Welsley.

Swami Agnivesh and Valson Thampu, "Mastering Materialism", July 15th 2001. The Hindu.

Swami Nihilananda, Vivekananda - A biography, Advaita Ashrama, 1992.

Walker, Body and Larrehe, Marketing Strategy Planning and Implementation Tata Mc Graw Hill 1999 edn. pp.

THE CRISIS OF UNEMPLOYMENT IN THE NEW ECONOMY

*G.S. Mohan Krishna, & Uday***

Conventional ecojnomic theory divides econmies into three broad categories. By the beginning of 20th century the pulse of the most rich economics had shifted from Farm to Factories. Particularly in the later half has been transformation from an emphasis on the manufacture of physical goods to the production of intangible services the world over.

In India however, the age of the Industry never really arrived the largest the industry could grow was up to 22.7% GDP of the economy in 1997-98. India has thus leap frogged into services more by default than design. India has moved from agriculture to services without going through and enjoying the broadened industrialisation. Today service sector dominates the economy of even developing country like India as well.

As a result of such domination of service sector the winds of change are battering the very core of the socio-psycho-economic values, around which Indian society has been knit for hundreds of years. The change in value system is forcing the emergence of new life styles and consequently overhauling our consumption pattern.

After 1966 over the next 30 years India became the only one developing country that systematically ignored creating of jobs, gave it not even cursory attention in its plans and policies, framed its objectives solely in terms of GDP. The country's rulers thus systematically neglected employment opportunities for employable

---

* PGDBA 2000-02, Times Management, School, Tirupati.
** Faculty, Times Management School, Tirupati.

age category population, especially in the organised category by neglecting the growth of industrial sector especially because of leap frogging. Thus most of the organised labour entered into service sector. As a result service sector is major employer of over 60% while industry offered 36% and agriculture continue, to hover around 4% of organized labour. Out of 10% employed in the organised sector 2/5th are public employed.

Today there is a silent crisis of unemployment -- a huge but silent crisis is overtaking the country- failure to create jobs has been obvious for more than a decade.

India's employment of manpower can be broadly classified into organized sector or unorganized sector. 90 per cent of total employment is from the unorganised sector. The organised workforce is around ten per cent. The unorganised work force which is basically starting from rural areas in the form of agricultural workers. Than the unorganised workforce in the urban areas are contract, sub contract as well as migratory agricultural labour. Among them about 60 per cent are self employed and most of them are very poor. When they get work they work. Casual workers are about 30%, they are able to get jobs and ramain unpaid for the rest of the days. Most of the work force are either illiterate or below primary education levels. The unorganised workforce is characterised by large scale underemployment and poor quality of employment.

The crisis of unemployment is among organized sector

Successive governments were able to get away with GDP oriented planning till the end of 1980s because the increase in job seekers was only marginally higher than the increase in jobs. The reason for the above is namely 2/3 of the job created in the organised sector were in the government and public sector enterprises. The employment in the state sector 1951-61 seven million 1961-71 11 million 1971-81 15 millions by 1981-91 19 million. By 1991 there is a crisis in government employment. In the state sector employment stopped growing. However till 1997 the explosion in private sector took up some of the shock. But with the disappearance of private investment in 1997 and return to the 5 per cent hindu growth rate of economy, even this has come to an end.

During 1997-2000 India added just under 2 million young people to the educated unemployed. Only one in every 24 young job seekers succeeded in getting a job in the organised sector. By the past trend by now another 2 million young educated people will have failed to secure jobs in the organised sector. It is said that with the 100 crores population the country is not even ultising the energies and capacities of 10 crores of its total population. Having been educated in Institutions of higher education and unable to find a role to discharge by the educated unemployed youth today. For eg, in Andhra Pradesh it is reported having got good ranks in Engineering Entrance Tests and having completed their Engineering Education several hundreds of such graduates are roaming in the roads in the State capital, which is not an exaggaration.

The status of unorganized sector

Trends are likely to worsen in the unorganized sector for it depends on growth in the organized sector for its own survival. The fact is quite significant and alarming. It reported that an estimated 350 millions of our one billion plus reach bed without food that day often. A State which abdicates its responsibility towards it poor and unorganized in preference to highly organized communities becomes only an instrument of these organized communities private power. If the development has to have any meaning the poor, the illiterate, the hungry, the sick, the ignorant villagers and the victims of social injustice -- those who are the backbone of the nation, the farmer -- the industrial worker -- the soldier.

Unless these above categories of weak, unorganized are targeted and their empowerment is achieved through education, organisation and their discipline, it will not produce any tangible gains nor inspire the confidence of citizens especially these underprivileged about the ability of the state to be their benefactor.

References

Mohan Krishna G.S. Indias employment perspective at the seminar.
Pramshankar Jha The Crisis of unemployment, August 22, 2001. The Hindu.
Jayaprakash Narayan, Janavijnan Vedika a session on valueless education, Eenadu 9th Sunday 2002.

MANAGEMENT CHALLENGES FACED BY WOMEN IN MANAGEMENT IN THE SERVICE SECTOR:
A CASE STUDY OF INDIAN AIRLINES AND AIR INDIA

** Ms. V. Shanthi Latha*

*** Dr. C.S.G. Krishnamacharyulu*

The service sector at present is poised to reach the peak in a decade. One of the industries in this sector that is growing at almost the same rate is the transport industry, with special emphasis on the aviation industry.

The past decade in the aviation history of India has witnessed many changes. There have been many new entrants in both the domestic and international airline divisions.

The spurt of competition in the industry has changed the entire concept of flying. The whole package of traveling has been throughly revised to meet both competion and also international standards, even for the domestic sector.

While the customers benefit, comfort and satisfaction is what every ai.line states their goal, is all this change has been to achieve larger market share, higher profits and greater customer loyalty. The relentless effort of each and every employee in the industry has led to some outstanding performances. Yet the people employed to provide these services and make them better are still coping with day-to-day challenges. This is all the more true in the case of

---

* Research Scholar, School of Business Management, S.V. University, Tirupati-517502.

** Professor, School of Business Management, S.V. University, Tirupati 517502.

women managers. This present study tries to focus on a few such problems encountered in the two most important airlines of India i.e., Air India (AI) and Indian Airlines (IA).

Objectives and Methodology

The study aimed at not just identifying the challenges faced by the women managers of these two organizations i.e., AI, and IA, but also what the organizations are providing. It also tries to suggest a few new/alternative remedial measures to reduce/ eliminate these problems.

The study was undertaken using two questionnaries. The first was administered among 24 women managers of Air India and 17 in Indian Airlines. The Human resources managers of the respective organizations filled the second questionnarie. Simple percentages were calculated form the data available.

Analysis and Interpretation of Data

The profile of the respondents, 24 from Air India and 17 from Indian Airlines, is given in the table below.

Table 1: Profile of Respondents

Profile	Air India (N=24)	Indian Airlines N=17)
1. AGE (Yrs.)		
21-30	12 (50)	7 (41.2)
31-40	11 (45.8)	8 (47.1)
41-50	1 (4.2)	2 (11.7)
>50	-	-
2. MARITAL STATUS		
Unmarried	9 (37.5)	6 (35.5)
Married	15 (62.5)	11 (64.7)
3. HEALTH AILMENTS (Which affect work)		
Yes	3 (12.5)	1 (5.9)
No	21 (87.5)	16 (94.1)

Contd......

4. EDUCATIONAL QUALIFICATION		
<Under Graduation	-	-
Under Graduation	3 (12.5)	4 (23.5)
Post Graduation	21 (87.5)	13 (76.5)
5. INDIVIDUAL INCOME (Rs.)		
< 10000	-	4 (23.5)
10000-20000	20 (83.3)	12 (70.6)
20001-30000	3 (2.5)	1 (5.9)
>30000	1 (4.2)	-
6. JOINT INCOME (Rs.)		
<15000	-	1 (5.9)
15000-25000	4 (16.7)	7 (41.2)
25001-35000	13 (54.2)	5 (29.4)
>35000	7 (29.1)	4 (23.5)
7. INVESTMENT		
Bonds/Deposits	24 (100)	17 (100)
Share/Stock	10 (41.7)	5 (29.4)
Gold	24 (100)	17 (100)
Durables	4 (54.2)	4 (23.5)

Notes: Figures in parentheses are percentage.

The following aspects were observed from the data.

Table 2: Work Profile of the Respondents

Profile	**Air India (N=24)**	**Indian Airlines (N=17)**
1. JOB TITLE		
Officer grade I	5 (20.8)	5 (29.4)
Officer grade II	7 (29.2)	3 (17.7)
Deputy/Asst. Manager	9 (37.5)	7 (41.2)
Manager	3 (12.5)	2 (11.7)
2. TYPE OF WORK		
Administrative (general)	5 (20.8)	2 (11.7)
Sales and Marketing	4 (16.7)	4 (23.5)
Finance	5 (20.8)	4 (23.5)
Human Resources	3 (12.5)	1 (5.9)
Systems	7 (29.2)	6 (35.4)

Contd....

3. NUMBER OF POSITION CHANGED		
None	9 (37.5)	8 (47.1)
One	8 (33.3)	4 (23.5)
Two	3 (12.5)	3 (17.7)
Three	4 (16.7)	2 (11.7)
4. NUMBER OF ORGANIZATIONS CHANGED		
None	20 (83.4)	15 (88.2)
One	3 (12.5)	1 (5.9)
Two	1 (4.1)	1 (5.9)
Three	-	-
4. REASON		
Temporary/Government job	3 (75)	2 (100)
Marriage	1 (25)	-

Note: Figures in parentheses are percentages

The challenges or job related problems and issues faced by these women managers are shown in the table 3 given below.

Table 3: Profile of Issues/Problems Faced by Women Managers at Work Place

Issues	*Air India (N=24)*	*Indian Airlines (N=17)*
1. DISCRIMINATION		
Yes	7 (29.2)	5 (29.4)
No	17 (70.8)	12 (70.6)
2. CONTEXT*		
Promotion	5 (29.4)	3 (25)
Salary	7 (41.2)	5 (41.6)
Responsibility	1 (5.9)	2 (16.7)
Evaluation At Job	4 (23.5)	2 (16.7)
3. HARASSMENT		
Yes	2 (8.3)	1 (5.9)
No	22 (91.7)	16 (94.1)
4. ACTION TAKEN WHEN REPORTED		
Yes	2 (100)	1 (100)
No	-	-

Contd..

Issues	*Air India (N=24)*	*Indian Airlines (N=17)*
5. SATISFIED WITH THE JOB		
Yes	19 (79.2)	15 (88.2)
No	5 (20.8)	2 (11.8)
6. REASON FOR CONTINUING		
Permanent Job	4 (80)	2 (100)
Location of the Job	1 (20)	-
7. SEEKING OPPORTUNITIES ELSEWHERE		
Yes	5 (100)	2 (100)
No	-	-
8. WILL CONTINUE IF DISCRIMINATION IS ELIMINATED		
Yes	4 (80)	2 (100)
No	1 (20)	-
9. SUPERVISED BY		
Male	21 (87.5)	16 (94.1)
Female	3 (12.5)	1 (5.8)
10. PROBLEMS FACED FROM FEMALE SUBORDINATES		
Jealousy	3 (100)	1 (100)
Ego	1 (33.3)	1 (100)
Family Problems	1 (33.3)	1 (100)
11. PROBLEMS FACE FROM MALE SUBORDINATES		
Male Chauvinism	1 (100)	1 (100)
Rejection	1 (100)	-
Lack of Understanding	1 (100)	1 (100)
12. STRESS AT WORK		
Yes	17 (70.8)	12 (70.6)
No	7 (29.2)	5 (29.4)
13. TYPE OF STRESS		
Heavy	1 (5.8)	-
Moderate	7 (41.3)	4 (33.3)
Light	1 (5.8)	-
Consistent	3 (17.7)	2 (16.7)

Contd....

Issues	*Air India (N=24)*	*Indian Airlines (N=17)*
Sporadic	5 (29.4)	6 (50)
14. REASON		
Role overload	21 (87.5)	14 (82.4)
Role Conflict	7 (29.2)	2 (11.8)
Responsibility	10 (41.7)	7 (41.2)
15. SATISFACTION		
Performance Appraisal	19 (79.2)	12 (70.6)
Career Opportunities	21 (87.5)	15 (88.2)
Career Advancement	20 (83.3)	16 (94.1)
Work Assignments	17 (70.8)	10 (70.6)
Expatriate Assignment	19 (79.2)	-
Power and Authority	24 (100)	17 (100)

The following aspects were observed from the data

1. Most of the women managers are post graduates (87.5% AI, 76.5% IA) with an individual income between Rs.10000 and Rs.20000 (83.3% AI, 70.6% IA).

2. They are distributed almost evenly across all the types of work areas. Administrative (20.8% AI, 11.7% IA), sales and marketing (16.7% AI, 23.5% IA), finance (20.8% AI, 23.5% IA), systems (29.2% AI, 35.4% IA) which usually is the area where more women are present. So this general impression has been proved other wise here in these two organizations.

3. Most of the women managers had changed positions i.e., promotions within the organizations, but a very few had changed organizations. Most of the women (83.4% AI, 88.2% IA) have been first employed by these very organizations and still continue to work.

4. The context of discrimination at work place (29.2% AI, 29.4% IA) has been felt mainly in the areas of salary (41.2% AI, 41.6% IA) followed by promotion (29.4% AI, 25% IA), job evaluation (23.5% AI, 16.7% IA) and job task responsibility (5.9% AI, 16.7% IA).

5. While harassment has been reported in both the organizations (8.3% AI, 5.9% IA), the women were satisfied with the anti sexual harassment policy as prompt action was taken up soon after reporting.

6. Most of the women (79.2% AI, 88.2% IA) were satisfied with the present job they were in.

7. The remaining however dissatified still continued in the existing job as it was either a permanent job (80% AI, 100% IA) or due to location of the ob (20% AI). However all the dissatisfied women managers were seeking opportunities elsewhere.

8. More women managers were supervised by male (87.5% AI, 94.1% IA) than females (12.5% AI, 5.8% IA).

9. In the experience of female supervisors jealousy (100% AI, 100% IA), ego (33.3% AI, 33.3% IA) and escaping stating family problems (33.3% AI, 100% IA) were the major problems faced from female subordinates. Male chauvinism (100% AI,100% IA), rejection of female superior (33.3% AI) and lack of understanding (33.3% AI, 100% ia) were the problems faced from male subordinates.

10. Majority of the women (70% AI, 70.6% IA) faced stress at work. The stress levels being moderate (41.3% AI, 33.3% IA), sporadic (29.4% AI, 50% IA), consistent (17.7% AI, 16.7% IA,) heavy (5.8% AI) and light (5.8% AI).

11. The major cause of stress at work was role overload (87.5% AI, 82.4% IA) followed by responsibility (41.7% AI, 41.2% IA) and role conflict (29.2% AI, 11.8% IA).

12. The satisfaction of women managers was found to be high on power and authroity given to an individual (100% AI, 100% IA) followed by career opportunities (87.5% AI, 88.2% IA), career advancement (83.3% ai, 94.1% IA), performance appraisal (79.2% AI, 70.6% IA) expatriate assignment (79.2 AI) and

work assignment (70.8% AI 70.6 IA).

The other questionnarie filled by the HR managers shed some light on the organizations procedures and activities; these are discussed in the table 4 given below.

Table 4: Organizational Activities

Information	*AIR India*	*Indian Airlines*
1. SPECIFIC POLICY FOR EMPLOYING WOMEN	Yes	Yes
2. EXISTING FACILITIES		
Job rotation	Yes	Yes
Job sharing	Yes	Yes
3. FACILITIES TO BE PROVIDED		
Flexi time	Yes	-
Compressed work week	Yes	-
Legal Assistance	Yes	-
4. INCLUDE THE CLAUSE OF GENDER IN APPRAISAL FORM	Yes	Yes
5. STEPS TAKEN TO PREVENT STRESS		
Health camps	Yes	Yes
Try to find the cause and solving it	Yes	-
6. OTHER FACILITIES		
Medical insurance	Yes	Yes
Loan facility	Yes	Yes
Leave travel concesssion	Yes	Yes
Loan for higher education	Yes	Yes
7. SEXUAL HARASSMENT		
Existenc	Yes	Yes
Policy against it	Yes	Yes
Practiced strictly	Yes	Yes
8. ACTION TAKEN		
Employee dismissed after fine	Yes	Yes
Follow up taken	Yes	Yes
9. PROVIDE TRAINING	Yes	Yes
10. HELP PROMOTE WOMEN TO LEADERSHIP POSITION	Yes	Yes

Contd....

Information	*Air India*	*Indian Airlines*
11. WOMEN ONLY RECRUITMENT AND SELECTION	Yes	Yes
12. WOMEN EMPLOYEES AWARDED/REWARDED/ RECOGNIZED/HONORED	Yes	Yes
13. PROMOTION (10-30%)	Yes	Yes
14. EXISTENCE OF EMPLOYEE ASSOCIATION	Yes	Yes
15. EXISTENCE OF SUGGESTION SYSTEM	Yes	Yes

From the above data the following was observed.

1. Both the organizations have a specific policy for employing women as these are government bodies and need to follow the rules of the government.

2. While job sharing and job rotation exist in Air India and the organization is thinking of providing flexitime, compressed work week and legal assistance, Indian Airlines does not have and is not in the plan of providing any of the facilities.

3. Both the organizations include the clause of gender in their job evaluation/performance appraisal forms.

4. While medical insurance and health caps are being taken up by Air India, health camps have not been taken up in recent years in Indian Airlines. Besides only Air India is trying to solve the problem of stress be identifying the cause.

5. Both the organizations however provide loan facilities, loan for higher education, leave travel concessions along with medical insurance.

6. As sexual harassment cases have been reported in both the organizations, a policy against harassment at work does exist in

both. This is being practiced strictly.

7. The previous cases of harassment were dealt with strictly and the harassers dismissed promptly after paying a heavy fine. Follow up action too was taken.

8. Both the organizations had in-house, off-the-job training. However there was no 'women only' training, even though there was 'women only' recruitment and selection.

9. Help is extended to women to promote them to leadership positions in both the organizations. The exact nature of the help was however not revealed.

10. Women employes were previously awarded/honoured/ recognized in both the organizations, for their performance,

11. Air India had a promotion rate of 10.305 among women managers in the past 5 years. The data was not available for Indian Airlines.

12. If there were any problems, women managers could take it to the employees association, or drop a note in the suggestion system available in both the organizations.

Suggestions

The organizations have centralized decision making, thus these suggestions addressed to the central decision making body.

1. The clause of gender has to be eliminated in the performance appraisal/job evaluations, promotions assignments etc.

2. Expatriate assignments should be addressed/extended to women managers too, especially if they are for a short duration (say months). This is because many married women did want expatriate assignment as they count for job experience,

evaluations and promotions, but preferred shorter assignments due to familial reasons.

3. Equality has been practiced in the distribution of power and authority. The same has to be done in the case of career opportunities and advancements.

4. Stringent rules to eradicate discrimination in all the aspects of the job.

5. Continue to practice the constant monitoring of the sexual harassment policy at work.

6. Encourage more number of meritorious women into leadership positions and supervisory roles to reduce/eliminate the problems faced from male and female subordinates. While promoting make their merit clear to eliminate conflicts (harassment, silly talk, rumours) which may arise later.

7. Start program/procedures to monitor stress, find the cause and try to reduce/eliminate it.

8. Legal and financial advice to be extended to women so as to make them more independent and stress free, as many women sought help from their husbands and strangers for investmeents and legal advice.

9. Introduce work concepts like flexi time, part time, compressed work week, as early as possible to help reduce work related pressures and stress.

Conclusion

As the gap between the problems faced by the women mangers and the organizational efforts has been identified to some extent, it is hoped and expected that these organizations may consider the suggestions to further improve the existing situation and make the organizations more customer oriented and truly service oriented inside and outside.

SECTION-II

INDIAN SERVICE ECONOMY UNDER POLITICO LEGAL PRESSURES OF GLOBAL LOCAL LEVELS

OVERVIEW

In view of vast potential of Service Industry in the country like India the role of two more crucial Service Organisation have to be highlighted. They are first the role of government at the commanding height of the economy in the capacity as the world`s largest democratic nation and as a major service provider of the developing country in many areas of service. Secondly the role of political parties as a major category of Service Organisation is thedirection of government formation as per the role of law and as a watchdog of government performance leading to its impact on the economy. There are five papers that explore the issues under the above sub theme of the book. The first paper highlights the changing global environment and its impact on the nation. Prof. Chomsky Lecture based article examines the issues of nature of globalisation, liberalisation that are taking place and their impact on the country sovereignty. Terrorism raising its ugly head and counter terrorism especially state terrorism and its impact on democracy is explained succinctly. The second paper is yet another example of dominant countries attitude and relationship with developing nations especially with regard to trade, Nuclear policy and the brinkmanship in the international bodies like security council, Dr. Rao explains. The third paper examines the management of conflict within and across the border. Being yet another area of challenge to the nation's sovereignty and integrity. The issues include the cost of peace and war across the border, management of conflict within the nation through the practice of federalism and facing the challenges of terrorism which is even cross border affecting very core of our nation such as attack on Parliament. The fourth paper examines the political and administrative leadership capacity for a balancing act in the economic affairs of the country which includes neglect or support (inferred through a deductive logic) a policy bias towards IT and tourism sectors in the promotion of the new economy. The fifth paper examines the very core dimension of spirit of constitution and political aspirations and legal or other hurdles. The paper looks at the evidence of rising friction between the above.

PROF. CHOMSKY ON THE TREND OF LIBERALISATION, GLOBALISATION, DEMOCRACY, TERRORISM AND SEPTEMBER 11TH AND ITS AFTERMATH

Ms. Amulya and Dr. P. Balaji Prasad***

This article is based on excerpts from the review of lectures reported in the press. Prof. Noam Chomsky, renowned linguist, scholar, writer, thinker, visited India in the month of November 2001, toured and lectured at different cities of India including New Delhi, Nov. 5 Chennai Nov. 10th and Tiruvanthapuram on Nov. 11th participated in Seminars delivered lectures on "Sept. 11th and its aftermath where is the world heading? Globalisation and Human Survival coalition for peace and democracy etc. The other important persons who participated in these lectures include Booker prize winner Ms. Arundhati Roy at Delhi, Mr. Sashi Kumar, Media development Foundation at Chennai, Prof. K N Panickkar, V.C. Sree Sankara University of Sanskrit at EMS Akademy Tiruvanthapuram are dignitaries who accompanied the scholar.

US strikes on Afghan had no reaction with in America because the information is controlled in the name of patriotism. It is considered normal in Western countries to kill 1 1/2 million people.

The US launch of war on Afghan constitutes state terrorism because the bombing of sewage systems, electricity lines and other civil facility amounted to a form of bio-terrorism. Afghans several of them fleeing to areas covered with mines and dropping of duster bombs also worsened the situation. The bombs which have not exploded which enhances fears what may be in store for future of the Afghan people.

---

* MBA, 2001-03.

** Associate Prfess, School of Business Management S.V. University, Tirupati.

Thus according to Chomsky war on Afghan constitute a greater terrorist act than September 11th attacks on the United States. Attack on Afghan was criminal; it had no sanction of international law. The US could have taken the attack on legally with the approval of UN security council. However it did not want to do that because that would mean that you need authorisation, "The mafia don would not seek a court order for extortion."

He described all states as Terrorist states barring the weak ones which are incapable of aggression. According to him India is also practicing state terrorism. What the country was facing in Kashmir was a resistance movement. State terrorism had nothing surprising about it as states are not moral agents. The world was being governed by force, not by law. The war on Afghan waged by US it did not want to legitamize the need to approach the council. The US wanted to reserve its right to act unilaterally.

The war on terrorism was being led by a coalition of terrorist states. The US had started its international terrorist activities with the killing of an archibishop in Latin America. Nicaragua was another victim; there was even a verdict of International court of justice asking the US to pay reparations for attacks.

"Rogue State" was the term used by the US to identify its enemies. This status could shift. Mr. Saddam Hussain of Iraq was once a good guy.

September 11th and its aftermath

US adapts double standards; while it wanted the extradition of Osama bin Laden in connection with the attacks, it was unwilling to grant Haiti's request for the extradition of a criminal wanted in connection with atrocities committed in the Nineties.

The September 11th attacks were a historic point, not because of their scale but for the choice of target. The National territory of the US itself became the target of attack.

The war on terrorism was not a clash between civilisations as the US was fighting its own creation. The Al-queda network of Osma bin Laden was one nurtured by the Central Intelligence Agency (CIA), the British Intelligence, Egypt and Saudi Arabia in their own interest.

The US was not fighting Al-queda because it turned against the country. That was no clash of civilisations. Neither was the US fighting Islamic fundamentalism, for its ally Saudi Arabia was the most fundamentalist of Islamic regimes.

On globalisation

Drawing similarlity between the process of colonisation in the past and the ongoing policies of the US, Prof. Choksky said the problem of terrorism could not be seen apart from the kind of globalisation taking place. Globalisation in literal sense was not bad. However in its 'Propagandistic" sense it was designed to protect the interest of those who hold power. When used in this sense, those who oppose it like the left are seen as primitive forces opposing a progressive process.

While voicing support for genuine "free trade' says this should not be done at the cost of states abdicating their social responsibilities. This was the advantage of the Bretton woods system which allowed regulating the flow of capital among countries, making it possible for them to pursue social goals.

However, globalisation agenda set out by neo-liberals according to him had replaced the old system "What we have today is a combinaiton of State power and imposed liberlaisation. This is similar to policy followed by Britain in India. Criticizing the US hegemony in the world, he said the moves for extending the defence system and for total domination would only increase with the attempts toward globaliation. The forms which globalisation took were intended to benefit the West and the corporates and not the people.

Globalisation benefited only a section of the society in various countries including in the US. The divided between the rich and the poor had widened. Convergence of markets and wages did not happen as expected.

Public opinion against globalisation increased in the nineties in countries such as India. Globalisation has only widened inequalities. There was not a broad alliance of labour unions, social democrats and others against specific forms of globalisaiton. There was also greater awarness of human rights and civil liberaties from the sixties onwards.

Liberalisation and Democracy

Liberalisation of capital was undermining democracy as it created virtual parliament of business that can veto decisions. On one side there would be the voters and on the other the speculators with unaccounted concentration of power.

On India's efforts to liberalise its economy Prof. Chomsky said, "If India wants to return to 18th century liberalisation, then it is its choice. Those days too the British - controlled Indian economy was both liberalised and run by Indians themselves. The political class wanted to reduce the domain of democratic choices. Major decisions were not taken in the public arena.

Insisting that US was not a democracy, he said that the political system in that country was meant to protect the opulent classes against the majority of the people. The "permanent interests" of the country was defined as the interests of the property holders. Pointing to the alienation from the political process in the case of a vast majority of people he said these sections were indoctrinated with a consumerist culture of sports, music and purchasing. The propaganda tools reached their highest forms in the more democratic societies.

On civil human rights and socialism

He said the growth of civil and human rights movement would have restraining effect on terror by states. If the movement is sustained it would strenghten solidarity and sympathy.

He remarks that Soviet Union had nothing to with Marxian ideology. Lenin was a Marxist. But Trotsky was not. What he introduced was a kind of state capitalism. Marxian ideology becomes harmful when people believe in it in a religious manner. The collapse of the Soviet Union and the emergence of a unipolar world has increased American hegemony. The collapse of Soviet Union was in effect a removal of a barrier to the emergence of Socialism. However the existence of two super powers left some manouvering room for the rest of the world and the non aligned movement, as the victims of one super power were supported by the other.

GOVERNMENT SERVICES - TECHNOLOGY MANAGEMENT AND HUMAN WELFARE

Dr. V.V. Satyanarayana & B. Munirathnam
Faculty Members, JBIT, Renigunta, Tirupati.

Governments are regulating the industries and their policies according to their requirements. In almost all nations government policies are designed according to the convenience of their people. But it is varying in the developing world. The third world countries are not able to design their administrative policies according to their people. They are enforced by the UN dominant nations, particularly the members of the Security Council. The implementation of WTO policies all around the world, the implementation of non-proliferation policies, migration acts, etc., are highly biased. With these imbalances the poor nations, particularly the most populous nation India is struggling due to inadequacy on several Fronts. Nation's budget is biased on the global demands. Particularly the defense sector is consuming the maximum resources due to security threat from eternal aggressors. If India secures a permanent position in the Security Council by sitting with US, Russia, U.K., France and China, India can take right decisions in their budget presentations.

The role of technology advancement is keeping more pace on Indian soil by securing patent rights through WTO. The gap between developed nations and developing nations is always wider and the rich countries are making it wider. For example when we took an example of a maize seed which possesses 30,000 genes, just by adding gene more one which may sustain at high temperature, the bio tech corporates are procuring the patent rights and they are holding the complete seed and are keeping more price on the poor farmer. WTO is supporting these corporates and making farmers too penurious. The seed was developed from thousands of years and finally the false organizations are holding the rights. It is not a service. It is a business without ethics. Similarly the World Bank Policies are also not appropriate. The rupee value is completely depending on the US dollar image and with this high inflation is exuding every year in this populous nation. The banking sector became vulnerable to dominant currencies and they became syndicate in regulating the world currency. The foreign corporates are pludering the Indian society. The rich nations like U.K., France, Italy and Switzerland are using the most populous nation on the globe i.e., India by experimenting on various grounds like, Pharmaceuticals, Chemicals, Bio-technology products. Ours is a democratic one unlike China or other Kingdoms like Islamic. Our Indian policies are highly vulnerable to the foreign corporates and our political system should be changed in order to sustain at salubrious conditions.

China became the member of WTO after careful consideration and understanding only. The key players, namely US, Russia, UK, France & China of UN Security Council, are selfish and are not working for human welfare.

US continues to pressure non members of security council to go for non-proliferation treaty. NPT was designed only for the sake of protecting the interest of member countries of the security council only these five nations have veto power till now 279 times these nations applied their veto power on poor nations.

US is the first country which conducted the nuclear test in 1945 followed by USSR in 1949. Britain in 1952, France in 1960 China in 1964 while India conducted the nuclear test in 1974. Thermal Nuclear Bomb is more than 100 times effective than the general nuclear bomb. USA conducted thermal nuclear test in 1952, followed by USSR in 1953 Britain in 1957 China 1967 while India conducted the thermal nuclear test on 11th May 1998 only. USA used the nuclear bomb on hiroshima on 6th August 1945 with explosive capacity of 12 kilotonnes. Which is very meagre when compared to the present capacity of 58,000 kilotonnes. The nuclear test was conducted by USA within the water in 1946 which is yet to be conducted by India.

With regard to frequency of conducting the nuclear test USA conducts once per every 18 days followed by fomrer USSR once per every 22 days, France for every 61 days, China once per every 284 days Britain. Once per every 7300 days. Till now USA conducted 1032 nuclear tests and still continuing followed by Russia 715, France 210, Britian 45, China 45.

US is the first nation which sent the satellite for defence purpose in 1960. India tested the prudhvi missile in 1988 for which USA applied super 301 power on India. US has thus conducted while pressurizing NPT dedication by the other nations and taking the other countries for its nuclear design. In 1971 USA warned India by atomic bombarding at the time of Indo-Pak war. Congo producing above 50% of world total uranium production, which is under the clutches of USA.

INS Chakra, a nuclear submarine, was sent back to Russia at the time of Chandrasehar's regime by USA though the lease time is existing. Canadian president Jane Cheriteen cancelled his attendance on the Republic day Parade in 1996 only for the cause of NPT enforced by USA.

India needs to elect a powerful regime in order to hold the grip of UNO and to secure the position in security council, with which they can control the economies. If Nehru had not signed on NPT in 1963 India could have demonstrated its nuclear capability in 1964 itself according to Indira Gandhi.

Also to get permanent efficiency of nuclear arsenal India has to conduct the thermal atomic knowlege. Morarji Desai was the first man who opposed the nuclear test severely than anybody in India due to USA's interest and is the only Indian who accepted a foreign award from Pakistan by Name Nishan - A-Pakistan.

Although every year India is spending more than 20% of the annual budget for defense purpose it is nowhere near in the global context. These liberalisation, privitsation, globalisation and digitalisation policies that would only lead to cannibalisation. The

Indian Public therefore should be made aware of the global policies and should adopt a right government which can fight for permanent membership in UN security council so that rich nations cannot apply their veto power on poor and liberal communities. Though India has 1/6th of world population it is painful in its ability to secure the permanent membership in security council. Indian blood has no good price in international amrket.

Human welfare is possible only when there is stability of the nations economics, with the help of right business policies and right balance of power of the security council that could regulate the national government health and wealth generaton.

For eg. India should be in a position to a convert the automic power towards the electricity generation without causing for security council in order to feed its 100 crore population with the nuclear tests we can derive the electric power. Worldwide, the total electricity came from the nuclear tests is 18% where as India is able to produce only 2% USA produced, 1,00,000 mega watts of atomic electricity through its 109 atomic electric reactors. Hence it is essential to make the entire population of India exposed to developments on International politics so that these 100 crore democrats will elect a wise government which can honor and respect the dignity of the nation in the world.

Conclusion

Political remedies are to be taken in the service sector of political services.

* Educational Industry
* Defence Services
* WTO
* Ministry of Commerce and Industry
* Research and Consultancy Services.

THE CHALLENGE OF MANAGING CONFLICT WITHIN AND ACROSS THE BORDER

Karimullah and Dr. P. Balaji Prasad***

Introduction

This paper presents the challenges of managing intra and inter state conflicts in the form of defence, security and internal stability related problems. It is divided in two parts first challenge across the border and second challenge within the country.

Meeting the Challenge Across the Border

According to Prof. Rajan Harshe who edited the book "Intra and Inter State Conflicts in South Asia", South Asia over the year has become a theatre of diverse kinds of conflict. These conflicts in their turn are the by products of unresolved and ongoing ethnic, regional, ecologial, linguistic and border related tensions within the states as well as between the States of South Asia.

Most distinguished former military men expressed their views at a seminar organised by the Leslie Sawhney Programme on Sunday at Mumbai on December Third 2001 on "India's Security Strategy - Historical Lessons and Future responses".

According to this India should be on its guard and not lulled by the present tranquility and peace on the border and line of control. Md. Ali Jinnah - an enigma - Ambivalent Wizard - He is dead - his inglorius ghost -stalks Pakistan still with democracy gagged and

---

* MBA student 2000-02.

** Associate Professor, School of Business Management, S.V.University, Tirupati.

thugged. The historic blunder was committed and the victims of partition are still reaping the bitter harvest of that seed of hatred sown by Jinnah. The blood, sweat, toil and tears suffered by the numberless people of South Asia, loss of life, human rights of which history has rarely parallel.

According to Vice Admiral Manohar Awati, History was replete with examples which supported the fact that the Indian mindset was not comfortable with hard military and security decision. The Indian rulers have shown little inclination to grasp the concept of national security and majority of our parliamentarians are ignorant of the subject.

Lack of state security and economic strategy was India's Achilles heel according to HD. Moddie noted scholar. The rulers in New Delhi were not realisitic in understanding history and contemporary International relations what they meant to Indian State.

On China

China has been building new roads in Tibet leading to the Indian territory and improving the existing one, even while laying a railway line to facilitate movement of larger number of troops and their maintenance in the forward areas. The Chinese working for total supremacy in Asia had found India to be only rival in the race. Though they are already leading in many areas. But now they want time so that their economic development progressed and their military strengthened. Maj. Gen. D Souza who thought that Chinese might wait till 2007 when they will be hosting olympics. China was working for having an airbase in Myanmar and Bangladesh. According to Lt. Gen. K.S. Brar who maintained that the Chinese need not take any road to India and they could easily exploit the unrest in the North East. He called for sustained and proactive measures to settle the differences. he blamed the rulers of past, and present for the disunity and disaffection and alienation of the local people. This is the time for them to show what the good governance is about. The fault is lying in New Delhi.

Outlining the geopolitical situation around India that the country was surrounded by "Green Crescent" and while all SAARC countries bordered India among themselves they did not have any common border. No matter whether a civilian or military government ruled Pakistan the neighbour would remain inimical to the Indian security interest for it thought that India could be wrecked and fragmented that would serve its national interests.

Ideological, economic and social security should become an integral part of the security doctrine of the States of the region as military security in the region has more or less reached a saturation point.

Meeting the Challenges from Within

With regional parties at the helm the demand for greater political autonomy for the states often clashes with the desire to have a strong and stable government at the centre. No federal system thrives exclusively on constitutional and institutional arrangements, guaranteed rights, judicial protection and efficiency of the bureaucracy. Federalism implies political accomodation of a heterogeneous people. It is a sort of political gregariousness, a faith in the political values and the will to live together called political culture. Federalism at the moment stands at the cross roads in India.

Siege of parliament

In terms of scale or number of casualities, it is far from being the worst terrorist attack India had suffered. But in terms of purposes or sheer audacity of the choice when the outrage was perpetrated, there are clearly no parallels.

The bloody siege of Parliament represents an attack on the citadel of the very symbol of India's democracy. The attack was conducted at a time when the sizable number of the country's top political leadership was present in Parliament house; the cataclysmic potential of such an attack is mind boggling.

The act of brutality committed within the four walls of the parliament complex is an ugly reminder of the extreme vulnerability of India. Even its most secure and fortified places to the menace of terrorism, particularly the suicide attacks.

Parallels have been drawn with the attack on the Jammu & Kashmir assembly a few months ago and attention has been directed to the Al-queda plot to attack parliament house. The attack demands immediate responses first to radically upgrade the existing security arrangements inside parlament second to determine the identity of the organisation behind the attack and bring the conspirator to book.

Conclusion

South Asia over the years has become a theatre of diverse kinds of conflict. These conflicts are the byproducts of unresolved and ongoing ethnic, regional, ecological and linguistic and border related tensions within the states as well as between the States of South Asia.

Ideological, economic and social security should became an integral part of the security doctrine of the States of the region as military security in the region has more or less reached a saturation point.

Federalism at the moment stands at the crossroads in India. Federalism implies political accommodation of a heterogeneous people.

Siege of parliament represents an attack on the citadel of symbol of democracy. The attack demands immediate responses first to radically upgrade the existing security arrangements, secondly to expedite bringing the conspirators to book.

The Indian constitution is likely to face further amendments in the near future and the demand for presidential form of government is likely to gain momentum with more and more individuals and political parties getting war or the operation of Indian constitution.

References

Sudhir Jacob George, Review of Theatre of conflict, Intra & Inter State Conflicts in South Asia ed. by Prof. Rajan Harshe, Nov. 28, 2001.

Krishna Iyer, Review of the Man who divided India Ed. by Rafiq Zakaria, Nov. 21, 2001.

Arun Kumar Bhatt, 'India should be watchful' Dec. 4th 2001, The Hindu.

Editorial on "the ugly terror strikes again" Dec. 14, 2001, The Hindu.

ECONOMIC POLICY IMBALANCES - SLUMP AND SLIDE - THE CASE OF IT & TOURISM

Madhava Krishna Reddy and Dr. P. Balaji Prasad***

The paper highlights the major reasons why service sector has grown on its own in the economy. Neglect of economy priorities resulted in imbalances in agriculture and industrial sectors and growth of service sector almost in an unhealthy manner at the cost of rural and small scale sectors while paying more attention on urban areas and urban biased services. Free information and communication facilites have resulted in increased complexity of governance and need for strong police state.

The bias of the State is much more vivid and glaring in no other than in the service sector of IT and Tourism Industry as can be seen from the below. The World Travel and Tourism Council's (WTTC) Tourism Satellite Accounting Research (TSAR) which measured tourism's share in the national economy in 160 countries over the last 10 years has found a global shift away from Europe to Asia and the far East in the last 10 years.

Indian Tourism Industry

India can become number one in tourism: The world travel and tourism council has predicted that India could have been number one tourist destination in the world with demand growing at 10.1 per cent per annum. But what is required: Prioritising Tourism and Investment in the sector. The government's response in the form of government spending on tourism is 153 rd in the world at 0.9 per cent. China spends 3.8 of its budget on tourism and rates fifth in

---

* MBA Student 2000-02.

** Associate Professor, School of Business Management, S.V. University, Tirupati.

receiving the largest tourist arrivals with 31.2 million after France, US, Spain and Italy. India gets only 2.6 million tourists on an average per annum.

TSAR developed a measure in terms of share in personal and business consumption, government. expenditure on tourism, capital investment total demand for tourism and travel, share in GDP & employment generated both in the industry as well as in the economy.

According to WTTC the demand for travel and tourism had to be satisfied by matching supply. Failure to meet the demand would lead to overcrowding of existing facilities, shortage in basic infrastructure, environmental imbalance, driving away of Foreign visitors and excessive outgo of domestic traffic. The WTTC study showed that while outbound tourism had grown over last 10 years from 76 million to 179 (with the boom in the economy), the inbound traffic has remained almost static at 2.6 million arrivals.

The only way to counter the threat of outbound tourism was to develop and promote tourism within the country to make India competitive internationally as a destination. The potential of toruism's contribution was more than realised. Given the breathtaking range of tourist products, tourism could become the largest industry in India, the report said.

The WTTC said that the infrastructure dictated by the domestic demand would also serve to attract foriegn visitors and to make India internationally attractive, changes were necessary in the visa regime, the aviation sector, taxation policies and marketing initiatives. Business travel, and tourism were also similarly poised to grow in the coming decade, but because business travel had unique features of high spending, requirement of services, higher expectations, world class standards, telecommunications, efficient and convenient travel schedules, the public sector must assess this growth and plan its services and policies to serve the growing segment.

India's comparative advantage was its mystical attraction with its ancient civilisation and culture with a history of going back to 50,000 years, the report said. India had much to by offer by way of spiritual and mental rejuvenation. Other attractions were the world's highest mountains, miles of coastlines with excellent beaches, tropical forests and wild life, desert, safari, lagoon backwaters, ancient monuments, forest and palaces, adventure tourism and the Taj Mahal. The tropical forests in Uttaranchal, Madhya Pradesh, Karnataka, Orissa, Kerala and Rajasthan could be developed into major tourist attractions.

India's Strategic Advantage

Being located virtually midway between Europe and the far east, Europe and South East Asia/Australia, India had a strategic advantage. Since all international flights have to out of necessicity fly over India, the country could develop one or two international airports with the best of transit facilities inducing passengers to break journey and thereby facilitating visitor export.

The report suggested that the Indira Gandhi International Airport "which today ranks amongst the worst in the world" could be converted into a modern state-of-the art airport with luxury lounges visa on arrivals, hotels and restaurants, extended shopping, sports, and entertainment facilities and superfast corridors to Agra and Jaipur.

Indian IT Industry

The Indian IT Industry must have a **product focus** and look at establishing a local market to recover the ground it has lost in the wake of a slowdown in the American economy. Said Mr. Allan L. Fisher President and CEO of Carnegie Technology Education, an arm of the Carnegie Melon University. Fisher said the Indian IT industry felt the severity of US slow down the most since it focussed on **contract services.** IT as industry must be seen more than just services. The problem of Indian IT Industry was confounded as it had **an Export oriented focus,** worse still it had an American-Centric thrust. In his reckoning the severity of down turn was felt most by the Indian IT companies because they grew rapidly during the up turn.

It is time that industry migrated towards product direction and established domestic market. The fact that it acquired visibility in the global market place spoke of its traffic achivements. On the current slowdown: he felt it is temporary - IT is fundamental to all areas of Commerce. Even to any emerging technolgoies be it biotech or new energy processes. The real opportunity in IT according to experts come from IT enabled services, also called business process outsourcing (BPO) activities, covering a range of activities such as call centres, transcriptions, geograhic information system and even consulting. Today people world wide have realized that getting a person on site is much costlier than having the job done in India itself. India would be a major force to reckon with in the field of IT enabled services.

Analysis and Discussion

Firstly, the IT industry has been encouraged unduly. There is a sudden shift of emphasis in the last one decade by the government and its agencies which has resulted in present predicament for the manpower entered into the Industry. Secondly, the other service sectors, which would have long term potential with a great employment potential and other long term benefits leading to strengthening of the economy like tourism industry as one of the prime service sector have been neglected can be seen. As a result such a sector lagged much behind many countries. Even a small island country like Maldives has been immensely benefitted by a planned emphasis on their most potential sector like tourism in their economy to their advantage. We in India with a short sighted and biased apporach have sacrificed our long term interest for the benefit of few of the categories of people. The result is self evident in both the sectors is only the tip of ice berg of our service economy with such imbalances produced by the ruling elites whims and fancies.

Conclusion

In globalising world, the quest for generation of wealth than promotion of human welfare given prcedence by the rulers of the day. Had there been a change of mind if not heart preparing the national economy to the global opportunities would have been proactive rather than reactive. The priorities set and policies pursued by the government towards export oriented information technology industry, which was intially bitten by Y2K bug to the neglect of most potential and promising industry like tourism sector, are just the pointers to cite expediency prevailing over the government approach. The above two service sector industries illustrates the gaps that need to be plugged in the policy making aspects of government in the macro economic management and political dimensions of it.

References

India can become number one in Tourism, August 17, 2001, The Hindu, p.11.

Mr. Allan L. Fisher, Carnegie CEO Tips to Indian IT Industry, August 19 2001. The Hindu p.13.

Krishna Iyer, A tryst betrayed November 11, 1999 The Hindu.

Venkat Kumar S., Strategic Management - IT enabled services industry, August 24, 2001 Ph.D. proposal seminar to SV University, Tirupati.

SHOULD WE BE GOVERNED BY IRON RULE OR THUMB RULE?

Ramasastry* and Dr. P. Balaji Prasad**

This paper highlights the importance of political environment for society in general and economy in particular. It also reviews the changing political environment for the benefit of citizen and economy. The paper examines whether the evolution of politics since Independence for better or worse? If certain cues from the happenings taken into consideration for the economy.

Introduction

Despite the reservations expressed by George Washington & Roussey about the truthfulness of democracy through indirect and representative politics through party system and party politics, the survey of modern International Political Scene will reveal that political parties have come to stay.[1] According to Duverger they are a necessity of the democratic system and never more than today because the modern party system in modern. It is the twentieth century mechanism designed to solve the problem of how to bring the people the new mass of voters into political community.[2] In India too even though some of the noblest spirits like Gandhi, Jayaprakash Narayan expressed in favor of partyless democracy[3] party based democracy has become a reality due to practical and historical reasons.

The world politics conjures up to the common man often on the wrong side of its traditional cousins namely constitution, caste communalism, crime and corruption from the infamous politician's tool kit. However there appears a change now to see on the right side some of its new cousins in the eyes of citizen as a hope on horizon. A few of them may include culture, violence, election,

* MBA 2000-02.

** Associated Professor, School of Business Management, S.V. University, Tirupati.

cinema, backwardness and women to capture some of the issues and trends of the Service Economy from the discipline of business management.

Culture and Politics

Indians in all walks of life gained more exposure to the world these last 10 years than in the 40 years before that. An imagination for good quality of life as a result of exposure which is a collective social activity. it may not always lead to an action, it is a prelude to action. This cultural shift also owes its existence to the changing politics of India. There has been a churning in caste politics and the rise of Mayawati and Mulayam are visible symbols of it. Laloo's success sends out the signal that "to reach power you do not have to become like them" and wear a gentleman's dress. It's okay to come riding on your cow.

Violence and Politics

It should not be mistaken even with the increasing frequency of criminals, communalisation, and corruption political means are leading to increasing incidence of violence in politics. Because politics is about countrolling violence and relegating it to margins. Accoring to English political philosopher Thomas Hobbes, violence is the hypothetical pre-political and pre-social state of nature and is so immediately threatening and vicious that any kind of political order that can contain it is better than none.

A Leviathan vested with all power by his constituents is preferable to the anarchic state of nature when individuals possess absolute liberty. Recognising the soul destroying potential of violence, people opt to give up their liberty in return for security of life and property. Correspondingly Leviathan cedes all claims to loyalty and obligation if he violates the basic premise of the contract provision of security and the control of violence.

After all, politics is the art of negotiation as the technique of neturalising tensions, as the way of creatively engaging with the aspiratiosn of ordinary people as the art of achieving what seems to be impossible, has been swept aside in favor of naked and unashmed use of violence.

Election and Politics

In 1996 parliamentary elections unique mandate is given by Indian electorate in the post independent Indian political hitory.3 It signifies the end of the one party dominance and beginning of a new coalition era in parliamentary democracy. The mandate therefore makes the political parties to sit up and introspect rather seriously vis-a-vis electorate whom do they serve, by adopting to reduce the gap between what they promise to what they deliver. With the maturity of democracy the party managers must realise that there is need to formulate people friendly policies in the context of rising expectations of people. People cannot be taken for granted any more.[4]

Cinema and Politics

Noted film maker and fiction writer Mr. Randor Guy has said that film actors proved to be better rulers and administrators compared to their non-film counterparts. "They are intelligent in turning events in their favour."

Delivering a talk on "Cinema and Politics" organised jointly by Madabhushi Ananthasayanam Institute of Public Affairs (MAIPA) and the local branch of the Indian Institute of Public Administration IIPA, he showed NTR and MGR to drive his point. Mr. Guy recalled the situation when NTR climbed the ladder of his political career as fast as he could with the catch word 'Atmagouravam' or self-respect, when Rajiv Gandhi was said to have insulted the then CM. Anjaiah. Finding that the congress was at its low ebb at that time, he turned the situation to his favour, thus proving his intelligence. The craze among the film goers and belief in the minds of his fans that NTR was the re-incarnation of Lord Rama and Krishna also played a role in determining the Assembly Poll results at that time as he cleverly encashed his reputation.

Former Tamil Nadu State Chief Minister MGR as a film hero in his pre-political period during his meeting with congress leader Kamaraj had to earn his displeasure, when the later burst out that, "Cinema people are loafers" This comment which spread wild fire turned the wheels of the TN politics a full circle and made MGR the CM. It can thus be said they are intelligent in turning events in their favour. Both NTR, MGR were good actors, orators, kind-hearted both used film techniques like dialogues, lyrics and titles to influence the viewers. The story of Jayalalita in TN much recently. The latter could turn the tide in her favour and even at her estranged relationship with the party at the centre and at the height of legal controversy.

CN Annadurai the founder of DMK also had a celluloid background as he was a film script writer. He was very successful in turning national level events to his favour though it amounted to whipping up of emotions on North South Divide. His dig at the centre when Prime Minister Nehru inaugurated Bhakra Nangal Project in Punjab and Sindri Project in Pune evoked a roaring response thus making possible to tilt the vote balance.

Backwardness and Politics

In the recently held seminar in Tirupati on the theme of development of Rayalseema, Politicians were balmed for the backwardness of the region. It is observed in this connections that education was the prime factor which could give a thrust to development of the underdeveloped area ridden with factions, perennial drought and naxalism. It is pointed out that six out of twelve Chief Minsiters who ruled the State were from this region. Except Chittoor the other districts of the region Cuddapah, Kurnool, Anantapur did not see any kind of progress because of person or a group of persons who were wielding the stick and dictating terms even to district administration.

Women and Politics

Is the Chief Minister of Bihar a puppet, the strings being pulled by her predecessor and husband? Or is she making the best of a situation that she had no role in creating? Is there more to this woman that than most people assume?

Nature of persons: Former Chief Minister Laloo Prasad Yadav deliberately plays to the gallery, using his assumed role of State jester to cock a snook at those, especially outside. "The Republic of Bihar," who underestimate his political prowess. His wife and present Chief Minister Rabri Devi does not. In sharp contrast to her seemingly irrepressible husband, she continues to retain the sober demeanour and quiet dignity that were evident from the moment she was catapulated into public life four years ago.

Woman the under dog: Her husband's colourful image and reputation, her sudden and controversial appointment as Chief Minsiter, her political inexperience and lack of preparedness for her new role, together with her State's obvious and despearate need for good governance, may have all contributed to the derisive and dismissive manner in which she has been dealt with in the public realm. That she is a woman -- and one who makes no bones about the fact that she is a wife, mother and housewife above all -- has clearly not helped her to be taken more seriously.

She has often been referred to as "Laloo's seat- warmer" and seen as a mere puppet on a string pulled by her wily husband. She has been widely ridiculed for having produced a "brood" of nine children in a State notorious for its galloping population growth rate. Only rarely has she been acknowledged and appreciated for -- if nothing else - the serene self -- confidence that has enabled her to remain true to herself and resist the temptation to reinvent herself in some body else's image. Forgotten now it seems is the fact that a few months after she took over the government in 1997 she was described as "Bihar's most dignified Chief Minister in living memory" by India Today. The gender stereotypes implict in those descriptions would not have bothered Rabri Devi. Even today she is unabashed about her wife-mother housewife image.

Conclusion

The challenge before today's democratic government is to change the concept of governance. For the people "government represented by officials and greedy people's representatives as alien, inflexible and corrupt. It is possible to change this image through induction of trustworthy people's representatives as an interface between the faceless government machine and voiceless majority of the ignorant mass of voters this calls for making it binding on the part of the political parties capable of functioning in the positions of power professionally yet democratically.

References

1. Sirsikar V.M. Fernandes, L. Indian Political Parties, Meenakshi Prakashan, p.4.
2. Duverger Maurice, Political Parties, Mathew & Co. Ltd., Third edn. reprint 1978 p.viii.
3. Pran Chopra, The brighter side of 1996, The Hindu p.12. 25 May 1996.
4. Uday Pareek and T.V. Rao, Designing and Managing Human Resource Oxford IBH 1981. p.1.
5. News report, Politicians blamed for backwardness of Rayalseema, p.3. The Hindu Sept. 9th 2001.
6. News report, Men from films prove to be better rulers, July 19, 2002. The Hindu p.3.
7. Ammu Joseph, Rabridevi revisited, profile, Sunday Magazine p. V., Sept 9th 2001. The Hindu.
8. Rama Bijapurkar & Titoo Ahlawalia in Business Today Anniversary Issue 2002. p. 190.
9. Neera Chandhoke, Politics as violence, June 1, 2002 Central Article, The Hindu.

SECTION - III

INDIA SERVICE ECONOMY UNDER MACRO/MICRO SOCIO-CULTURAL IMPACT

Overview

Though the third section has only two papers to boot, the section highlights the social-cultural dimension of the service economy. Paper two examines the changing trend of Indian cinema in particular Telugu cinema under the influence of the new economy. The salient features of the change involves film making going digital while making the producers more empowered rendering the thinking revolutionaries of the early 80s redundant. With a narrative course without story accent on glitter and gloss - enjoy the life as the credo with no social coherence, no economic rationale and no political responsibility. The first paper under the section deals with changing social reality for worse-changing relationship of individual with outside world, the influence of market related culture of consumerism and the rise of religiousity and communalism contributing to the myopic vision of man who is losing peace of mind. With a prescription for cultural action in order to create conditions of life free from domination, to bring back the individual into social fold under creative and constructive realm. Underscoring the role of spiritualism as the essence of the action.

RELIGION, SPIRITUALISM, MATERIALISM AND TERRORISM--AN AGENDA FOR CULTURAL ACTION

N. Anil Kumar and Dr. P. Balaji Prasad***

(This paper attempts to bring out the impact of man's material progress through the economic development in his socio-cultural well being. The authors feel that the service economy is affected by culture and counter cultural activities. They also stress the spiritualisation and counter cultural actions are necessary to ward off the twin threats posed by globalisation, communalisation in the service economy).

Introduction

Man is losing peace of mind. The spiritual head of Tibet, Dalai Lama, has blamed material progress sans spiritualism for the increasing conflicts in the world and said such technological sophistication sometimes brought in its wake, fear, suspicion and destruction.

Inaugurating a three-day national seminar on "Buddhism" organized by the Salar Jung Museum in Hyderabad on December 17th, he said modern technology and sophistication of the human mind bred negative human emotions that were leading to destruction and disaster. Such material progress needed to be tempered with a warm heart, compassion and respect for each other's traditions. Spiritualism within oneself eliminated such negative emotions.

He said while basic principles like, love compassion, mutual respect, forgiveness, tolerance were common to all shades of spiritualism, religions and teachings, the difference was in philosophy. The Governor, Dr. C. Rangarajan, said the Dalai Lama had been tirelessly working to propagate Buddha's message of truth, non-violence and compassion

* MBA 2000-02.
** Associate Professor, School of Business Management, S.V.University, Tirupati.

to a world which is becoming increasingly fractious and prone to violence. He said religion acts on the people at various levels, but the ultimate tests by any relation was the impact it had on the daily lives of people. it was here that the Buddhism scored over other religions by placing emphasis on the noble "Eightfold path", which led to the promotion of ethical conduct, mental discipline and wisdom.

At the root of all tensions that prevailed in the world today, lay hatred, intolerance and ill will, he said. Nations have come closure measured by the time it takes to travel. But has this "end of geography" or "death of distance" brought people closer together in their minds?

The spiritual message of Sri Satya Sai on his birthday. He advised man to redeem faith in himself and make an attempt to know the love and divnity and inturn attain peace of mind. Discourse delivered in the Sai Kulwanth Hall in Prashanti Nilayam called the man to develop spirit of love and divinity and spread it all. He said joy and sorrow were not permanent but the man had to find his origin. Then alone he would attain peace of mind.

If man had no faith in himself he would never relish the life, that was why man must have faith in himself always. Become master of mind, then you are not affected by anything. Fathom the sorrow with equal mindedness by treating the joy and sorrow alike, then you will get the ultimate happiness love and divinity. Self-respect was the noblest of properties of man as it was uniform among all irrespective of rich and poor. The man who had self respect would respect others and get it back from others. So man should develop self respect in order to respect others. Saibaba termed man's experience of comfort and miseries as perversion of mind. It would happen due to dual thinking. The bliss man could attain from sadness was greater than what he would get from happiness.

Invite problems every now and then to experience the ultimate joy of love and divinity. The bliss man could get from happiness was momentary but from miseries it would be permanent. Divinity is nothing but loving everybody.

Happiness and god are not separate. They were always found in union. Emphasizing the truth and god were found everywhere. There was no difference between god and man if the latter attains divinity.

There Principles

Fear of sin, love of god and morality in life that would always bring man closer to the almightly. The Indian culture would it stray with passage of time.

Indian Social reality is fast changing; changing for the worse. The hopes of a social transformation, not bridled by external constraints, which the national liberalation movement had raised, seem to be dwindling everyday. As Antonio Negri and Michael Hart, authors of a widely discussed work on globalization, have recently observed, imperalism is dead, but the empre is forming before our eyes.

Globalization

The name of the empire is globalization, which seeks to subjugate the world for the interest of transnational capital. The 'virtues' of the new 'empire' and the paradigm of development they offer from the hegemonic public discourse in India today. The message of the 'empire' is the market transmitted though the cultural network, of which the implicit purpose is the creation of a modern, read capitalist, taste and the making of an uncritical mind. It promises to usher in modernity and affluence, but actually promotes social obscurantism and cultural backwardness.

Communalism

No other phenomenon is a stronger statement of obscurantism and backwardness than communalism, reinforced in recent times by the cultural crisis that the 'empire' has generated.

Communalism and globalization have thus become mutually complementary with commonly shared interest. The recent development in the wake of the Afghan war have established beyond doubt the uncritical acceptance of the 'empire' by the Indian ruling classes. Any attempt at social engineering is, therefore, a multi-pronged effort-cultural, ideoloical and political-which should aim initially to change the nature of the hegemonic public discourse. Cultural ation is at the centre of this effort.

Cultural action is an intervention in daily life, directed to the transformation of social consciousness. It is not a performance or spectacle based on various art forms, though they are not ruled out as a means of communication. Instead, it is conceived as a continuous social activity capable of activting the 'cultural' in everyday life. It is a form of intervention directed towards the radicalization of civil society. The purpose of cultural action, therefore, is to foreground the human agency for what Antonio Gramesi has described as unsettling the existing equlibrium' in order to create conditions of life free from domination. A rearticulation of cultural action, both in form and content, is called for, to effectively interrogate the existing social conditions. Such a rearticulation should bring continuous intervention in daily life practices.

Factors, which impede such a cultural action

However, the contemporary social and ideological conditions are beset with several factors, which impede such a cultural action. Three of them, which are of particular importance, deserve some eleboration; the changing relationship of the individual with the outside world, the influence of the market and the related cultural of consumerism and the rise of religiosity and communalism. All the three contribute towards a myopic vision insensitive to the social reality.

The changing relationship of the individual with the outside world

The social problems are increasingly becoming alien to the concern of the individual. Society is no more in the mind of the individual, possibly because of the competitive spirit fostered by capitalism. The personal has replaced the public and as a consequence the problem of the self has become the most serious concern. The individual is more and more involved in seeking solutions to his own crisis that he has become insensitive to the social good. This is in contrast to the past when during the Renaissance and Nationalism movements, the individual surrendered the self for common public interest. The presence of socially sensitive individuals who could promote cultural action in the public sphere is therefore becoming scarce.

The influence of the market and the related culture of consumerism

The crisis of the individual has been further deepened by the changes in the material life during the last few years. The character of the market has changed dramatically and globalization has opened up the possibility of unprecedented access to consumer goods. The transnational capital has created a new market and along with that a new culture which the individual imbibes not by his choice; it is forced upon him. as in advanced capitalist societies, the market is becoming so irresistibly powerful that consumerism tends to be the ideology and culture of the masses, creating material aspirations not commensurate with their real situation.

The main agenda of cultural action

The main agenda of cultural action is to bring the individual, who is increasingly being alienated, into the social fold through two possible areas of activity. The first, the creative realm and second, the constructive realm.

The creative realm

Using art forms for social and political campaigns has been a long tried method, going back to the peirod of the anti-colonial struggle. In contemporary India, several art forms in their public campaings. SAHMAT, for instance, has conducted its campaign against communalism very effectively during the past several years by using painting, music, street plays and so on as means of communication. Considerable work by several organisations, though uncoordinated, is taking place in this field, which over the years has made some impact on social consciousness. A drawback of these effort is that they are sporadic in nature and do not constantly engaged the attention of the masses.

The constructive realm

In contrast, the constructive realm has the potential to provide for continuous activity and this make cultural action an integral part of everyday life. Gandhiji had set an admirable and effective example through spinning, Khadi and the organisation of life in the ashrams and turning into symbols of mass mobilization.

The creation of cultural communities

The main feature of cultural action through the constructive realm is the creation of cultural communities. Two types of communities are possible imagined communities and local communities.

Imagined communities

The imagined communities internalize certain common values and interests and their members relate themselves to a common source of origin.

The educational intervention of Ekalavya in Madhya Pradesh is good example, as through an educational experiment it has created a cultural sharing certain common ideas, even if the members do not act together or communicated with each other in a formal manner. Ekalavya has brought into being an abiding but invisible cultural community drawn from the influence of an organization working in a selected field.

Local communities

The local communities function at an entirely different level. Not because they address local issues, but because of the manner in which they function. What they do is to localise for action issues which are universally valid. Environmental issues which underline man-nature relationship, for instance. Environmental degradation is a problem that has already alarming dimensions and is likely worsen in countries like India in the conditions of globalziation. Both at the level of social sensitisation and for evolving alternative strategies local communities can be constructed around environmental issues. The local is likely to generate greater interest to people rather than something distant. Yet, environmentalism being a common problems present in almost every part of the country, the local become part of a larger whole. The local community, however, is not an organisation, but a collectivity, of which the participation is not through membership but through activity, which is limited to the intervention at the local level. Innumerable such areas can be identified according to the specificities of each locality. The local communities, however, are not isolated communities, but are to be located within the larger cultural, social and political ambience.

The significance of local communities is the posssibilities they offer for continuous engagement, a necessary condition for the creation of social consciousness. the agitprop methods that are generally adopted by the political parties and their front organisaitons are limited to sporadic or spontaneous action, which does not have an abiding impact. Moreover, their reach is generally limited to their own followers and in most cases they do not even generate sympathy among others. Although demostrative actions are necessary part of democratic struggles it is time to reconsider their effectivness in the prevailing social situation. In constrast, the work of the local communities is silent and unobtrusive, providing a platform for people to forge bonds of solidarity around chosen issues.

To radicalise civil society and initiating counter cultural action

The main purpose of cultural action is to radicalise civil society. Towards that end, the preliminary step is to de-ideologise civil society from the influence of globalization and the logic of communalism. A powerful and influential public discourse in favour of both is current in Indian society.

Creation of a counter culture through constructive undertakings

The purpose of cultural action is, therefore, to influence and change the character of the public discourse in civil society. It cannot be achieved thorugh rejection, resistance and opposition alone. All the three are necessary, but not sufficient. What is required is the creation of a counter culture through constructive undertakings, which would alter the existing public discourse generated by globalization and communalism. This can be achieved only though the revitalisation of indigenous cultural resources, remoulding them to face the contemporary challenges, at the same time without being obscurantist and revivalist. The formation of local communties with the ability to intimately intervene in the cultural life of the people is the necessary beginning for the creation of counter culture.

Inevitable conflict with the dominant social and political power

Implicit in the counter is the inevitable conflict with the dominant social and political power. Such a conflict has both local and national dimensions. Locally, the engagement of the communities will be in a variety of cultural issues, ranging from access to water and firewood to claims over shared history and tradition. The local also extends to the national as it impinges upon the way the national is constructed. The culture the local commuities invoke draws upon the plural tradition variously articulated in different localities. Such emphasis on the local, without being localized, is likely to be a major challenge to the emerging tendencies of homogenisation which both communalism and globalisation, though in entirely different ways, seek to realise.

Conclusions

1. Man is losing peace of mind with material progress sans spiritualism.
2. At the root of all tensions lay hatred, intolereance and ill will.
3. Indian society, rich in diversity, is polluted by twin evil trends of globalisation and communalism.

4. Cultural action is intended to radicalize civil society and initiate counter culture to deideologise to reduce the impurity to tolerant levels.

References

Dalailama "Material Progress Sans Spiritualism is futile" The Hindu Dec. 18 2001.

Saibaba on his birthday message (p.156) Nov. 24th 2001 The Hindu.

K.N. Panikkar: An Agenda for cultural action 1 & 2 January 9th & 10th 2002 The Hindu.

THE FUTURE OF INDIAN AND TELUGU CINEMA UNDER THE NEW ECONOMY

Sriram and Dr. P. Balaji Prasad***

Introduction

Firstly the paper reviews the past decade developments in Indian cinema. Secondly it focusses on the secrets of success and failure and its analysis with reference to Telugu cinema for meaningful conclusions.

Indian Film Industry

A film critic can be heard mournfully asking as to what happened to those simple, yet revolutionary, narrators of the early 1980s like Bharatiraja, Balu Mahendra, Bhagyaraj, Mahendran, Rudriah or R.C. Sakthi, and somebody replies that television, big budget movies and digital technology have driven them all into oblivion.

Virtually no film is shot in order that is finally presented on the screen, which means that the actors and the technicians have to rely entirely on the director and hope that the film will ultimately make sense when put together on the editing table. The production of cinema was therefore vitrually in the digital domain from day one although it recorded itself on a filmstrip or videotape, which is actually in the analog domain.

In film making today, going digital is the Buzz word. But is it really superior to existing technology? What has gone wrong with Indian cinema is almost parallel with what has gone wrong with the

---

* MBA 2000-02

** Associate Professor, School of Business Management, S.V.University, Tirupati.

bizarre bubbly world of information technology called the "New Economy". It spelt out a narrative course with no social coherence, no economic rationale, and with absolutely no political responsibility.

Coming back to the world of Indian cinema this bizarre exercise has taken its own toll. Thanks to digital technology, the music director can now record a song without having to assemble the entire music band. Each musician comes in separately and plays his or her piece without any idea of the final product. In fact it is seen as an act of idiocy if a film maker insists on having all of them present to get a "good effect".

Similarly, film scripts are constructed in terms of non-sequential items -- six songs of six minutes each of which two will be in Switzerland, two in Rajasthan, one at the wedding hall and one in a blue screen studio. These items are taken care of by the choreographer. And then there will be six items of comedy by Vivek or Manivannan or Senthil. These actors take care of that.

And then there will be two fights -- one in a ship yard and other in a chemical godown. The stuntman takes care of that. That accounts for over 75 minutes of film time. The screenplay writer or the director is now called to conceive the rest of the 45 minutes of screen time. And usually the cameraman takes care of that! The Net result is a pastiche done by several craftsmen with no cohesive grammar. It is impossible for one film maker to attain mastery of sreenplay, writing, cinematography, music composing, art direction, make-up, editing, location scouting, casting and directing the final work. Being multiskilled does not make one sensitive to the complex demands of the various branches of film making. The producer feels completely empowered thanks to a whole digital "itemised" thought process. Why will he need those "thinking" revolutionaries of the early 1980s?

In essence the bane of Indian cinema today is lack of story most of its whirs merrily along plotless, with little clue to theme or even direction. Often it is a lot of color and hype or meaningless movement and frenzy peppered liberally with violence. The whole idea behind a feature film seem to have narrating a tale. An interesting idea developed into equally gripping story is sacrificed midway for their sheer gimmicks that sometimes border on sadism.

The Telugu Film Industry

1. Quality of Films

Cinema to the Telugu Film Industry appears to be an instrument of money making plus keeping somehow busy. Gone are the days when cinemas has some social relevance. The social structure is no longer there. The story and other elements like career aspects of heroines, character actors and villains paled into insignificance. It is very clear that the future of the hero alone matters. The accent now is on glitter and gloss. Less on frailties and foibles. They all seem to have one mantra i.e. enjoy the life. Hedonism is the new credo. Films increasingly made for the urban college crowd -- guys and galls with everything provided for.

II. Production Trends

A look at the Telugu Film Industry production trends during 1997-2001. There is phenomenon of straight makes versus dubbed films from other language film industry. The trends in the last five year from the table 1 reveal A marginal rise in straight remakes is observed from the table 81 to 88 only. But it is the dubbing movies gain three times in the last three years from mere 35 in year 1997 to 103 in 2001 A 300 per cent rise! There are arguments that entertainment industry being saved by the dubbings alone. No doubt in 1999 the dub movies helped theatres for an easy run. When the straight movie making registered negative growth or slump. It is the dub movies which peaked and contributed for growth and health of industry. Out of 71 films nearly half of them helped distributors and exhibitors. However in the year 2000 and 2001 the situation with regard to dubbing films reversed with regards to profits of Industry. Probably this dimension of dub films must have

Table 1: Past five years the Ratio of Dubbing Versus Straight Makes in the Telugu Film Industry

S.No.	Year	Straight makes	Doubbed ones	Total
1	1997	81	35	116
2	1998	79	45	124
3	1999	67	71	138
4	2000	79	74	153
5	2001	88	103	191

contributed the film producers and directors and other relevant public to rediscover how to make straight make films viable. In other words Film makers having the commercial success of film in mind began to make conscious effort at discover the aspects of film making appealing to the audiences.

III. Changing Success Formula

It is increasingly realised by them the year 2001 proved that star image, graphics, heavy budgets are not yielding results. Rather story, narration and music are the winning attributes of success. Another major trend ushered in the industry in the year 2000 is small budget movies. Merit has appreciation. The year 2001 witnessed A. Two super duper hits, B. Seven super hits, C. There hits; D. Another three above average; E. Ten average; (almost 1/3rd are successful). F. Others have lost With stardom and image even though producers did not lost much buyers have lost.

IV. The Success Story

The following are the details of above mentioned film categories in the year 2001 ranged from most successful to least successful; details include the films, directors, Hero and Heroine and secrets of success if any.

A. Superduper hits category (Two):

1. Narasimha Naidu: Secret of Success variety story, screen play and action oriented. Director B. Gopal, Hero Balakrishna.

2. Khushi: Secret of Success Variety story, screen play Pavan Kalyan The Hero, attained stardom who had not agreed even for a single movie is another highlight. Director in fact New Director Surya Heroine Bhoomika.

B. Super hit category (Three):

1. Youthful love story "Nuvvu-Nenu" introduced last year through "Chitram" film Uday Kiran and new actress Anita; it belongs to Teja Production. 2. Director of "Nuvve - Kaavali" Vijaybhaskar, Venkatesh as Hero of Sravanti Ravi Kishore Suresh Productions banner Nuvvu-Naaku Nachchav Family background, love story - Tivikram Sreenivas screen play gave strength. 3. "Student No.1" made NTR (Junior) as mass hero after he was introduced in "Ninnnu chudalani". New Director Rajamouli, Gajala is the heroine.

C. Hits Category (Seven):

1. Mahesh Babu and Sonali Bendre in **"Murrari" 2. Priyamina Neeku** Tarun and Sneha Balasekharan the director introduced. 3. Usha Kiran movies Sreenu Vytla directed "Anandam" Aakash and Rekha Hero and Heroine. 4. **"Preminchu"** a blind girl Suresh Productions another one. heroine Laya Saikiran Hero selected from Indian Panorama Section, 5. **"Itlu Sraavani Subramanyam". "Baachi"** director Poori Jagannadh, Raviteja Hero, love story; 6. **"Manasanta Nuvve"** Srihari acted as hero, New Director; V.N. Aditya "Chitram" pair Udaya Kiran and Rima Sen 7. Bhadrachalam directed by N. Sankar: Story based on **sports.**

D. Above average Movies (Three)

1. Rajsekhar Hero supergood films **"Simharaasi"** In B & C centres received good support; 2. **"Sampangi"** Saana Yadi Reddy

direction conflict between two faiths Music is scoring; Editor Mohan's Son Raaja Director, 3. **"Hanuman Junction"** Arjun, Jagapati Babu and Venu acted in this.

E. Average category (Ten):

1. **"Deevinchandi"** Mutyala Subbaiah director Srikanth Hero. Ushakiran movies. 2. **Eduruleni Manishi** Nagarjuna's double role as brother. 3. **Ammayi Kosam:** Meena Heroine 4. **"Ninnu Chudalani"** NTR Ushakiran Movies 5. Sarat direction Rural atmosphere, love story **"Repallelo Raadha"** 6. Upendra Hero K.N. Nageswara Rao direction. **"Raa"** 7. EVV direction venu Hero **"Veedekkadi Mogudandi"** 8. Suresh Varma direction NTR acting, "Subbu" 9. Suresh Krishna direction Chiranjeevi **"Daddy"** 10. **"Sixteens".**

F. Flop Category:

Chiranjeevi **Mrugaraju;** Venkatesh **Deviputrudu, Premato Raa;** Nagarjuna **Bavanachchadu, Akasaveedhilo,** Balakrishna; **Bhalevadivi Baasu** EVV **Mi Aaavidamidottu Maa Aavida Chalamanchidi** Krishna's own **Pandanti Samsaram** Mohanbabu's **Adhipati** Jagapathi babu **Family Circus,** Tarun Chriujallu Srihari, Evadra **Rowdy.** All the above are straight remakes.

Among dubbed:

Sreemanjunatha, and Hollywood **"Mummy"** are Okay. Kamals Heavy Movie "Abhay", K. Balachander 100th directed movie **"Paravasam"** did not do well.

V. Hero Future Oriented Industry

While Telugu film industry centred around the hero the following table 2 to 7 will reveal the nature of this phenomenon. There are at present 8 senior most heroes exist in the film industry.

Krishna tops the list of seniority with fifth rank or star image (i.e. the rank enjoyed by their overall success in the industry by the year 2001). While Chiranjeevi the third in the seniority tops the star image. Balakrishna second rank with the fourth in seniority.

Table 2: **A Profile of Telugu Heroes Based on Seniority in the Film Industry (Source)**

S.No.	Name of the Heroes (Based on seniority)	Rank enjoyed in the year 2001
1.	Krishna	5
2	Mohanbabu	6
3	Chiranjivi	1
4	Balakrishna	2
5.	Arjun	27
6.	Suman	20
7.	Rajendra Prasad	22
8.	Rajeskhar	7

Table 3 gives the next generation heroes in the industry. Venkatesh heading the table of seven heroes with third rank while Nagarjuna enjoying fourth rank stands second.

Table 3: A Profile of Next Generation Telugu Heroes in the Film Industry (Source Eenadu Article)

S.No.	Name of the Heroes (Next generation heroes)	Rank enjoyed in the year 2001
1.	Venkatesh	3
2.	Nagarjuna	4
3.	Suresh	25
4.	Chakravarthy	19
5.	Srikanth	14
6.	Srihari	16
7.	Saikumar	17

The table 4 presents the next next generation with Pavan Kalyan with 8th position Mahesh Babu 9th position. Sumath 10th position.

Table 4: **A Profile of Next Next Generation Telugu Heroes in the Film Industry (Source Eenadu article)**

S.No.	Name of the Heroes (Next next generation heroes)	Rank enjoyed in the year 2001
1.	Pavan Kalyan	8
2.	Mahesh Babu	9
3.	Sumanth	10

The table 5 gives "the latest craze" with six heroes heading the table with Udaykiran with twelth position. Last but not the least in the table Junior NTR with position Unknown.

Table 5: A Profile of Latest Crazy Telugu Heroes in the Film Industry (Source Eenadu Articles)

S.No.	Name of the Heroes (Latest craze)	Rank enjoyed in the year 2001
1.	Uday Kiran	12
2.	Saikiran	13
3.	Tarum	11
4.	Naveen	21
5.	Raviteja	24
6.	NTR	?

Yet another table gives 'still latest" with Venu leading followed by three others.

Table 6: A profile of Still Latest Telugu Heroes in the Film Industry (Source Eenadu Article)

S.No.	Name of the Heroes (still latest)	Rank enjoyed in the Year 2001
1.	Venu	18
2.	Sivaji	23
3.	Upendra	26
4.	Akash	?

Finally Table 7 gives stars with pedigree. On the top of the table it is Mr. Balakrishna NTR's son who is oldest among these type of actors to get the patronage of the pedigree yet he is the box office Superhit Hero of year 2001 with Narasimha Naidu film breaking all the earlier records. Mr. Venkatesh, Dr. Rama Naidu's son, Nagarjuna ANR's son. etc. Mr. Venkatesh followed by Nagarjuna are the most successful heroes even though 2001 does not seem to give them much. With Venkatesh having only a super hit movie "Nuv Naaku Nachchau" to his credit.

Table 7: A profile of Telugu Heroes in the Film Industry (Stars with Pedigree)

S.No.	Name of the Heroes	Relationship	Rank enjoyed	Category of Heroes
1.	Balakrishna	NTR's son	2	Oldest
2.	Nagarjuna	ANR's son	4	Next generation
3.	Venkatesh	D.Rama Naidu's son	3	Next generation
4.	Pavan Kalyan	Chiranjivi's brother	8	Next generation
5.	Mahesh Babu	Krishna's son	9	Next generation
6.	Sumanth	Nagarjuna's Nephew	10	Next generation
7.	Tarun	Actress Roja Ramani's son	11	Latest craze
8.	NTR Junior	Harikrishna's son NTR's Grand son	?	Latest craze

The third category stars are next next generation they are three stars who had high potential? better pedgree. Prime among Mr.

Pavan Kalyan Chiranjivi's brother is with tremendous action potential who had tasted a super duper hit movie among two most successful film of year 2001 called *Kushi* the other one Mahesh Babu Krishna's son *Murari* a hit Sumanth Nagarjuna's Nephew though had potential not done well. Fourth category of heroes include six they being the latest craze category heroes. Chief among them Uday Kiran with two hits *Nuvvu - Nenu* and *Manasanta Nuvve* to his credit. Others who did not do well but towards the end there appears a rising star in this category who is Mr. NTR the NTR's grandson with great potential approved on the horizon.

Conclusion

> Film making today going digital is the buzz word today in contrast to normal mental sequential analog process under the impact of new economy.

> The producer feels completely empowered without any depended on those thinking revolutionaries of the early 1980s.

> Modern cinema spelt out a narrative course with no social coherence no economic rationale and with absoultely no political responsibility.

> In particular the Telugu film industry the future of hero alone matters accent now on glitter and gloss hedonism is the credo.

References

Gautam Bhasakaran, Friday review 24th April 2001, The Hindu.

Ziya us Salam, Friday review 24th August 2001, The Hindu.

The fate of Telugu Film Heroes, Friday Review January 4, 2002. The Hindu.

Digital Technology and Indian Cinema Friday Review, Article in the Hindu, January 2002.

SECTION-IV

SERVICE ECONOMY AND HEALTH CARE SYSTEMS

OVERVIEW

Section Four focusses on service economy and its impact on health care services. The first two papers are seminar presentations while the other paper is reprint. The paper on "Marketing of health care services by Naga Padmini dwells on increasing importance of health care marketing under the impact of services marketing. Paper suggests an increased scrope for private sector participation making service with a difference against government health care organisations approach. The second paper identifies the problems that exist in the management of hospitals which till recently did not recognise the importance of professional management which have come to realize the essentiality of sustaining and optimizing their resources. The other paper included under this section is maternity care service marketing a reprint the study limits to maternity care services among many areas of healthcare because of the paradoxical situation of continued low status enjoyed by women at the macro societal level and pivotal role to be played in the family. the immediate reasons for the attention continued high infant morality maternal mortality calling for urgent and special measures on this service.

MARKETING OF HEALTH CARE SERVICES

K. Naga Padmini

An economy on the basis of its evolution can be divided into segments; primary (Agriculture), secondary (Marketing) and Tertiary (Services).

The tradition of hospitality is the pride of our nation. In some homes even today, the host will give guests what the family cannot afford or is not accustomed to having. And yet our experience of the service industry is not a good one. Each one of us his/her own horror stories of the service, government hospitals and many other service industries. We will be pleasantly surprised if we get good service particularly from government institutions.

Services marketing is about placing the customer at the centre of our concern and develops systems, procedures, tools and techniques to ensure that the customer gets the service he wants. Services account for an increasing share of our gross doemstic product. As a nation with huge human resource, with high mental abilities, capable of being trained and with need for generating employment, this is a sector that has much to offer to India.

Service marketing made its presence felt in India some time in 1985 in the sector of financial services. Citibank took an initial lead in services marketing and Standard Chartered followed suit. The Indian computer education served as the next growth engine for service sector in India with NIIT & APTECH leading the pack. The real boost in services marketing came from marketing of cellular and telecom services. The private sector started playing a bigger role in 1990s in the development of infrastructure services such as banking, courier, telecommunications etc. services were marketed now as against sold earlier.

K. Naga Padmini is faculty in Department of Business Management Sri Padmavathi Mahila Visvavidyalaya, Tirupati.

Score card of Indian service Firms (Scale 0-5)

Advertising and Promotion Competence	3.6
After Sales service	2.3
Close links with customers	2.5
Company brand reputation	3.1
Close links with suppliers	3.0
Fin and Credit offered	2.4
Marketing info Systems	2.5
Personal selling effectiveness	3.5
Packaging	3.8

Health Care

Health care is an expression of concern for fellow human beings. It is defined as "Multitude of services rendered to individuals, families or communities by the agents of the health services or professionals, for the purpose of promoting, maintaining, monitoring or restoring health".

Health care has many characteristics.

* Appropriateness - i.e. whether the service is needed at all in relation to eventual human needs, priorities and poliices.
* Accessibility - This may be geographic accessibility, economic accessibility or cultural accessibility.
* Affordability - i.e. cost of health care should be within the means of individual and state.
* Feasibility - i.e. operational efficiency of certain procedures, logistic support, manpower and material resources etc.

The purpose of health services is to improve the health status of population. For ex. Immunization of children can influence the incidence/prevalence of particular diseases. Provision of safe water can prevent morality and morbidity from water borne diseases. To be effective, the health services must reach the social periphery, equitably distributed, accessible at a cost the country and community can afford & socially acceptable.

Health Care Delivery indicators

The following used indicators of health care delivery are

Doctor - Population Ratio

Doctor - Nurse ratio

Population - Bad ratio

Population per health centre

These indicators reflect the equity of distribution of health resources in different parts of country, and of the provision of the health care.

At the beginning of 20th century a new concept, the concept of health promotion' began to take shape. It was recognised that in both developed and developing countries, the standard of health services the public expected were not provided. The services do not cover the whole population. In developing country like India health care marketing has to play two important roles, viz.,

* To provide basic medical facilities and health coverage to the people in non-profit sector.

* To provide best medical facilities in the commercial sector.

Health Care Marketing

Health Care marketing has been assuming considerable importance in the recent times. Any one engaged in the delivery of health care has to be equipped adequately with information and still for involving the individual, client or commuunity in groups in a process of learning how to maintain the health, how and where to seek remedial action when afflicted with illness.

Health care service is in many ways different from other services and products. Here a person in need for a health care service does not know for sure where to search for relevant informaiton. He consults his family members, relations and friends first. The patients who come to a hospital generally have the old patients of that hospital referrals. This indicates that word of mouth is very critical in influencing the patients preference for a particular hospital.

Satisfied past patients of a hospital can bring more number of patients to that hosptial than a number of advertisements. In this light one organisation competing in such high pitch market has to take all possible measures to provide quality service consistently.

The principlal dimensions customers use to judge a firm's service are as follows. (Service Quality Dimensions)

1. ***Tangibles***	The physical facilities, equipments, personnel and communciation materials.
2. ***Reliability***	The ability to perform the promised service dependably and accurately.
3. ***Responsiveness***	The willingness to help patients and to provide prompt service.
4. ***Assurance***	The knowledge and courtesy of employees and their ability to convey trust and confidence.
5. ***Empathy***	The provision of caring individualized attention to patients.

Global expenditure on health care is $ 2.8 trillion, of which the US with population of 300 million account for $. 1.2 trillion. India, with one billion inhabitants, spends $ 17 billion (Rs. 73,950 crores) on health care which is just 4% of GDP. Through info tech health, delivery can be taken to remote centres and competencies can be delivered. Infotech, apart from enabling the use of tele medicine and maintenance of electronic records, would lead to paperless hospital.

Promotion

Communication plays a very effective role in health care marketing. Television with its wide network and coverage now is reaching 85 per cent of popualtion. Since a few years the prime times in television are reserved for advertising social issues like family planing, control of Aids, use of different types of contraceptive, care for the girl child and so on. Most of these commercials use the common man approach for reference group appeal. In case of health care products and services use for "common man" appeal is widely prevalent. The use of celebrities is not as effective as that of a common man. The identification with the common man is easy and quick.

Besides television, other media of promotion are to be used innovatively. In villages wall writings and hoardings, attract the attention of villages. These media can play crucial role in conveying ideas and issues. The communiation can be made effective through puppet shows and folk dances, which are more popular in rural areas. Family planning, child care and vaccination camps which held in school and village markets may attract more attention of the villages and they may feel that services are provided by experts and it motivate them to avail services immediately, as seen in the camps held by service organizations.

In a competitive market place, positioning plays a key role in the success of organisation in the absence of objectives and concentrate performance makers the image of the firms will affect their competitive standing. Many of the hospital chains are spending a lot on corporate advertising for image building. In the coming years branches of big hospital chains which will proliferate in cities and towns would compete with local professional clinics. With among a change in people's attitude increasing population towards health, apprearance and life, the health care market is going to have increased demand as well as increased competition in the coming years.

Price

Price is another important tool in health care marketing. Most of the services provided by the government are perceived to be inferior than services provided by private professionals, who charge for it. So therefore it is necessary to carry out market research to find out the exact perception of people and take corrective actions.

The up -- market group has a large discretionary income. These consumers are very careful in choosing health care services. The last decade has witnessed a health, appearance and nutrition conscious population. Indian doctors who have work experience in highly sophisiticated hospitals abroad are coming back to set up hospitals in India. Apollo Hospitals, Birla Hospital of heart surgery, Sankar Nethralaya, Madras Medical Mission, Fortis Heart Institute and many such hospitals and nursing homes have appeared in Indian health care scene.

The health care field has become very competitive. The patients of upper middle and upper income group have a wide choice to make from a number of clinics and hospitals. So, many hospitals have abandoned traditions and adopted marketing strategies to woo more and more patients to their clinics.

For example Madras Medical Mission offers free services or services at concessional rates. Services are categoriesed into three groups. The first group includes patients who are treated at concessional rates based on income. In second group the services of doctors, nurses and paramedical staff are given free of cost.

Patients pay for disposables and consumables. For third group all services and counsumables are free, patients pay for diet and transport charges. For the last two groups the income should be below Rs.500/- per month.

At Sankar Netralaya, any patient with family income less than Rs. 1750/- per month can avail free surgery. It is the first eye hospital in Asia to be awarded ISO 9002 certification.

Place

The demand for health care in rural India can be hardly understated - according to NCAER survey, prevalence rate of illness for mean is higher in the rural areas at 105.5 per 1000 population as against 98.2 in urban areas. For women it is that similar levels in urban and rural at 108.4 per 1000 population. With the services market becoming firecely competitive, service institutions have an incentive to explore the rural potential. But the road of success could be a bumpy one.

Most health care providers target their services to older individuals the segment consisting of individuals aged above 50 years is growing at a faster rater than other age groups segments. This segments offers opportunity for helath care providers. Some health care chains are focusing on institutions. As many public and private sector companies are becoming more professional and are providing better perquisites and amenities to their employees, many of them have positively responded to the proposals put forward by hospital chains in providing health coverage and other medical facilities. This is one segment which will grow faster in the coming years.

Conclusion

In India we are just entering the era of services marketing. Since we are on the threshold of services marketing era a great deal of work still needs to be done to get the marketers understand, appreciate and to perfect the art of marketing services. The size of services market is bround to increase rapidly. Like products, services will go from sophisticated metros to towns to villages - a greater variety of services and more of them. This wave cannot be stopped.

In the marketing of services more than any other marketing, you need to, want to build continuing relationships, something, which is at the very centre of marketing contept.

References

1. Dr. John Everett Park, ***Preventive and Social Medicine,*** 14th Edition.
2. Philip Kotler, ***Marketing Management,*** Millennium edition.
3. *Journal of Services Research, Vol.1* - Number 1 (April September 2001)
4. *Advertising and Marketing* Volume 12, issue 9 (August 2001).

HOSPITAL MANAGEMENT-CHALLENGES AND STRATEGIES

Dr. Talluru Srinivas
Lecturer, Department of Management Sciences
R.V.R. & J.C. College of Engineering
Guntur-522109 (A.P.)

Professor G. Prasad
Department of Commerce and Business Administration
Nagarnuja University, Guntur-522510

Dr. R. Sivaramaprasad
Dept.of Computer Science & Engg.
Nagarjuna University,
Guntur

A number of health problems required intensive medical treatment and personal care which normally are not available at the patients's home or in the clinic of a doctor.The hospital, a major social institution, offers considerable advantage to both patient and society. It is the place where a large number of professionally and technically skilled people apply their knowledge and skill with the help of world class expertise, advanced and sophisticated equipment and appliances. Thus, the first and foremost function of a hospital is to give proper care to the sick and injured without any social, economic or racial discrimination. In the past, the hospitals were set up as charity institutions, especially for poor and weaker sections of the society. Of late, the hospitals are set up with a motto to serve all sections of the society. The development of healthcare facilities is influenced not only by the opening of hospitals or healthcare centres but more so by their administrtion and management. If hospitals or healthcare centres are managed properly, there would be expansion in the medical care facilities, even with the least possible investment.

The 20th century has been a period during which hospitals have been called on to provide an ever increasing number of services to the patients, resources for the education of physicians, nurses and other members of the health team and facilities for medical research. In recent decades, significant contributions to the improvement of hospital care have come from professional nursing leaders. The development of medical science from symptom-centred to people-centred is given in the following Chart.

Development of Medical Science up to the year 2000 From the empirical era to the era of political health science

	Empirical Health era	*Basic Science Era*	*Clinical Science Era*	*Public Health Science Era*	*Political Health Science Era*
	1850	*1900*	*1950*	*1975*	*2000*
Purpose & Philosophy	Symptoms centered Empirical diagnosis and treatement of symptoms	Bacteria or disease centered Diagnosis and treatment of disease	Patient centered Diagnosis and treatment of the individual	Community centered Diagnosis and treatment of the community	People centered Diagnosis and treatment of total body politics
Education	Lectures, authoritarian instruction	Laboratory instruction	Clinical instruction besides teaching	Clinical public health instruction community side teaching	Social experience, learning, social & economic understanding Managerial, Political Psychology & Process country health programming

1. World Health Organisation, Technical report series No.122. Geneva, quoted in Mrs. A. Dalal's research thesis on hospital administration in Bombay with respect to Bombay's Municipal Teaching Hospital.
2. Goyal R.C. Handbook of Hospital Personnel Management, New Delhi, Prentice Hall International Inc. 1993 pp.3.4.

Research	Historical	Basic laboratory, Development of new tools	Clinical Development of clinical techniques	Community Development of community measurement and criteria planning technique	Social economic indices for health development subject indices for quality for life intersectoral activity process,networking, process.
Behavioural Science	Unknown	•Not needed individual activity	Ancillary social science-an adjunct to medicine specially group activity	Integrated social sciences sophsticated skills equal with public health science inter-disciplinary team activity.	Inter-related social , health economic and political, sciences, intersectoral team activity

Source: WHO World Health July, 1974, p.14. cited in Goel S.L. **Public Health Administration,** Sterling Publishers Pvt.Ltd.

Present Status of Hospitals in India

The most recent statistics available on health care is dated January, 1993 and the number of hospitals and beds catering to the population at that time and their ownership were distributed as shown in Table. 1.

Table 1: Ownership of Hospitals and Beds

Ownership	*Hospitals*	*Per cent*	*Beds*	*Per cent*
Government	4,235	31.0	3,65,696	61.3
Local bodies	344	2.5	19,520	3.3
Private and voluntary organisation	9,113	66.5	2,10,987	35.4
Total	13,962	100	5,96,203	100

It is interesting to note that the government owned one-third of the hospitals, but provided two-thirds of the total beds in the country. On the average, ignoring ownership, 1,412 persons are served by one hospital bed, and 70 hospitals provide service to one lakh persons. Between the year 1992 and 1993, growth in the number of hospitals and in the total number of beds seem to have been stagnant. The average fell in the year 1993, as compared to 1992. The average per bed in 1992 was 1,318 persons, and the hospitals were 76 per lakh population.

Growth of Hospital and Beds

In Table 2 we have presented the data on the growth of hospitals and beds over the years. They are unitised to per lakh population in order to trace their growth. During this decade, the population had an annual growth rate of 2.24 per cent. If this is taken as a reference factor, the health care facilities did not keep up with the increase in population. In all likelihood, the spurt in the number of hospitals in the year 1993 could have been from the nongovernment sector, since this was around the time that private hosptials entered into the health care sector in large numbers.

Table 2: Hospital and Beds per Lakh Population over the Years

Year	*Number Hospital*	*Per lakh Population*	*Per cent Growth*	*Number Beds*	*Per Lakh Population*	*Per cent Growth*
1988	9,803	1.2	-	5,85,889	74	-
1989	10,840	1.3	8.3	5,98,059	74	0
1990	11,079	1.3	0	6,02,490	74	0
1991	11,571	1.3	0	6,29,453	75	1.3
1992	11,174	1.3	0	6,42,103	75	0
1993	13,692	1.6	23.1	5,96,203	70	(6.7)

Basic information relating to Health of Different countries along with India can be observed from the following tables.

Table 4: Health expenditure in Some selected countries: 1990

Country	*Total Health Expenditure (Official exchange rate)*		*Health expenditure as a % of GDP*		
	Million 1990	***Percapita 1990***	***Total 1990***	***Public Sector 1990***	***Private Sector 1990***
High income countries (per capita GNP $ 9,500 and above)					
United States	6.90,667	2,763	12.7	5.6	7.0
Switzerland	16,916	2,520	7.5	5.1	2.4
Canada	51,594	1,945	9.1	6.8	2.4
France	1,05,467	1,869	8.9	6.6	2.3
Japan	1,89,930	1,538	6.5	4.8	1.6
Germany	1,20,072	1,511	8.0	5.8	2.2
Italy	82,214	1,426	7.5	5.8	1.7
Australia	22,736	1,331	7.7	5.8	1.7
United Kingdom	59,623	1,039	6.1	5.2	0.9
Hong Kong	4,060	699	5.7	1.1	4.6
Singapore	658	219	1.9	1.1	0.8
Middle Income Countries (per capital GNP between $ 750 and 9500)					
Korea Republic	16,130	377	6.6	2.7	3.9
Saudi Arabia	4,784	322	4.8	3.1	1.7
South Africa	5,671	158	5.6	3.2	2.4
Russia Fed	23,527	157	3.0	2.0	1.0
Brazil	19,871	132	4.2	2.8	1.4
Mexico	7,648	89	3.2	1.6	1.6
Thailand	4,061	73	5.0	1.1	3.9
Phillippines	883	14	2.0	1.0.	1.0
Indonesia	2,148	12	2.0	0.7	1.3
Low Income Countries (per capita GNP $ 750 and below)					
India	17,740	21	6.0	1.3	4.7
Srilanka	305	18	3.7	1.8	1.9
Pakistan	1,394	12	3.4	1.8	1.6
China	12,969	11	3.5	2.1	1.4
Nigeria	906	9	2.7	1.2	1.6
Bangladesh	715	7	3.2	1.4	1.8

Source: World Bank, World Development 1993: Investing in Health.

Table 3 Basic Information Relating to Health

Item	*Bangla desh*	*Burma*	*India*	*Indonesia*	*Maldives*	*Mongolia*	*Nepal*	*Srilanka*	*Thailand*
Population (in thousands)	80.560	32.206	625.820	143.280	140	1.555	13.136	13.970	44.160
Urban population%	8.8	20.0	20.6	18.2	11.3	46.0	4.0	22.4	15.8
Annual population growth rate	2.4	2.2	2.1	2.6	2.0	2.7	2.3	2.2	2.6
Expectation of life at birth (male)	45.8	48.6	48.6	47.0	-	64	46.0	64.2	57.6
(Female)	46.6	51.5	51.6	47.0	64	46.0	42.5	67.6	61.0
Population under 15 years%	43.5	40.5	40.1	44.1	44.9	46.2	41.2	39.0	43.7
Crude birth rate	49.5	32.9	35.2	42.9	45.3	37.1	44.7	27.6	35.0
Crude death rate	28.1	11.9	15.9	16.9	11.5	9.9	19.5	8.0	9.0
Infant mortality	153.0	77.0	122.0	137.0	106.2	80.0	M141.2 F132.0	-	-
Maternal mortality rate	30.0	1.0	-	8977	11.9	-	-	1.0	2.6
Number of doctors	6.508	5.700	154.000	15553	9	3.184	378	4.427	6.000
Population per doctor	12.379	5.409	3.884	0.64	15.444	488	34.751	3.156	7.160

Contd..

Item	Bangla desh	Burma	India	Indonesia	Maldives	Mongolia	Nepal	Srilanka	Thailand
Doctors per 10000 population	0.81	1.85	2.60	-	0.64	20.5	0.29	3.17	1.40
No.of nurses/midwives	-								
(a) professional	1749	5.878	113.455	1.683	8	-	249	6.022	11.832
(b) auxilliary	-	10.949	162.671	41.192	43	6.871	582	3.482	15.816
Population per nurses									
(a) professional	46.061	5.245	5.377	80.832	16.250	-	52.755	2.320	3.339
(b) Auxilliary	-	2816	-	3.303	3.023	226	22.570	4.012	2.647
Nurses per 10000 population									
(a) professional	0.22	1.91	1.86	0.12	0.62	-	0.19	4.31	2.83
(b) Auxiliary	-	3.56	-	3.03	3.31	44.19	0.44	2.49	3.78

Source: Arun Kumar, Encyclopaedia of Hospital Administration and Development Vol.2, Anmol Publications Pvt.Ltd., New Delhi.

The table given below presents the information about health expenditure and its percentage in GDP in some selected countries in 1990.

Challenges in the present day context

There are numerous problems before the policy makers. Some of them are explained below:

(1) **Increase in Size:** The pressure on the hospital administration has been increasing considerably over the years owing to rapid growth in the size of the hospitals over the last three decades in terms of number of doctors, number of patients, etc. There has been sizeable increase in the volume of work in the administration which was created primarily to monitor the required administrative services. However, planning that is resorted to currently in hospitals take care only of day to day operational matters. As a result making adhoc and interim arrangements becomes necessary from time to time to meet the immediate requirements.

Another problem relating to planning includes defective construction of the words. At present wards are made of brick cubicles. At present the sanitary arrangements are not sufficient to meet the needs of the patients. because of large ward size. It becomes difficult for doctors and ward sisters to supervise and co-ordinate the activities to ensure smooth functioning.

(2) **Grouping of Unrelated Activities:** The existing division of diferent working units has not been done by following established principles. The present set up in most of hospitals is based on convenience. As a result, a number of unrealted activities counstituent the working section. This has contributed to considerable delays and problems of coordination between different sections. From the structure of government hospitals, it can be observed that in most of cases it is centralised and at the same time the span is so wide where one cannot manage the operations effectively.

(3) **Lack of Clarity in Duties and Resonsibilities:** Through casual observation, it can be said that the duties, responsibilities and

roles of different categories of staff have not been clearly defined and made known to them. As a result, there is no proper distribution of work, which often results in duplication. The researcher, Goel[3] states that there are many duties which are clerical and can be performed by non-technical personnel. Most of the nursing personnel in the wrard had forty percent of their work which was non-nursing. This results in the wastage of resources.

(4) **Faulty Staffing Procedures:** A hospital should be staffed with personnel who are capable of thinking and have a perspective of developmental directions with proper orientation. The major weaknesses of our hospitals are largely related to personnel. This includes shortage of staff at higher levels, lack of specialised staff, unsatisfactory methods of recruitment, inadequate provision of in-service education. Promotions are being initiated on time-scale basis. These practices are demoralising the staff concerned. This is observed by eminent researchers earlier.

(5) **Ineffective Leadership:** Leadership stands as an instrument for bringing about stability and control to the system. But unfortunately those who become the heads of the institutions are unable to lead the people effectively towards the common goal owing to lack of knowledge of the skills which are required for a leader. It is found that often the leaders in the hospitals choose to be autocratic rather than participative, which is necessary for institutions like hospitals.

(6) **Lack of Coordination among Different Specialties:** It is observed that a Class-IV employee is deciding to which department a patient should go. For vague problems, he suggests medicine department, for head-ache and for associated complaints he suggest the E.N.T. The patient is exhausted in his trials to get the correct ticket. Moreover, the outpatient departments in the hospitals resemble conveyor belts. Patients stand in serpentine queeues and they are disposed off in a minute or two with instant diagnosis or referred to some other speciality. This is demoralsing to the patient. Apparently a high degree of team work with proper coordination is

---

3 Goel S.L. Adminisration of Outpatient and Inpatient Services, Hospital Administration and Management, Vol.2, Deep and Deep Publications New Delhi, p.19.

needed to fulfil the objectives of the hospitals effectively. Unfortunately, these factors are absent in modern hospitals which leads to lack of proper coordination.

(7) **Equipment Idled Owing to Neglect:** Though along with leading private hospitals, medical college hospitals too boast of sophisticated equipment for diagnosis and surgery, many of them are defunct owing to lack of timely and proper maintenance. Huge equipment with labels 'not working' or 'under repair' can be seen stacked for months together in a hospital. To a large extent bureaucracy too contributes to the lack of maintenance of equipment.

(8) **Absence of Public Relations Department:** At present, maintaining of public relations department is totally neglected in most of the government hospitals. There is every need to strengthen public relations department because, hospitals receive a number of complaints from the public, patients and the employees on various aspects. It is the responsibility of the Public Relations Department to sort out these grievances. Similarly, if there is no department to look after the publicity regarding various achievements and outstanding contributions made by the staff, the individual employees concerned may be demotivated.

(9) **Lack of Formal Control Mechanism:** There is no formal control mechanism currently existing in the administration of hospitals in India. The present hospital system is not providing check over the performance of the subordinates, prepare budgets but no budgetary control will be applied. They publish annual reports as a ritual every year but speak nothing about standards for measuring performance. Most of the hospitals, both government and private do not maintain proper records of the medical check-ups done from time to time.

(10) **Political Interference:** Political interfence or ministerial interference is the major curse on the working of government hospitals. Every ministry wants to retain tight control over these bodies; and no hospital was ever permitted to function as an

autonomous body in the matter of appointments of Director and higher officials to these hospitals and in policy formulation, etc. political interference is generally seen.

(11) **High Treatment costs:** Now healthcare has become sheer business. Heavy investments public limited companies have made in the health business make them profit oriented and hence they tend to unnecessarily hositalize patients. Moreover, there are innumerable instances where even for common illness the helpless patient has to undergo a list of tests After the completion of these tests a patient become poorer by thousands of rupees. For example, at a corporate hospital, a person, despite presenting classic clinical symptoms of T.B. was asked to undergo numerous tests including C.T. Scan before doing in normal, inexpensive X-ray sputum or montous test.

From the above discussion, it may be concluded that the traditional concept of managing hospitals will not serve the purpose. There is need of structural transformation. Every hospital has to come up with new and innovative ways to decrease their costs, to provide a high quality care with strong patient orientation. Now let us observe the historical background and prevailing Management Systems in sample hospital, Osmania General Hospital.

New Environment

The severe constraints, the selfish and flimsy staff relations demand an entirely new environment for the present day hospitals. Now-a-days there are many criticism levelled at the hospital industry such as pricing structure, costs and productivity. In order to survive in the ensuring decades a metamorphosis of the hospitals is imperative. Every hospital has to come up with new and innovative ways to decrease their costs while continuing to provide a high quality of care and strong patient orientation. The hospital executives have to create and maintain a competitive advantage for their hospital. Some of the strategies every hospital has to adopt include (a) Technology Leadership (b) Quality Leadership (c) Cost

Leadership. This can be achieved through application of modern Management Principles' which rationalize and standardize the services.

Suggestions for betterment of hospitals:

The following are some of the general suggestions made to the administrators of the different types of the hospitals.

(1) **Work Redesign:** Work redesign is changing the actual structure of the jobs people perform. It involves changing the work and job parameters of staff of a hospital. Presently, there is a need of structural transformation in all cadres of the employees in the hospital.

(2) **Patient Focussed Care:** Hospital organisations should develop patient focussed care for its long-term survival. Hospitals have to increase their efforts in response to drastic and rapid changes in healthcare environment. It should foucs on the co-ordination of patient care in order to achieve desired outcomes.

(3) **Managing the Quality Care:** Recent market place realities and trends have forced healthcare settings to adopt strategic orientations that stress a customer focus. Central to such strategic orientations is the effective utilisation of service quality practices and philosophies. The ultimate aim of quality is zero defects. The quality of medical care refers to the degree of excellence of the care delivered to the entire satisfaction of the patient. Quality care is not a temporary effort but should aim at continous improvement in patient care.

(4) **Quality Circles:** There is plenty of scope for application of the concept of quality circles in the hospital which is a labour intensive organisaiton. A small group of six to eight functionaries with similar or related assignments are called

quality circles. Quality circles enhance the morale of the employees, reduces costs, and provides quality medical care to patients.

(5) **Rewards and Recognition:** The workers are to be duly recognised and rewarded with suitable incentives to keep them motivated for ongoing quality management performance. Rewards are essential for excellence. Coercion and threats will do worse. So that hospitals must offer deliberate and identifiable rewards for loyalty, for participation, and for contribution to increased market share. Installing intangible rewards and monitoring rewards in a hospital is a matter of further use.

(6) **Implementation of Business Process Reengineering:** Due to financial constraints and scarce resources, now hospital has to use Business Process Reengineering (BPR) as a tool. BPR is a problem solving approach. It emphasizes on the fundamental rethinking and radical redesign of business processes to achieve dramatic improvements in critical contemporary measures of performance such as cost, quality service and speed. This tool has already given positive results in US hospitals and Canadian hospitals. So, it is one of the techniques which can be implemented in Indian hospitals.

(7) **Private Medical Insurance:** It is one of the new development in the field of healthcare sector. The General insurance corporation, one of the insurance companies in the nationalised sector started its "Mediclaim" policy in 1986. Some corporate hospitals are already having tie ups with these insurance companies. Government also should think in this direction to help the poor in providing hospital care facilities.

(8) **Creation of Public Relations and Information branch:** A pubic relations and information branch should be created. It should be headed by an officer who should be in-charge of

the co-ordination activity. The Public Relations Officer should report to the Superintendent. The creation of information and enquiry service will result in considerable saving of time of the officers in the administration who are currently spending a lot of time in attending to queries from patients, visitors, etc.

(9) **Establishment of Legal Branch:** Every year there are a number of litigation cases with patients, employees and suppliers/contractors. The hospitals are generally hiring services of 'Legal Counsel' to represent such cases before the Court. Most of there litigations arise out of absence of foolproof ordinances, statues, rules, regulations, etc. based on which decisions are taken by the authorities. At present, in most of the hospitals there is no officer in the administration to offer option on legal implications of various decisions taken from time to time and to provide all relevant information to the Legal Counsel. In the absence of this, the hospitals tend to lose most of their cases in the Courts.

(10) **Hospital Information System:** The slogan in industry and business, 'the more the information, the better the decision" is equally valied in hospital adminsitration, with of course, a major qualification that the right kind of information should be available to the administrator at the time he needs it is a form in which he can use it. Right from the formualtion of policies to their time honoured and cost, effective implementation, we need different types of information to improve the quality of decisions. Moreover, hospitals are supposed to be aware of the latest developemts in all areas and to improve the quality of services. It is, therefor,e of the utmost importance that all the hospitals should give the highest priority to develop Hospital Information System (HIS) for proper policy planning, monitoring, evaluation and feedback.

(11) **Total Cost Management:** 'Conquer your costs before they

conquer you'. This statement makes clear to the policy makes regarding its importance. Now a days, organisations are forced to cut costs for their survival. The conventional approaches to cost reduction were arbitrary and failed to improve structures and processes. As a part of Total Cost Management, one has to benchmark the costs and it should be followed by analysis. This help in differentiating the activities that add value and those that do not. Thus Total Quality Management acts as a perfect vehicle in managing total costs.

(12) Privatisation of Services: In order to facilitate the top level executives to concentrate on core areas of administration, it is suggested to privatize some of the peripheral services in the hospital such as sanitation work, clearance of garbage, house-keeping services, dietary services etc.

Conclusion

The problems of hospitals in India are many and varied. These problems can only be solved when authorities take appropriate and bold decisions without caring for troubles. Unpleasantness and threats. Further, the follow-up action is more important than taking many decisions. If one is determined to solve the problems, it may not be so very diffcult to resolve the problems of the hospitals and achieve the objectives for which they were established. From the above discussion, one can conclude that Management is an important feature of all developed nations and knowledge of management helps organise every human enteprise. It can be applied to all levels of an organisation. A sound, efficient and well planned Management programme is very important for stable and meaningful growth of patient care and development in a hospital. It is necessary that hospitals should advance from their present state of a "Semi-Handicraft' to a process of modernization in management area.

MATERNITY SERVICE MARKETING
Estimation of Demand for Maternity Care through Logit Regression

*P. Balaji Prasad**

ABSTRACT

Marketing is an important business function found to be applicable beyond the realm of business organisations. health care services can gain a lot by bringing marketing orientation in their adminsitration of services whether they are under Government or private management and for profit or nonprofit. The marketing orientation enables health administrators to serve their customers (Health seekers) better by identifying their clientele effectively, mobilising resources efficiently for their activities and becoming responsible for their performance.

However the scope of the present study is limited to maternity care services among many areas of health care services becuse among many other reasons, the paradoxical situation of continued low status enjoyed by women and their pivotal role to be played in the family and society in general. The immediate reasons being high infant mortality, maternal mortality calling for special attention on these services.

The paper therefore aims firstly at identifying the maternity care users for maternity services such as prenatal and intra-natal care by different centres such as private hospitals, Government hospitals and home deliveries especially for intra-natal care in the urban

---

* Dr. P. Balaji Prasad is faculty member in School of Business Management, S.V. University, Tirupat.

This article is a reprint from the volume titled Management Research Contemporary Issues Ed. Nirmal K. Gupta and Abad Ahmed 1994 South Asia publications Delhi, pp. 147-60.

context because of their potential for marketing orientation. Secondly to investigate the facotrs that significantly differ for the users different choices of centres. Thirdly, it constructs a model of such significant factors for the prediction of demand through regression analysis by idenfiying the intercept and slope of the factors in the equation and finally, suggests appropriate action strategy for satisfying such maternity care user groups by redesigning and restructuring the maternity care services and resources.

While using multiple regression technique the recurrent problem is that of dichotomous dependent variable sufficiently skewed to violate assumptions underlyig ordinary least squares regression which impairs the statistical efficiency of estimates. To overcome the above in recent years data analysis methods have been developed which employ maximum livelihood estimates to solve this problem. One such method is that of logit regression. The study therefore made use of Duncan Walker logit regression.

The paper offers suggestions to policy makers in the maternity care field include users of different delivery options as different segments for understanding their needs and expectations e.g. user of home delivery option, government hospital delivery etc. It also identifies the broad socio-economic and other relevant factors of each segments accordingly planning the maternity services in the respective segments. It also provides the basis for promotion of certain services specific to certain disadvantaged groups by estimating their need, practical approach to locate and serving them in better way.

Introduction

Health is wealth, search for health and happiness has been the endeavour of all human beings. Yet it is often taken for granted and its value is not realised until it is lost. The principles of management are universal and hence have an important role to play in the task of ensuring health for all.

Among many areas of health care, maternity care is considered important because of continued low status of women, but their crucial role to be played in family especially with their offspring, society and humanity, of the fact of high infant mortality-especially of less than 28 days new born and high maternal mortality.

Marketing is an important business managment function and discipline that is found to be effective beyond Business Organisation including health care organisations. The health care organisations with marketing orientation found to satisfy their customers better, mobilise more resources for their operations and bring in quality, efficiency and effectiveness in their activities.

Maternity care is the expression of need for pregnancy and child birth which involves care before and during pregnancy during and after child birth. The role of marketing is to orient maternity care from the perspective of user- pregnant women or mother rather than that of producer/doctor. The marketing of maternity care therefore invovles analysing the needs of users, designing organisations and programmes in terms of users or target markets needs and desires by evolving appropriate market mix viz., Product, Place, Priicng and Promotion strategies, Evaluation and Controlling the effort as an ongoing process (Kotler, Clark; Sanchez and Prasad).

In India an overwhelming majority of deliveries are conducted by Traditional Birth Attendants (TBAs) (Bhatia, 1982, 1985 b). About 44 million women in urban areas, 116 million women in the rural areas are of reproductive age group. While there is one doctor for 176 women of the reprdouctive age in the urban areas, there is only 1 (one) doctor serving nearly 5,216 women in the rural areas obviously calling for better expension of medical facilities in rural areas.

The Maternal Mortality Rate (MMR) of 4 to 5 per thousand live-births per week when compared to same rate of mortlaity for entire Europe in one year. Further maternal mortality was only tip of the huge iceberg of maternal morbidity. Some of the causes for the above situations relates to poor medical and health services, reproductive factors, socio-cultural, economic and administrative (Royston and Armstrong).

Maternity Care in Urban Areas

Even in urban areas to a small extent deliveries are handled by midwives, but most of the deliveries take place in hospitals run by the Government. An increasing number of deliveries are being handled by the private doctors especially Gyneacs.

The maternity care interventions at different stages follow a sequence much earlier to pregnancy (Park and Park, 1977 et al., P.80) and can be divided into the following states - (a) Health Care before pregnancy; (b) During pregnancy: promotion screening and monitoring; (c) During child birth; and (d) After child birth.

Planning for Maternity Care services must take into account the wide variety of influences on women's decision making process to make use of services effectively.

Finding out who are the consumers using optimise different delivery centres will reveal what is to be done and evolve a plan of action to cater to different types of customers depending on the need as well as capacities. Therefore the study addressed itself to the respondent in an urban context and finding out what factors are important to different categories of Maternity Care with regard to delivery options and suggest ways and means to satisfy such groups of customers.

Objectives

1. to identify the customers in terms of different delivery centres;

2. to identify the factors that significantly differ for their different choices;

3. to construct a model of factors for different customer groups; and

4. to suggest appropriate measures or plan of action, action strategy for satisfying such groups.

Methodology

Two groups of users of Maternity Services viz., pregnant women and mothers with child under one year were considered for enquiry. The study was undertaken in the context of populace in the urban area. Since the marketing concept would be more relevant in this geographical area to start with. A total sample of 225 in the ratio of 1.2 with respect to the above two categories was analysed.

Data Analysis

The data so obtained was analysed in two phases. In the first phase the socio-economic background of respondents was investigated through a computer package to obtain cross tabulations of socio-economic variable against prenatal, intra-natal and post-natal behaviours and to analyse users perceptions, experience and expectations. In the second phase of analysis important socio-economic, psychographic variables were identified through statistical tests of significance. The factors so identified were regressed to determine their impact on particular maternity facility by using computer software 'Logic Regression' and the extend of influence was found out by identifying the intercept and slope of the factors.

Results and Discussion

Maternity Care respondents surveyed in the sample consists of largely from nuclear families (76 per cent). They belong to generally higher social strata (57 per cent), and form a Hindu majority (92 per cent). They beong to 21-25 years of age group (50 per cent) and are in general housewives (93 per cent) hailing from urban and sub-urban areas. Their education ranges from Nil to Intermediate (82 per cent). The respondents, husbands are in the age group of 26-30 years (80 per cent) engaged in low level to medium level occupations (87 per cent), earning an income of Rs. 12,000/- to Rs.36,000/- (58 per cent).

In the cross tabulation analysis it was found that there is a significant association between delivery intention and social status ($p<0.0001$), occupation of husband ($p<0.0001$), education of respondent ($p<0.001$), education of respondents' husband ($p<0.0001$). The present delivery is very much dependent on previous delivery experience in terms of number of issues and nature of earlier delivery and place of delivery. For example, from the sample 57 per cent of previous home deliveries 91 per cent of previous Government hospital deliveries, 60 per cent of private hospitals preferred similar delivery again. The percentage of those who go to private hospital has decreased with increased previous delivery experience. "Doctor's Care", "All facilities under one Roof", "Capacity to take care of emergencies" are the chief considerations among most of the respondents stated for their reasons of selection.

Through Multiple Regression Analysis one can predict future demand for a given product or service provided their dependent factors are known. By finding out the nature and strength of a relationship between Independent variables demand determinants and dependent variables such as the product or a given service. However the recurrent problem using regression is that of dichotomous variable sufficiently skewed to violate assumptions under-lying ordinary least squares (OLS) regression and impair the statistical efficiency of estimates. Data analysis metods in recent past have been developed to address this problem. This study makes use of the logit regression approach to identify the factors that effect the choice of delivery centre for maternity care thus enabling policy formulation for planning maternity service centres.

Duncan Walker Logit Regression used in this study has the following model:

$$Y = 1/ \{1 + \exp [-(A + Bx)]\}$$

Where, Y is the dependent risk variable, A and the Vector B are the regression coefficient and 'x' is a vector of dependent predictor or control variables. An iterative method is used to seek convergence of coefficients with discriminant function coefficients, calculated by Truett-Cornfield discriminant function analysis, used as initial estimates (Loon, Byung, Cohen 1985).

The following tables present how logit analysis is carried out to know the factors influencing the delivery intention for one centre in comparison with the other to know the extent of various factors influence on the decision related to choice of a given centre.

The Table 1 presents the list of independent variables used in one or the other Logit regression models presented. For example, in the logit regression model 1 the following factors that were found to be significantly associated to fit the model: 'Nature of previous delivery, Birth centre of previous delivery", "education of the respondent", Family income, and "social status".

The table also present each of these independent varibles that were defined to fit the model. For example, nature of previous delivery has been defined 1 = Normal delivery; 2 = Forceps delivery; and 3 = Caesarean delivery.

In Table 2 the list of dependent varible or Events/Non-events for each of the logit regression runs were presented. There were six logit regression runs. L.r.r. 1 is model to fit the respondents of having previous delivery experience either to private or to Government hospitals. While entering the dependent variables visit to private hospital was shown as 1; visit to Government hospital as 2; and Home delivery as 3. Since the Logit regression used is binary model this has been to find out the choice as dichotomous options at a time. Hence, L.r.m. - A: used to run the choice between private hospital and Government hospital visitors with previous delivery experience for prenatal care. L.r.m. B: used to run for the choice between private and Government hospital visitors without previous delivery experience for prenatal care.

Logit regression model (L.r.m.) I used to run for the choice between private and Government hospital visitors with previous delivery experience. While L.r.m. II used to run for the same categories without previous delivery experience. L.r.m. III used for choice between Government Hospital and home delivery and finally L.r.m. IV used between visit to private hospital verus home delivery. However the dependent varible, where a value of 1 = indicates a case or event of say visit to private hospital and a value of 0 indicates a noncase or nonevent as a visit to Government hospital. The total no. of records considered as cases in L.r.m.I are 12 and non cases 71.

Table 3 through 6 present the maximum likelihood fit typical of the Logit regression model (e.g.: L.r.m.1). In the second column of the table it shows the intercept denoted by 'a' in the equation and the other independent variables selected for the regression model. The third comumn of the table gives the estimate of the values for the intercept and independent varibales. The column four gives the standard error of the estimate corresponding to estimates of B value of the variables in the second column. The fifth column gives the probabilities values to indicate the significance of the predictor values. The significance of the value considered were at various levels ($p<0.01$, $p<0.05$).

Table 1: The List of Independent Varibales used in Combinations to fit the Logit Regression Models for Delivery Intention of an their Descriptions

Sl.no.	*Independent variables*	*Definitions*
1.	Nature of previous delivery	1 = Normal 2 = Forceps 3 = Caesarean
2.	Birth centres of previosu delivery	1 = Caesarean 2 = Govt. Hospital 3 = Private Hospital
3.	Education of the respondent	1 = Illiterate 2 = Matriculate 3 = Graduate 4 = Postgraduate

Sl.no.	Independent variables	Definitions
4.	Family income	1 = Below Rs.12000
		2 = Rs. 12000-24000
		3 = Rs. 24000-36000
		4 = Rs. 36000 and above
5	Social Status	1 = Upper Castes
		2 = Middle Castes
		3 = Lower Castes
6.	Prenatal Care visits	1 = Govt. Hospital
		2 = Private Hospital
		3 = Other hospitals
7.	Family status	1 = Joint family
		2 = Nuclear family
8.	Religion	1 = Hindu
		2 = Muslim
9.	Age of the respondent	1 = Upto 20 years
		2 = 21-25 years
		3 = 26-30 years
		4 = 30 years and above
10.	Occupation of husband	1 = No work
		2 = Low level
		3 = Medium level
		4 = High level

Table 2: List of Dependent Variables used in Different fits of Logit Regression Models for Delivery Intention

S. No.	Dependent variables	Definitons	Case/Events Vs. Noncases or non-events	No.of Respondents
1.	Logit Regression Model-I (with previous delivery experience)	1= Visit to Pvt hospital	1=Case	12
		2 = Visit to Govt. hospital	0=Noncase	71
2.	Logit regression Model-II (without previous delivery exerience	1= visit to Pvt. hospital	1= Case	32
		2= visit to Govt. hospital	0= Noncase	54
3.	Logit regression Model-III	2= visit to Govt. Hospital	1=case	136

S. No.	*Dependent variables*	*Definitons*	*Case/Events Vs. Noncases or non-events*	*No.of Respondents*
		3 = Home delivery	0 = Noncase	38
4.	Logit regression Model-IV	1 = visit to Pvt. hospital	1 =Case	49
		3 = Home delivery	0 = Noncase	37
5.	Logit regression Model A (with previous delivery experience)	1 = visit to Pvt. hospital	1=case	50
		2 = visit to Govt. hospital	0 = noncase	53
6.	Logit regression Model-B (without previous delivery experience)	1 = visit to pvt. hospital	1 = Case	63
		2 = visit to Govt. hospital	0 = Noncase	35

Table 3: Typical Logit Regression Model run for Logit Regression Model I (C=12) + (N=71)++

S.No	*Variables*	*Estimate of B-values*	*SE of the estimate*	*Probability*
1.	Intecept	-19.94	7.13	0.005
2.	Nature of previous delivery	3.17*	1.45	0.030
3.	Birth centre of previous delivery	4.12**	1.5	0.006
4.	Education of the respondent	1.61*	0.82	0.05
5.	Family income	2.54*	1.19	0.03
6.	Social status	-4.7*	2.3	0.04

** p 0.01

* p 0.05

1. All the above factors with stars are significant
2. While + = Number of cases that visited private hospital for delivery
   ++ = Number of NOn-cases visited Government hospital for delivery.
3. $ = Respondents delivery intentions with previous delivery experience.

Conclusions and Recommendations Based on Logit Regression Results

1. When people without previous delivery experience go for prenatal care their "educational level" has greater influence on their choice of hospital. But, among the people with previous delivery experience, the previous centre of birth along with their "education" has greater influence on their choice.

   Therefore while predicting the demand for prenatal care among the two segments of experienced and first times the level of education can provide the basis for the extent of utilisation and type of prenatal care centre. So, the Government can plan the appropriate facilities according to the need and level of utilisation. While assessing the demand among experienced, knowledge of previous centre of birth details such as Home, Govt./private hospital also enriches the demand measurement for these sgement of the population.

2. In the case of delivery choice between private and government hospital. People without previous delivery experience are found to be more influenced by their earlier "Choice of prenatal care" as well as the "annual family income".

   "Hence the data related to PNC visit regarding the choice of delivery place and their income status would be helpful in projecting the demand in the immediate context.

3. While among those with previous delivery experience "birth centre of previous delivery", "nature of previous delivery", "Sociȧl status" and "educational level" all of them have strong influence in their choice of intra-natal centre.

   "It is suggested that a birth record could be maintained and in which the "nature of delivery" and "birth centre of the previous deliveries", "status of the child" could be entered into which will be useful for prediction of future utilisation of delivery centres. Since the choice of delivery also based on income consideration, the income levels of respondents would be helpful in projection of future demand. Also with the rise in the education people are preferring personalised and specialised deliveries. Therefore above factors would collectively help in deciding on the demand for delivery centres at various levels of use.

4. When the choice is between government and Home deliveries among the both categories of experienced and first time users "Social Status", "religious background" and "family" have a strong bearing on their mind.

   Home delivery practice which is on the decline however still followed among a few lower social status groups and muslims especially if they are from joint families. Government can concentrate for better maternity care facilities reaching, these groups of people where they located most. To prevent certain negative practices with regard to maternity care they can promote better practices of maternity care. e.g., Discouraging breast feeding, female infanticide, female circumscision, abortions by force etc., Government hospital or home delivery seekng population belong to under and middle income group, lower and middle level of occupation, little to moderate education who constitute a majority needs to be separately addressed.

5. When there is a choice between private hospital and home delivery "education of respondent" and social status together found to have greater influence.

   Among the social groups upper castes, Muslims have high probability to visit private hospital while lower and intermediate castes are more likely to opt for home delivery. When those respondents who are educated likely to visit private hospitals then who are not educated. It is clear from the above, therefore that promoting education as a long term strategy among these groups would enhance their utilisation of both government and private hospitals for their delivery choice. Particularly utilisation of private hospitals would increase when income is not a barrier. Further it also helps to make them give-up negative practices of maternity care if it is included as part of their functional literacy among these women.

References

1. Balaji Prasad, "Marketing of Health Services in Maternity Care- A managerial approach". 1993, Ph.D. Thesis.
2. Bhatia, J.C., 1982, "Evaluation of Traditional birth attendants (Dais)" Training Scheme in the State of Karnataka, Bangalore, Indian Institute of Management.
3. Royston, E & Armstrong, S. (ed.) 1989, Preventing Maternal deaths, WHO, Geneva.
4. Park, J.F. and Park, K., 1977, Text Book of Preventive and Social Medicine - A treatise on Community helath, Jabalpur Banarasidas, Bharat, 758 pp.
5. Kotler Philip, 1990, Marketing Management, Analysis, Planning Implementation and Control, 6th Edn., New Delhi Prentice Hall Inc.
6. Kotler & Clark, 1987, "Marketing for Health Care Organisations", Englewood Diff. J.J., Prentice Hall Inc.
7. Sanchez, Peter, M., 1983 Marketing in the Health Care Arena Some comments on 'O' cannols, Evaluation of discipline, Journal of Health Care Marketing, III, 1, 24-30.
8. Lson, David, 1985, Logit Regression Analysis, Operating Model of the Logit Regression Package.
9. Byung - Ryenkirm 1990, "A Logit Analysis of Hosptial choice behaviour in cohollabukdo province of Korea", Social Science Medicine, pp. 1119-1129.
10. Cohen, A. Lee, L., 1985, "The determinants of spatial distribution of hospital utilisation in a region medicare."

Section - V

SERVICE ECONOMY AND EDUCATION SYSTEMS

Overview

Section five discussses the service economy and its impact on education systems. The section has four papers. The first paper by Prof. Murali and Prasad touches ailing higher education with the trend of rapid expansion, perverse incentives, insulation from the reality of job markets in the midst of financial and pedagogical mess. An honest attempt to integrate the vital issues from the prism of management by objectives (MBO) a managerial tool for performance appraisal of the sector as a whole. Second paper on similar mission with exhaustive study of system. The present day system of education often confined to the citadels of elites content with narrow specialisation and remaining aloof from the problems of larger society. Mr. Ramprasad suggests the key to meeting the present challenges are to ensure quality assurance, cost effectiveness and remain globally competitive. The third paper by Dr. Lalita and Prof. C.S.G.K. look at education service in the context of world trade organisation and the agreement among the WTO member countries with respect to education with a thrust on quality, subsidy and funding. The fourth paper by Ms. Bhanusree underscores the importance of knowledge management as a fifth discipline after business strategy, accounting, marketing and human resources and its application to service sector. KM as highly centralized information system enriched with individual interpretation and expertise as a valuable asset.

LOWERING THE AILMENTS OF HIGHER EDUCATION- An MBO Approach

Prof. P. Murali,
Vice-Chancellor, S.V.University, Tirupati
and
Dr. P.Balaji Prasad
Associate Professor,
School of Business Management, S.V. University, Tirupati.

"Education is not a way to escape poverty -- it is a way of fighting it" -- Julius Nyerere, former President of the United Republic of Tanzania.

Introduction to higher education in India

The higher education is at the cross roads in India today. The features of crisis include complex causes: rapid expansion, perverse incentive structures, insulation from the realities of job markets. But there can be little doubt that the system is in the midst of a financial and pedagogical crisis. We would like to carry on the present debate on Higher education from the prism of management by objectives (MBO) the various issues discussed by experts in the field to process further concerning all of us in the higher education to bear.

According to the great living legend of management movement Peter F Drucker in his famous book, "The Practice of Management" Objectives are needed in every area where performance and results directly and vitally affect the survival and prosperity of the business. The search for the single objective is essentially a search for a magic formula is always irrational. There are Eight areas of objectives in any field to target for results. They are Market standing, Innovation, physical and financial resources, Productivity, Profitability, Managers performance and development, Workers (Teacher and Student) performance and attitude and Public responsibility.

Objectives in the key area should enable us to five things. I To organise and explain the whole range of business phenomena in a small no. of general statements 2. To test the statements in actual experience. 3. To predict the behaviour. 4. To appraise the soundness of decisions while they are still being made and. 5. To enable businessmen to enlarge their own experience and as a result to improve their performance.

Market standing

Changing job market; the rapid changes in the economy leading to shifts in the job availability and course preferences. This seems an unending story of history repeating itself overproduction of graduates and a corresponding increase in the number of unemployed youth in those disciplines. It happened in every decade after Independence and it is happening even now. Shifts from manufacturing, state or public sector employment to a predominantly service-oriented, and private sector job market. Even in the private sector, only those with a degree in information technology and software have jobs.

The way the UG courses run it is difficult to imagine that under current dispensation the structure of UG education which is the heart of any university system, can be overhauled. Second is the curricular dimension or pattern of existing and new courses in higher education. The IT revolution, Distance education and internet shrunk the role of teacher. The third is the examination pattern, for example univerisities would like to move to a credit - based system of evaluation and teaching rather than end of the year papers.

Productivity and Diversity

Measuring productivity i.e. how well resources are utilized and how much they yield. One of the most important and broad based challenges currently facing higher education is adapting to people who different as the institutions are becoming more heterogenous. There is a growing tendency today that both teachers and students are increasingly divided on caste and political lines. Increasingly campus are witnessing the impact of localization threatening the positive effects of diversity on the campus. Managing this diversity in higher education has productivity implications too. Over the years though each of the educational institutions has been undertaking efforts in realising unity in diversity', they could not make the students understand the complexity of diversity.

Physical and Financial Resources

Planning for good facilities especially physical facilities like class rooms, labs, administrative building offices etc., Objectives should aim at providing physical infrastructure needed to attain the goals set for market standing and innovation. If the students need to exhibit pro-social citizenship behaviour and activities in their post college life they need to have a pleasurable and profitable learning experience on the campus during their stay. The challenge is daunting and that needs tapping of many more resources not only from existing public finance but from many more by fostering the partnership on a self-sustaining basis. There is no reason why some of the vast sums that are going into ill thought philanthropy cannot be again brought into the university system. It is here some existing experiments that needs to be watched for understanding the spirit of partnership after all, institutions such as the Delhi School of Economics and the Tata Institutes were products of wonderful public private partnerships. Arguably, the creation of independent endowments or even private universities will increase rather than decrease university autonomy.

Profitability and Autonomy

Profit for business serves three purposes. First purpose is to show the net effectiveness and soundness of business efforts.

Second is as the cost of staying in business such as cost of replacement, cost of obsolescence, market risk and cost against uncertainty. Lastly the profits ensure the supply of future capital for innovation and expansion. It is difficult to imagine how universities will retain any autonomy without seriously thinking of their financial independence. The question is not whether private funds should be mobilised but how. Can these be mobilised to ensure that quality education remains widely available, the subjects such as the basic sciences and social sciences continue to flourish, and the state system is able to mobilise those resources that are draining to bad institutions in the private sector anyway? Therefore the issue of mobilising private resources should address the following concerns in higher education. First, one ought to worry about uhpholding academic standards. Second, there have to be mechanisms for ensuring access to the economically disadvantaged, And third, academics rather than entrepreneurs masquerading as such must control educational decisions.

Managerial Performance and Development

The best talent is leaving faster than it arrives. Entrepreneurs rather than Academicians are at the control of educational decisions. University autonomy is being daily abdicated by a combination of a heavy-handed UGC and weak Vice-Chancellors. The UGC and most of the teaching community have their heads in the sand about the actual state of education. Is the present system of education irrelevant. If higher education is handed over to the private sector, will its problems melt away? These views are a major challenge to those manning higher education institutions.

Teachers and Students Performance and Attitude

The objective of education is to train and condition the mind to function effectively in a contemporary context. The two chief constituents of higher education are the teachers and students. The changing composition of student's and teachers: The main beneficiaries of state subsidies are still largely the upper and middle classes. The Indian middle class, like the middle class anywhere in the world, is differentiated in terms of the occupation, income and education. But the peculiarity in India is its diversity in terms of language, caste and religion.

The affirmative action and its Impact: While affirmative action has broadened the social base of the student body, most univeristies cannot do much for the students once they get there. With the demand out matching the means and resources the quality of education and individual attention to the people has suffered. The stduents are like rudderless boats on the high seas. The Campus unrest: wide gaps existed in the socialisation patterns and processes among the students. What we lacked all these years was the planned development and concern for diveristy and multiculturalism in higher education and led to conflict, confrontation and unrest on various campuses. *The curricular content and quality of education:* Teachers should make learning a pleasure, by going beyond textbooks and focus on improving competencies of students in such a way that it makes learning a fun. Teachers should have a spark in them. Through training programmes teachers to take to classrooms in order to make them "places of discovery" for them. *The outcome purpose and motivation for education:* The students are encouraged to become members of the global village, rather than members of their own villages and towns. The marks based evaluation in vogue and the general tendency to get somehow passed is leading only to get cheated at the end. Students seeking shortcut methods and teachers imparting syllabus from the examination point of view are the signs of a lurking danger to the very foundation of the education system in the country. It is desirable to change the general curriculum learner-centre, activity oriented and centred around improving the knowledge base of the learner.

Abdication of Public Responsibility and What are its Consequences?

Strength of the society is the strength of the enterprise. Most of those who canot afford private education are strack in third rate state institutions. Do our systems of higher education prepare students to cope with situations in their post-college life in a culture completely different from theirs? Amartya sen decries the sectarian outlook to education. He advocates openness of the curriculum and secular and inclusive approach that cultivates reasoning and scrutiny as the central to promote the human security.

Conclusion

An honest attempt to integrate the vital issues of higher education from the prism of MBO concept -- A managerial tool for performance appraisal through objectives in every area of performance and result concerning the higher education. In other words, the attempts to reform te higher education sstem should focus more on farming something relevant for the local as well as the global. This may seem idealistic or hypothetical, but certainly essential if we wish to establish a healthy and peaceful civil society. further economic independence means strengthening autonomy. The debate ought to have, by now, moved to a different set of questions. The question is not whether private funds should be mobilised but how. Education, thus, influences and is influenced by the context in which it is developed. This synergistic relationship implies that education must be in a constant state of change as it responds to changing social and economic needs and that education in itself is a force for social and economic change as people become more empowered and more productive.

References

Amartya Sen, Two day workshop in Education, Facility and Human Security by UNICEF Harvard University, The Commission on Human Security and Pratyahi Trust at Kolkata, Janyar 5, p.12.

Amrik Singh, The milch cow of higher education, the Hindu, Tuesday, Friday, October 5, 2001.

Amrik Singh, The UGC behind the times; The Hindu, Tuesday, June 5, 2001.

Drucker, P.F. The Practice of Management, Indian edn. 197 Ninth reprint 1985, pp.62-85.

Luthans Fred Organisation behaviour, Tata McGraw Hill Publications, New Delhi.

Panikkar, K N Eduation for fundamentalism, The Hindu, Saturday, April, 21, 2001.

Pratap Bhanu Mehta, Private funding and higher education, the Hindu, Wednesday, Dec. 26, 2001.

Ramamurthy, P.V. Present day predicaments of a teacher, Education The Hindu, Nov 13, 2001 OB-2.

Srinivasa Rao, S. Diversity concerns in higher education, The Hindu, Saturday, Dec. 15, 2001.

Stephen Robins Organisation behaviour, Prentice Hall, India Ltd., New Delhi.

Subba Rao, I.V. Secretary, Education Govt. of Andhra Pradesh, UGC Refresher Course on General Sanskrit and Pedagogy at Rastriya Sanskrit Vidyapeetha Tirupai January 4-5th P-5.

Venkatasubramanian, K. Education and Poverty, The Hindu, Tuesday, Dec. 4, 2001.

INDIAN EDUCATION SECTOR-- CHALLENGES AHEAD

M.V. Ramprasad
Assistant Professor, GITAM, Visakhapatnam

Introduction

The Education system of any nation is a mirror through which can be seen the image of the nation being shaped and likely to be shaped. education has been and will continue to be the potential cause of change in any society. Societies today are in a state of flux being divided and subdivided on the basis of caste, color, creed, religion, language, ethinic and national identities. This has resulted in pluralistic societies characterized by a multiplicity of needs each pulling in different directions. Our Indian Society is no different. At the moment we are passing through very critical phase of a battle between the best potentialities and the worst possibilities.

At a time when Science & Technology has turned the world into a global village, when its benefits can be used to abolish poverty and deprivation, precisely at this time the forces of violence of religious bigotry, of narrow sectarianism and gravitational pulls of the lower human nature are pressing forward on a global scale. Rationality, in which humanity has placed great trust for solving its problems for arriving at fulfilment of its ideal of true and comprehensive knowledge, appears to be overtaken by the forces of irrationality.

It has therefore become imperative to review education and its content in order to locate the malady, to find out how best, the education system can be geared to face these challenges and meet the requirements of this new millennium.

Present state of Indian Education sector

Students no longer have confidence in its ability to prepare them for entering the world of work as the nature of occupations have been constantly changing with rapid developments in Science and Technology, but curricula have practically remained unchanged.

The state is no longer the principal employer of the educated youth in the country. The hard reality is that majority of the employment opportunities now are in the private sector and this sector is very choosy, to say the least. The private sector employs only those who possess skills and competencies required by it. Its requirements are continually changing because this sector has to keep pace with its global competition. Education now has to be tailor made to the requirements of Private sector. Also under the World trade Organisation (WTO) agreement, Foreign institutions will make in roads in the higher education sector by providing alternative learning opportunities that lead to the award of degrees of their Universities. They claim that their certification will be preferred by multinationals to the degrees awarded by our universities. Such a scenario there is an urgent need to re-engineer the road of the education from its dead end. The need of the hour is to give a fresh look at the education and introduce such changes as it will restore confidence in the ability of the State Universities and colleges for providing education relevant to the present context cost effectively.

Education Sector - Marketing Orientation

Customer satisfaction is the key for upgrading the quality, as without full customer satisfaction it is not possible to increase the market share. The customers of education are students. Decline of interest in general education courses has hit 'the universities and colleges. It is perhaps due to dissatisfaction with the present education system.

Student Satisfaction

Students seeking tertiary education clamour for joining profesisonal courses of study this courses in general education. General education: the widespread impression is that unlike the professional education courses general education courses have failed to keep pace with the changes that are taking place in the world of work. The courses offered by general education colleges are determined by a traditional mindset and have continued to remain infleixible. Students complain that they are not able to exercise choice in selecting what they would like to study. They want to study what would suit their aptitude and also meet their future needs. Also, the general perception is that contents of courses that are being offered at present may not be helpful to them in acquiring the skills and abilities required by their future employees.

Students satsifaction may have to be used as an effective instrument for raising the quality of programmes of study. This will require acceptance of the sovereignty of learners by the education system. New courses and course combinations may have to be offered for meeting varying learning needs of students. The other driving force for raising quality will be the commitment of teahcers to their students and to the pursuit of excellence. The main task of teachers will be bringing out the inner potential of their students and chiseling of mental facilities.

Quality control - Education

There are innumerable examples of institutions in our country and abroad that stand out in the midst of mediocrity as centres of excellence. The challenge from within and without that should now drive each institution is to strive to obtain an ISO type of certification of quality. For that it may be helpful to learn from institutions both from within the country and abroad that have achieved unequivocal standards of high quality. There are many outstanding examples of role models.

Role of Teachers

Therefore the kingpin of an institution are its teachers. If good teachers have joined teaching profession in an institution. It is because they value academic freedom, enjoy teaching - learning and have made pursuit of excellence their mission. The quality automatically follows. It is generally belived that just and fair system in rewarding good performance is crucial for teacher motivation. But if one were to ask teachers of insittutions that are highly rated, it would be found that they set their own goals and drive themselves with self discipline for performing at the peak of their capability. The source of their motivation may be self determined goals peer apreciation, publishing articles in journals of repute invitation for sharing their research work in conferences and seminars etc. and not the desire for obtainin worldly gain such as rapid promotion in service or positions of authority. Rewards and Recognition follow them because of their hardwork.

Recruitment of higher calibre teachers is necessary but may not be sufficient for ensuring quality in their performance. They would require the support of infrastructure such as good library, laboratories equipped with modern faciliteis essential for carrying out teaching and reasearch at international standards and more than anything else, a sympathetic understanding of their academic needs by the administration. Only then they may be able to work at the frontiers of knowledge by keeping themselves updated with the latest developments in their field.

In our country there are outstanding examples of persons who made world-class contributions to knowledge without the support of advanced laboratories or research faciltieis that were available to their peers. There is not substitute for hard and serious thinking, and with sustained and serious effort we should be able to go a long way even with our meagre resources and capital. It will therefore be an anachronism to continue to use the human brain for memorising information when it should be used for solving problems, creative thinking the skill attributes of knowledge workers. Therefore unless any system of education is learner centred, is flexible, is around developing thinking skills and is able to help learners in acquiring the ability of learning how to learn will gradually lose if relevance. Therefore there is now urgent need to reorient teaching learning in the universities to meet the requirements of the youth for living and contributing effectively in the 21st century.

Information technology has placed us Indians ahead in the world, yet it has not provided a level playing field where equal pay for equal work is concerned. Much of the IT work is outsourced to India becuase of the cheap and skilled workforce. Education must seek to dispel this negative attitude of the developed nations towards the developing nations.

Population control and better healthcare in the wake of diseases that threaten to engulf the entire human race, proper management of fast depleting resources such as energy and fresh water, forest cover and mineral wealth which are necessary for the total economy of the country are other vital issues to be addressed by education in order to promote quality of life in the future. That the total economy of the country is linked with these vital issues and with the contemporary world, and that our relations with other nations are influenced by our economic position is reason enough for education to redefine its goals as to equip the young generation with the awarness of these issues and the knowledge to combat them.

Future challenges to Education Sector

A dynamic education must be futuristic in outlook, must keep pace with the changing times and be responsive to individual, social, and national aspirations. It must aspire to bring out the hidden potential of each and every individual to foster respect for national values, national culture, judicious use of natural resources, care for the small-family-norm and appreciation of the contemporary issues facing the world.

Social Justice: In order to meet the challenges of an undemocratic social scale education must be developing consideration for others by makig them realise the unscientific character of the prejudice against the disadvantaged. For this education will aim at developing individuals who accpet willingly the ideas of liberty, equality, responsibility for the common good, respect for personality of others treating them as ends and never as means. Education by providing equal opportunity to all will also aim at developing in the future a social scale, which is democratic, flexible and based on merit. A social scale thus will strive to provide good life to all.

Hence the aims of education would be:

- To develop citizenship owing allegiance to the constitution and respect for its ideals of justice, liberty, equality and fraternity and compassion for those low on the scale.
- To develop world citizens capable of fostering bonds between different cultures and different people.
- To develop self directed extrovert, creative, rational individuals open to novel and logical ideas, capable of becoming a resource rather than a liability to the nation.
- Positive feeling towards the national culture and appreciation of this 'Unity' in diversity.
- Creating awarness of rights and duties and operationalising them in education in order to impart human values.
- To develop a positive attitude towards small family norms and an understanding that the quality of life is linked directly to the size of the family.
- To develop capacity to manage the resources of clean water, energy and mineral wealth for the benefit of mankind today and with proper concern for future generation too.

- To tackle the problems posed by dangerous ailments like AIDS, TB, Cancer and Hepatits by educating the general public on the means of preventing their spread.

- To inculcate the judicious use of nuclear advancement for the energy of mankind and to educate against the dangers of nuclear proliferation of the environment and to the human race.

- Education must protect the natural environment to leave the world a better place to live in for future generations hence it will aim at imparting knowledge about the ways and means of environmental protection.

Role for women: Education as an instrument of human development must not discriminate between the men and women it seeks to develop. No society can progress if half of its members are uneducated especially that half upon whom rests the responsibility of upbringing the future generations.

2. Identifying excellent Leadership

It is essential, however, to identify the characteristics of the effective leader. These include openness and clarity, well-informed and fair in judgement a well developed strategic sense and capacity to build staffs commitment to institutional goals.

It is important to recognize the need and value of life long learning. Administrators must serve for themselves and their staff continuing opportunities to learn, in a period of unprecedented technolgoical, economic, social change and knowledge expansion.

3. Team Work

The most procedure approach to uncover the developmental opportunities for administrators themselves, for staff and for achieving the goals of the institutions. Hence administrators must work together with colleagues.

4. Professional development of Personnel

Series of activities for personal professional development such as skill analysis, workshops and mentoring in the contet of the strategic priorities of the participants. Organisations need to be targeted viz., workshop for accessing their own strengths and identifying their own developmental needs, followed by face-to-face workshop. Electronic communication, participants needs and priorities.

5. Seminars and Workshops

Seminars and Workshops on management and leadership issues be arranged for identified core participants. Seminars and Workshops should also be designed to strengthen international networks as Universities can send respresentatives to other countries. States for a national conference or workshop. In addition National seminars should be held and designed to provide up-to-date management theory and high quality training.

6. Academic audit (AA)

Academic audit should enhance application value which will in turn increase the operational value of good governance. We have least resources for education for education from the overall resources. We have to be very efficient and effective so as to accomplish the desired objectives. It will pave the way for effective utilisation of the resources allotted to higher education as it will not do the thing right but will only do the right things. The exercise would be with it only when it does not meet the same fate as most of the critical studies produced at our universities about other organisations every year when the studies do not even reach the concerned organisaitons or are considered in their policy making.

7. Quality Audit

The University with a model for carrying the assessment exercise, the success of the model in achieving the above stated objectives and abolishing the maladies prevailing in the Universities is yet to be realized.

The UGC should have classified university and encouraged and invited the selected ones for coming out with different models in applying their own tests and experiments instead of giving its own format in the beginning. The NAAC has evolved parameters for each parameter criterion statement of healthy practice have been identified serving as benchmarks. Freedom to have indepedent models initially would have provided a big push for both 'benchmark practices' and facts deserving adjutments for discredits. By this aproach ideal models can be developed for different clases of Universities. This exercise will make the problem once more specific and the model would be effective in sorting out the problems of governance segment of the study, as it will give boost to the experiments in different groups resulting in definite qualitiative indicies for grading and regulation. The model so formed may consider the following attributes.

* A university could assess itself without much difficulty but highly objectively as that produces sound quality audit.

* A governance quality index is constructed and the university awareded grades like in credit rating service for financial institutions.

* Grading awarded should stand valid for three seasors.

* It must be obligatory on the part of the universities rather than voluntary to project prominently the quality grade they fill in on all their marks sheets; information booklets, degreees, certificates, publications, academic proceedings, letterheads, sign boards, other documents and by the UGC on its outlets, directories etc.

* It must be binding on the Human Resources forces of the University to work collectively for goals with a sense of belongingness which is missing altogether at present where a

teacher works in unity and hormony with the administration and so does the administrators.

8. Good Governance

Institutions have personalities just like the individuals have. Institutions develop their identity by and by. The personality develops not casually but by actions and reactions in its perception, vision, planning and execution. Every little thing will count to make up the excellence with which the personality of an institution is moulded. Therefore the following parameters can be laid down to judge the efficiency of a model for acadmeic and governance audit.

* Capable of leading the system to Cost Effectiveness.
* Generating operational value of good governance.
* Making higher education accountable and socially relevant.
* Inbuilt provisions and autoforce generating system for quality maintenance not only by the universities themselves but primarily their regulating and fund providing agencies like the state governments.
* Generating a system in the University which creates loyalty to the system and not to the individual so as to do away with the frequently accused problem of fractionalism and politicisation. This type of leadership culture is to prevail at every level as a result of such an audit.

The key test of the presence of an ideal governance in a education institution may be as follows.

* Today we speak about independent directors in case of corporate governance. The composition of bodies and authorities in the universities like syndicate requires to be still more democratic, free from politicisation and partiality.

The present inconsistencies in this regard need to be eradicated eg. nomination of Professors, Deans etc. to the syndicate should be in a fixed order instead of the wish of the vice-chancellor.

* Existence of the well defined policies with suitablility as regards giving extra assignments and positions to the teachers by the VC, Deans, and Registrars.

* Policies noted above are fair and eauitable and communicated to all concerned that ensure the chance for every one without inviting group influences.

Existence of an independent standing performance improvement monitoring cell.

10. Curriculum

Another area which requires immediate attention is the change in course programme. The course programme does not respond to changes in the society. In most of the cases, it is found that the content of education programmes reflect the value of the dominant class. The training and skills imparted in the colleges and universities perpetuate the economic and social system instead of making any attempt to change the education programme and make it more relevant for developmental needs. We cannot implant an education system which is prevalent in developed countries. Each society must try to orient its own programme of education activities to solve their basic problems of development. India's major problems are poverty unemployment, illeteracy squalor etc. It is said that university is a liberal and liberating agency for individuals and social transformations. But if the education programmes follow the traditional pattern which perputate the existing system of rigidity and assist the rich become richer the curriculum loses its importance as an agent of change. It is therefore imperative that course programmes should be in conformity with the real needs of the plural society. In other words the course programmes should provide students the knowledge, skill and ideas which will enable them to function efficiently and in their own environment.

The development of higher education in India during last five decade presents a picture of light and shade. In the garb of quantitative success there is qualitative failure.

This is evident from the huge pool of educated persons which indicates a massive problem of graduates and their lack of employability which in turn probably reveals a low standard of education or an education that lacks relevance. There has been a commendable quantitative expansion in terms of institutions enrolment and very poor allocation of funds.

Conclusion

How can we reorient the education system so as to meet the real requirements and aspirations of the people. At present Education is often consigned to the citadels of elites content with narrow specialisation and remaining aloof from the problems of larger society. Since eduation systems largely reflect, reproduce rather than alter the economic and social structure of the socieites in which they exist any programme or set of policy designed to make education more relevant for development becomes a failure. In ther words, it does not respond to the needs of the changing social structure. On the other hand the content of education reflects as pointed out by Malcom Adiseshaiah S. the values of the dominant class.

We require an education system which promote knowledge, discipline, equity, truth for developmnt of society. While education can be a pace setter for society equally and even more education including University is all alas a faithful mirror of society.

Though an improvement in the social system is an important problem requring number of revolutionary changes. The key to meeting the present challenges are to ensure quality assurance, cost effectiveness and remain globally competitive. Therefore we have to learn from the management experts how to ensure quality in education sector and its sustaining and enhancement.

References

Kipatrick W.H. 1971. Education for a changing civilisation.

Brar, Sardar H.S. 1996 Higher Education and Development, New Delhi University News.

Adiseshaiah Melcom, S. 1985 Role of universities as agents of change in Higher Education in the 80s opportunities and objectives, Lancer International, New Delhi.

Todaro Michael P. 1977 Economics for a developing world Longman.

Nigavekar A.S. 2000. Recent effects in assuming quality in Higher Education Journal of Higher Education, Vol.20, No.4.

EDUCATION SERVICES IN THE CONTEXT OF WTO

Dr. Lalita[1] & Prof. CSGK[2]

Services include all the intangibles delivered to the customer or client. The spectrum of services range between the degree of intangibility and tangibility offered to the user. Examples of intangibles include athletics, publishing cultural services, education services health services, professional services, information centre etc. Tangible services include computer hardware, automobiles transportation, catering, financial services, library services, research and development, courier services, recreation clubs etc. Services differ with products due to their special attributes as given under.

Intangibility

Inseparability of buyer and service provider (simulatenity)

Lack of inventory

Time sensitivity

Difficult in measuring and controlling quality

Risk averse

Difficulty in experimentation

Customization of offering

Marketing relationship

Personalized marketing

1. Dr. Lalitha Ramakrishnan, MBA, Ph.D. Academic Coordinator, Dept.of Business Management, Sri Padmavathi Mahila Viswa Vidyalayam, Tirupati.
2. Dr. CSG Krishnamacharyulu, BE, MBA, Ph.D., Professor, School of Business Management, S.V. University, Tirupati.

Global Change

There is a global change in services management and even developing countries like India are gearing up to services. In developed coutries like USA 75% of the population are employed in services. In India, however merely 10% are employed in services. However, there is spurt in growth due to emphasis on ISPs, tourism, courier, services etc and the % employed in services is likely to touch 30% of the employed in the year 2002.

WTO and education services

India is member of WTO countries and the agreement among the WTO member countries with respect to education includes:

Market access to higher education

Recognition of Indian degrees

Movement of natural persons supplying education services

Seeking most favoured nation (MFN) exemption status for providing technical and scientific services to the developing and least developing countries.

Provision of higher education services for general higher education, technical education, medical education, law and management education

Providing educational services to SAARC and aligned and Central Asian countries.

Quality assessment on mutually agreed criteria

Use of local partners

United states and other countries have made specific requests to WTO with regard to removing the obstacles to have free access to market in developing countries as well as enlargement of definition of the system of higher education. this raises a doubt that the MFN countries like USA, and UK may try to drain out foriegn exchange if we follow the WTO agreement in privatizing education services. The question here is do we require globalised education. If yes, in what fields, with what safeguards?

Specific Safeguards

An attempt is made in this paper to analyse the specific safeguards we need to take as a member of WTO countries in globalising education.

Training and testing services

Training services related to administrative positions and corporate managers may be opened to foreigners. However, the vernacular based jobs, which interact with rural and semi-urban people in terms of education, or public administration should be reserved to national players. Specifically, the adult education programmes, training of municipal, mandal and village level officials and field personnel (Anganwadi workers) should be done by national institutions. Testing services for admission into professional courses and higher education (including PG and UG courses) as well as for recruitment into administrative positivions at national and state level may be a free zone for entry of foreign institutions.

Adult Education

Adult education by foreign entries may be prohibited. This is a nation wide programme , which requires penetration by local people to enthuse and educate illiterate adults. This task may be given to social organizations and primary and secondary schools of the country. On the other hand, the higher education is one field which requires more global perspective and interaction. This should be open to foreign entities removing all obstalces. So is the case of testing services. However, there are certain problems.

(1) **Financial:** India has a vast majority of people who do not have resources to pay for higher education. With the entry of

foreign entitites, the cost of education will rise alarmingly. The government has to arrange loans or subsidies. Loans will help again the middle income groups but not the poor. Safeguards as such are necessary to protect the interests of the poor.

(ii) **Operational:** The entry of foreign entities will create competition and improve educational facilities and quality of educaional outputs. At the same time, a vast number of Indian institutions will face resource crunch. There will be centres of excellence serving the elite whereas the less privileged will have to study in mediocre institutions. In the educational hierachy, the premier courses will be in the hands sof foreign centries, and the less remunerative courses will be left to national organizations. As such, some obstacles are necessary to prevent foreign entities from invading the premier education market. Protection to reputed Indian institutes as matter of preserving our culural heritage becomes necessary.

Phase wise entry

Opportunities may be provided phase-wise to foreign entities to establish their own campuses to offer higher education in selective fields in which India has strong foothold and in those areas into which India could not forge for want of resources. This will create healthy competition and progress in higher education.

Degree granting institutions

The permission to grant degree can be given to those Universities which are accredited by the NAAC in our Country or any global accrediation agency recognized by India. This will provide level playing field for all the participants in this field without discrimination.

Economic needs test on suppliers

It is necessary to put up restrictions to entry throuh economic need tests on suppliers. Only capable and financially sound entities should be allowed to operate. The criteria may include:

- Investment capability

- Proposed courses

- Operating costs and mode (academic infrastructure, staff and others) Without testing if entry is permitted, there will be flood of institutions which jeopardize the interests of students and the image of the nation.

Strategic alliances with local partners

To start with the foreign entities may be asked to go for strategic alliance or partnership or joint ventures. The opening up of the field of education will create two types of competition

(i) Between equals like IIMS, IITs vs foreign entities.

(ii) Between unequals. Foreign entities vs Universities facing financial crunch.

When the local partenership condition is imposed, it helps in

- Safe guarding the interest of local suppliers.
- Improving the quality and spread of operations globally.

The condition may be there for a period of 5 years, which may be called the introductory phase. In this period, the nature of competition and its implications can be observed and understood and further policy guidelines can be evolved. The partnership may be of two types:

- Equal partnership in case of professional education.
- Unequal partnerhsip -- in case of general education domination of foreign entitites and local players in case of adult education.

Private sector suppliers

There is no question of denial of permission to private sector suppliers in India as there is already the dominance of private sector in all fields of education. Only area in which private sector has not entered in a big way is research. However, the entry and operation should be regulated by appropriate regulatory Agencies, as is being done through AICTE (Technlogy and Management), UGC (Higher education).

Reduce the tiers in education system

Wherever government approvals are involved there are delays, politics and corruption in our country. We have four-tier system in our country for professional courses to be started with the affiliation of University. The tiers are AICTE, State Council for Higher Education, State Government and University. The delays and hassles must be removed to pave way for convenience and wider acceptance. A egulatory agency, may be one-stop window to grant permission and settle all related wrangles.

Tax treatment against foreign suppliers

The member country may impose taxes or levy duties like, Licensing fee, Tax on income from royalties and operations, foreign exchange conversion tax on repatriation of income etc. To say that these canot be imposed may be disadvantageous to the developing nations. The twin benefits of such impositios are income and restricted (selective) entry of foreign operators. This will be good even for foreign participants as it will discourage less capable entering the market and vitiate the image of the foreign nation.

Until we arrive at same currency values, the unequal exchange rates will be hitting the equation philosophy. Countries having advantage in exchange while entering the country may be taxed more. Such taxation is based on the principle of progressive taxation rates.

This becomes essential to safeguard the country's balance of payments position, since globalization of education would lead to loss of foreign exchange. By taxing and collecting royalty, the country can maintain its national income.

Treat foreign partners different to that of local partners

This is required in a country like India which is developing and there is a need to subsidize education. When local partners can do it effectively foriegn partners cannot due to their overheads and quality of education. There will be favoured treatment to locals to protect the interest of the nation. However, there is a need for clear cut domestic laws which prescribe rules of the game.

Subsidies

Subsidies are not necessary for higher education and professional education. Loans and scholarships are important for backward sections on economic basis Adult education and training of social workers etc. need be subsidized.

Local hiring emphasising quality

The local hiring conditions may be there to safeguard the interest of the nationals. However, such conditions must be reasonable in the interest of the quality of services that the foreign entity offers and the viability.

Regulate visiting faculty and trainers

The number of persons visiting the country for the purpose of imparting training and education cannot be restricted. But, on the other hand, if it is not regulated institutions may solely depend upon the visiting faculty or triners and escalate costs of education and narrow down the employment opportunities to locals. There must be an assessment of how many foriegn nationals will be required to move in and out. For some time to come such observation is necessary to gain an understanding of the situation.

Commitments India should seek from WTO member countries

India needs to give a swadeshi thrust in globalsing education. In this context, the following specific commitments should be sought from WTO member countries having market access for education sector.

Principle of reciporcity

The participation should be based on the principle of reciprocity. There should be bilateral agreements between the local partner and foreign player in terms of exchange of faculty students and research. A faculty member working in an Indian university in which foreign university has a stake should have opportunity to visit and works in the foriegn university as much as his or her counterparts of the foriegn university are given opportunities to work in Indian University. Similarly, the students may be allowed to study anywhere by credit system.

Recognition of Indian degrees

Granting of the degree shall be in the joint name indicating the partnerhsip. There shall be an International Assessment and Accrediation council to rate the universities. In fact, World University Centres region-wise in which the universities of the region may be set up who can grant degrees to students who fulfil the requirements for qualifying to a degree.

Discourage one way traffic of natural persons

While free movement is desirable there are apprehensions that it may be used to the advantage of the foriegn country. The expenses involved one-way traffic of natural persons, the dominance of foreigners in the name of experts, etc., may erode credibility of the good intentions of foriegn participants. As such certain restrictions are necessary in this regard to avoid domination of foriegn units in less developed nations.

Seek MFN Status

In the Asian countries due to cultural similairities, India can play a key role in offering educational services. Further, there are fields like computers, engineering and medicine where Indian expertise is good. We may seek MFN exemption to operate in developing nations.

Modes of supply

In case of higher education and professional education, our country may commit partially for conventional and non-conventional system of education and for the four modes of supply, viz., cross-boarder supply, consumption abroad, presence of natural persons and commercial presence.

Encourge profit making institutions in higher education and profit.

India has already opened up education to private institutions. Though they operate in the name of trust or society, the intentions are clarly commercial and money is made through backdoors.

However, there is need to give subsides to primary and secondary education in view of the backwardness in the country.

Quality assessment on mutually agreed criteria

The entry be restricted to only quality educational institutions. Otherwise, the benefit of joint venture will be marginal. There may be International Educational Assessmnt and Accreditation Council to rate the universities and only the highly accredited institutions may be allowed to enter the country.

Conclusion

To conclude, I would say that India can follow current procedure for quality of education, restrict repatriation of funds and subsidize primary, secondary and adult education and increase scholarships to the pooor. A Swadeshi thrust to improve per capita incomes, literacy and increase in standard of living is to be given while entering into any memorandum of understanding (MOU) with foreign nations. Strict vigilance of beneficiaries since the benefits are reaching those with fake income and social status certificates. Education subsidy to be given based on economic criteria rather than others. Subsidize research in thrust areas like engineering, medicine, management and biotechnology.

USE OF KNOWLEDGE MANAGEMENT IN ORGANIZATIONS WITH SPECIAL REFERENCE TO SERVICE-TO SERVICE ORGANIZATIONS

Bhanushree Reddy

Knowledge is a concrete term, when compared to the vogue terms like "expert systems", "core competencies", "corporate memory" etc., which were meant to be the key assets of an organization. the real asset of a company lies in the people, their knowlege and skills. Knowledge is information. We lived in times where we needed more information about products, consumers and markets, to make an organization succesful. Now we are flooded with information successful and intelligent managers only realized the value of knowledge and able to fluid mix the experiences, values, information and expert analysis.

The London Times called knowledge management (K.M.) as fifth discipline as business strategy, accounting, marketing and human resources accounted as other four disciplines of management. Knowledge Management helps an organization to create, communicate, apply knowledge of all kinds at all levels to achieve business goals. Market shifts, technology proliferates, competitiors become more and today's products and services become obsolete and crate an uncertain environment. The success of a company lies in its ability to create new knowledge, analyse it embody it into new products and services, which gives them competitive edge over the others.

Now let us see how Knowledge Management helps an organization to be successful over competitors.

1. KM helps to increase corporate value in times of uncertainty.

2. Knowledge cannot be copied like technology by the competitors.

3. KM helps to avoid work duplication.

4. KM helps in competing through process, i.e., the process used to deliver a product/service to a consumer.

5. KM supports and structures the cross functional collaboration in an organization and provides the cultural change needed to make such colaborations work properly.

6. Usually companies go by assumptions of the people about markets, customer and business environment. KM helps top management to maintain and analyse the knowledge regarding such assumptions in critical times.

7. Time is money. Companies with increased responsibility to changing environments, dynamic competitors, new evolving markets, innovative products look for KM for push delivery of information to right people at the right time.

8. KM provides opportunities for creating tangible assets to organizations with the help of corporate knowledge.

9. KM combined with job mobility gives the company a superior edge over competitors.

KM IN THE CONTEXT OF SERVICE INDUSTRY

Service sector is increasingly important in the information age as its is much larger and holding a considerable share in advanced economics. The survial of service industry totally relies on the concept of customer satisfaction and the quality of the service provided. Service industry includes, hotels, hospitals, call centres financial services provided by banks etc. The process of service production involves the flow and program of the service procedure that take place. For example a customer who buys a Television is not interested in the manufacturing process but interested only in the service provided by the T.V. But a customer at a fine restraurant is not only interested in the end result ie., cessation of hunger but also in the service process that takes place when he orders something. The entire experience of a customer arriving at a restaurant, being seated, enjoying the ambiance, ordering, receiving finally eating the meal and coming out of the restaurant with mental and physical satisfaction is more important to the hotel industry.

The service process to less emotional and sensual services like getting a bank loan sanctioned is also very critical and important to the service provider. A customer who applies for a bank loan not only evaluates the loan amount and the rate of interest he is getting from a bank but also the speed and sensitivity of the approval process of the loan by the bank as well. Many multinational banks are taking care not to loose the customers by making them go through labourious approval procedures and paper work.

Now how can we apply KM to the so sensitivie service sector?

Using knowledge efficiently to create customer value depend on the organization's ability to respond to the imperatives and challenges posed in a rapid changing environment. To face the new challenges the idea flow both in and out of organization and exposing people to many different perspectives and possibilities is a must. The process "Learn" and "Contribute" are relatively new to organizations. The formal recognition of this process as a means of creating competitive advantage is new. The challenge for organizations is to find ways to embed learning into the way people work. This is a method of training people to face any challenges while working in the organization with the help of information and knowledge management.

First challenge the service sector faces is knowledge generation about customers before providing the service process. Ths process comprises of three important functions.

- Knowlege acquisition
- Knowledge synthesis and
- Knowledge creation

KNOWLEDGE ACQUISITION: This looks like a simple function of acquiring knowledge that is available somewhere from exiting documents. For service industry knowlege acquisition is capturing tacit knowlege of its people/customers into its repositiories. Identifying external sources of technology or process expertise, market intelligence, the ever changing needs of the people also contribute to the acquisition of knowledge.

KNOWLEDGE SYNTHESIS: This is a process of putting different kinds of information together to produce new pattern and ideas. The acquired knowledge, information about the peoples requirements in a service industry are stream lined and leads to generation of new ideas.

KNOWLEDGE CREATION: Under this process the organization tries to create innovative knowledge bases from the knowledge acquired and syntehsised earleir. The knowledge creation includes

- Determining the kind of knowledge relevant to the organisation.
- Knowledge storage
- Maintaining the knowledge bases.
- Creating knowledge strategies relavant to the business strategies.

KM IN SERVICE ORGANIZATIONS

DATA COLLECTED	*INFORMATION*	*KNOWLEDGE*	
Knowledge Acquired ----	**Knowledge Synsthesised----**	**Knowledge Creation---**	**Knowlede Management**

The data collected becomes valuable information by analysisng, correlating and summarising information becomes knowledge by adding experience, context interpretation and discussion values.

When organizations asses how well their knowledge based assets can be leveraged to create value for customers they cross a threshold between two activity flows of the overall knowledge management process. The process step that include get, use, learn and contribute lie on the tactical side of model and become activated by a sepcific and immediate opportunity or demand.

In an economy where value and competitive advantage are increasingly derived from the management of intangible assets, rather than the ownership of physical or financial capital, organizations are inventing new approaches to understanding and monitoring how well they build the right mix of knowlege based assets. To asses knowledge based assets so that delebarte, constructive intiatives can be strengthened or launched to build, sustain or divest them, organization must meet the imperatives and challanges.

The step in knowledge management process which ensure that future knowlege keeps the organization viable or competitive, requires a fresh look at what it means to manage organization will build knowledge through relationship with employees, suppliers, customers, the community in which they operate. Organizations must do more than get today job done well. They must also integrate the strategic activities of growth and renewal into the course of everyday work. To build and sustain knowledge, organisational management must take a fresh look at the following imperatives and challenges.

Resources are channeled in ways that replenish and create knowledge.

- Subordinate information technology to people.
- Structure positions that foucs organizational attention on knowledge based assets.

The organizations form relationships that further its knowledge management objectives.

- Preach cooperation among internal divisions.
- Partner in new ways with other organizations.
- Retain the right people.

The organization sees how to extract the value embedded in knowledge.

- Use knowledge to strengthen the customer relationship.
- Dis-assemble the organizational whole to take a fresh look at its parts.
    - Demonstrate that value certain is a value proportions.
    - Make room for the entire person to show up for work everyday.

IMPERATIVES AND CHALLENGES

- Unnecessary knowledge should not be acquired in the first place.
- Discriminate between the forms of knowledge that can be leveraged and those that are limited.

- Find alternatives to direct acquisition in order to experiment with knowledge. Knowledge that is drain on resources is converted into sources of value.

- Recognise and dispense with true resources drains.

- Avoid throwing out the baby with the bath water.

Conclusion

Knowledge management is highly contextualized information system enriched with individual interpretation and expertise and also is organizations valuable asset. Knowledge management is not a new concept in India. The Upanishads are the best examples of knowledge of entire civilisations and socieites and were passed on to the generations of scholars who can influence the thinking and living processes of society. When a society acquires knowledge that leads to happiness and finally self-actualisation unfolds in front of us a world where there will be no place for doubts, distrust and suspicion.

Dr. Bhanu Sree Reddy
M.A., M.B.A., Ph.D.

SECTION-VI

SERVICE ECONOMY AND FINANCIAL SERVICE SECTOR

OVERVIEW

Section Six opens up with financial service sector under the new service economy. There are three papers. Dr. K.V.G. Rao in his paper deals with financial services such as leasing, hire purchase, factoring, fund/asset based financial services while merchant banking services as fee based advisers services. The challenge faced by the sector under LPG pressures. The financial services include mutual funds, insurance and banking sector. Second paper by Dr. P. Malayadri focusses on banking sector for innovative techniques under the pressure of LPG. The paper suggests customer relationship management for effective customer retention by banks. Dr. Niranjan Reddy and Praash Reddy paper deals with merchant banking in India its crucial role in the liberalized era both Indian and Foreign banks posing unhealthy competion in the economy suggesting and streamlining their activity for better economic development.

MARKETING OF FINANCIAL SERVICES

Dr. K. Venugopal Rao
Associate Professor
S.K. Institute of Management
S.K. University, ANANTAPUR-515003

Prof. C.N. Krishna Naik
S.K. Institute of Managment
S.K. University, ANANTAPUR-515003

MARKETING OF FINANCIAL SERVICES

Since June 1991, the country has been going through a process which should ultimately lead to restructuring of the Indian Econmy. One of the results should be a considerable change in the structure of the GDP. Services have gone up as a percentage of GDP in India, from 16% in 1988 to 38.8% in 1991. This compares with the figures for 1988 in Japan of 56 per cent. Taiwan 50 per cent, Korea 55 per cent; and Indonesia - 40 per cent. On the other hand, in China, services account for only 10 per cent of the GDP. In more developed economics the contribution of services tend to become high as the population spends an increasing proportion of its income on entertainment and recreation, health, education, training and other such personal services.

Service Sector and Indian Economy

The services sector dominates the Indian econom today, contributing more than half of our national income. It's the fastest growing sector, with an average annual growth rate of 8 per cent in the 1990s. One in every two Indians earns his livelihood by providing services. Conventional economic theory divides economies into three broad sectors; agriculture, industry and service. In the beginning all the economies in the world were agriculture based. By the beginning of the 20th century, the pulse of most rich economies had shifted from farms to factories. The dominance of industry as a source of income and jobs - lasted 50-80 years, before it was taken over by services. In India, however, the age of industry never really arrived. The largest that industry could grow was up to 22.7 per cent of the economy in 1997-98. India has leapfrogged into services more by default than design. India is moving from agriculture to services without going through and enjoying the fruits of broad based industrialization.

Table 1: Composition of GDP

Year	*Agriculture*	*Industry*	*Services*
1950-51	55.4	12.8	31.8
1990-91	30.9	25.4	43.7
1999-2000	25.5	22.1	52.4

India's future lies in services, much more than industry. By global standards, India is a laggard in services. The share of services in GDP is a whopping 83 per cent in Hong Kong and 64 per cent in Singapore. India too is becoming a service economy, though slowly is 1995, the share of services in GDP was 41 per cent, well above the 29 per cent share of industry. What is more, the share of services has risen steadily from 36 per cent in 1980 to 41 per cent in 1995. Industry grew fast in this period, so services grew even faster. Yet the share of services in India's GDP remains lower than in its neighbours in South Asia. As against India's ratio of 41 per cent, that of Pakistan is 50 per cent. Bangladesh 52 per cent and Sri Lanka 52 per cent. India's ratio looks emasculated even in comparison with Sub-Saharan Africa (48 per cent) or Latin America (55 per cent).

India's greatest comparative advantage lies not in manufacturing but in services. There is much talk of harnessing our cheap, skilled manpower in manufacturing, but the scope for this is quite limited. The labour content of all manufacturing is dropping steadily with new automated technology. In Maruti Udyog, for instance, the labour content of a car is below 2.5 per cent. In the new steel plants like those of Essar Steel and Ispat India, wages and salaries amount to only 1.3 per cent of sales. Even in other organized industries the labour content in a modern factory is typically below 10 per cent.

The global shift from manufacturing to services implies that the scope for increasing exports of goods will steadily get squeezed over time. The boardrooms prefer to use sophisticated technologies in place of employing more personnel since they find it cost-effective. New generations of advanced technologies are found establishing an edge over the excellence of human resources. After year of neglecting exports, we must of course catch up. But we must also realize that we need increasingly to export services rather than goods.

Today, service sector dominates the economies of other developed nations as well. As countries develop, the role of agriculture in the economy declines and that of services rises. Highly developed countries all have more than 50% of GDP and employment derived from services.

The winds of change are battering the very core of the socio-psycho-economic values around which Indian society has been knit for hundreds of years. The change in the value system is forcing the emergence of new life styles, consequently overhauling our consumption pattern. The forces of technology, communication networks, flow of information, rising education levels, exposure to western life style and increase in incomes are some of the change agents.

Apart from the changes in life style, other factors which explain the increasing demand for services include increasing affluence which allows consumers to spend more on dry cleaning, repairs, security sevices, travel, entertainment, hotels, restaurants, personal care, etc. Career consciousness among the youth and children creates a demand for educational institutions, and tutorial bureaus. As more and more women join the work stream, there will be less and less time aailable for domestic jobs. This holds promise for childcare services, domestic and household services, nurseries and away-from home meal services. Growing life expectancy among Indians is a potential market for old peoples' homes, nursing homes, and health care institutes. As products become more complex, the need for technicians, skilled specialists, and repair shops will grow. Also as life in general becomes more complex because of complicated rules and regulations, the demand for professional services like lawyers, consultants, travel agents, marriage counsdlors, legal advisers, employment services, transportation, tele-communication and courier services will boom. Further, as people get more leisure, the demand for travel services, airlines, railways, taxis, hotels, restaurants, travel resorts, long distance communication entertainment, and game clubs will also increase.

Service sector has a stable demand as against fluctuating fortunes in the case of Agriculture and recession and boom conditions in Manufacturing sector. With increasing specialization in all fields, this trend has a tendency to proliferate in services also, as hiring of services is more economical than to undertake their own services.

Service Sector and Private Sector

The private sector is catering into many areas which were earlier reserved for the public sector. Entry of the private sector into airlines, bus services, hoteliering and restaurants, foreign banks as well as some Indian private banks, to name a few areas, gives the consumer choices which he did not have at all, or to any significant extent, before. As the consumer becomes more demanding because there is competition, even public enterprise providers will be compelled to improve the quality of their services, or face a loss of market, and subsequent decline in their fortunes.

Marketing of Financial Services

Financial services, as the name suggests, include the whole range of services which help in raising of finances in an effective and efficient manner. It includes both funds/assets based and fee based advisory services. The former includes, leasing, hire purchase, factoring etc., services while the latter includes basically the merchant banking services vic., project counselling, issue management credit rating etc. Non-banking finance companies, merchant bankers, and credit guaranteeing institutions are playing an important role in provision of these services.

Marketing orientation or placing the consumer at the center of the enterprise is an ideal that should be followed by all organizations. This is imperative in the case of services. Services and marketing are inseparable. Service marketers should break away from the traditional production-oriented mode and adopt the marketing-mode.

After the recent liberalization measures from 1992 onwards, involving deregulation, privatization and globalisation, the financial sector has witnessed a deepening and widening of its services. Expansion and diversifiation became the hallmarks of banking and non-banking financial sector. There was a mushroom growth of NBFCs. The problems in this transition period were many such as emergence of various spurious companies, increased competition with the weak and inefficient finding it difficult to survive and many malpractices are being tackled by the SEBI through its directives, inspection and audit of all the capital market intermediaries and by the RBI through its increased powers of registration, directives, inspection etc., of the NBFCs. In the process, many merchant bankers and some other capital market intermediaries closed their business due to lack of sufficient business, tough competion and the need for higher networth, which they could not muster. Similarly, many NBFCs below Rs.25 lakh networth, inefficient ones and corrupt units which were refused licence from the RBI had to close their doors.

In this new competitive environment and globalised trading practices, the marketing of financial services assumed greater significance. Today's financial services market requires new strategies to survive and continue to operate. They have to adopt new marketing strategies and tactices which enable them to capture the minimum opportunities with the lowest risks in order to enable them to survive and meet the tough competiton from global players of domestic and foreign origin.

New Challenges

The challenges posed to the financial sector in the market place are the following.

(1) Deregulation,
(2) Advanced Information technology,
(3) Globalised markets and growing volumes of financial transaction,
(4) Volatility of the markets and
(5) Increased customer demands and sophistication of markets and customers.

Many of the existing could not cope with this new environment. Most of them sought to strengthen themselves by mergers and acquisitions, diversification or closure of some business lines which are uneconomical. Others have met the challenges by better management talent, adoption of the new organization structure, strengthening of the information system and technology and drastic changes in their marketing strategies. Adoption of all risk management strategies, soundly formulated business plans, acquiring new innovative talents, SWOT analysis, and correction of weaknesses and threats while making full utilization of their strengths and opportunities.

The Financial Services Marketing Mix

The challenges facing the financial services industry mean that greater emphasis than ever before must be placed on developing and implementing successful marketing programmes to create and foster a customer orientation. True differentiation of financial products is virtually impossible to achieve because they are intrinsically the same, offering similar benefits and services to consumers. The degree of substitutability between brands is correspondingly very high at the outset (for example, at the supplier or product selection stage). Once a financial product has been sold, however, the customer is frequently tied in over a long period and may even face penalties if they wish to change supplier (as in the case of fixed rate mortgages) or if they wish to discontinue the service (terminating endowment or insurance agreements before the full term has expired for example).

Some key issues which must be taken into consideration in designing the most effective financial services marketing mix are as follows.

Product

There is little or no room for innovation in product design due to the case with which competitors can make similar offerings, for example by altering charges or interest rates to meet those of competitors. Additionally, many financial services are affected by other restrictions, such as government directives relating to income tax and investments or constraints on the amounts which can be invested. Differentiation, therefore, can best be achieved through the other elements of the marketing mix.

Price

The price in financial services terms relates to the costs involved to the customer in, say, bank charges or credit card interest rates. These prices scem to evoke low levels of customer sensitivity as many customers enjoy 'free' banking, by maintaining their current accounts in credit, for example, or paying their credit card balances off each month. The introduction of new charges, however, such as the annual credit card fee had a noticeable effect initially, however, and sparked off competitive reaction from lenders prepared to offer cards with no annual charge. Pricing can therefore be used to differentiate the offering and is likely to be used by customers in selecting a service.

Promotion

Major advertising campaigns are undertaken continuously by banks, and other major financial institutions such as insurance companies. The main purpose of the advertising is to strengthen awareness of the brand and company image and to inform the market about the services available.

Place

Place or location has always been regarded as critical in retail financial services where high street positions are maintained by most of the large institutions. For transaction services where regular and frequent branch contact is required this can be important. The telephone banking service, has proved that a bank without branches is possible though its customers still need access to convenient ATM outlets. Some consumers prefer personal, face-to-face contact within a branch and may be more likely to use a local branch. Changes in distribution systems, tecnology and consumer demands are all key influences on the evolution of the 'place' component of the marketing mix.

People

Customer care is at the forefront of both quality and differentiation in the financial services industry. Staff need to be highly trained not only in customer care but in how to respond to the rapidly changing market environment. Personnel can be used to develop competitive advantage in the marketplace and to build and maintain relationships with customers.

Process

This is the main area where technological advances have led to major change. Improvements in the process stem not only from the automation of many transactions and data handling within organizations but also from process re-engineering to reduce delays in processing mortgage applications for example, or the installation of automated queuing systems to cut down on waiting time.

Physical Evidence

The environment in banks is changing, moving away from austerity and formality to a more friendly approach reflected in more attractive branch layouts and decor. Other physical evidence plays an important part in financial transactions such as the documentation which must be presented by salespeople to prove that they are authorized to offer investment advice. This creates confidence and helps to build the relationship between customer and provider. Physical evidence is also widely used to tangibilise the service. Attractive brochures and policy documents, presented in glossy folders, cheque book and credit cared holders, 'gold' credit cards, chidlren's 'collectable' money boxes are all examples of physical evidence being used in this way.

Services are different and that too financial services are more different from products. Here consumer-oriented are the services and there are more specific to consumer and time. These cannot be standardized and are not easily reproducible. Human element in these services is more prominent and hence management talent and personnel skills counts. Each service activity needs a different type of market strategy and hence generalization is risky.

Mutual Funds

Selling by Mutual funds is also different. As per SEBI norms, they cannot promise a fixed return nor indulge in prohibited practices such as speculative trading. Many Mutual funds in India have underperformed party due to lack of expertise, stringent investment norms of SEBI and poor market conditions. In this scenario, their marketing strategies have limited alternatives. They can offer services, which may still fall short of the expectations of customers. They an at best promise safety of funds buyback arrangements and Trustworthiness. In fact, while mutual funds, venture funds, and offshore funds are amenable to proper sales strategies like road shows, advertisement and hoardings, but not so in the case of stock brokers and bankers, who cannot advertise their products as intermediaries. In the case of other intermediaries, like merchant bankers registrars, collecting bankers, etc., they can be customer friendly, meet the challenges by quick adaptive methods and management skills to adjust to the requirements of customers quickly and timely delivery and a serious commitment to quality. Their customers are companies and their requirements are specific.

Insurance

Unlike the above services, Life Insurance and general Insurance require a different kind of marketing strategy, namely, a diversified product range, a mix of products suitable to meet varying needs of consumers, combining life with endowment, or a combination of accident, health and unemployment, etc. Their approach and their talents are more powerful than the attributes of product range. This is direct selling. Letters to potential customers, personal approach through Telephone, visits, etc., are also a part of the marketing strategy.

Banking Sector

In commercial banking, marketing strategy has to meet the challenges by strengthening themselves by mergers or diversifications such as going to national from regional and from national to global level playing. They have to have a dynamic management team, modified value systems, suitable to the requirements of customers and a market thrust to meet the challenge of competitors. There is need for diversification of product range such as introduction of credit cards or debit cards, 24 hour banking. ATM and other computerized services, banking from home through the website of the internet, electronic transfer of funds and dematerialisation of all physical certificates. Banks may be prepared to service the customers as they desire, say by arranging Portfolio Management, Tax Payment, consultancy and personal investments. These are all called Market responsive management practices and customer oriented services.

The emphasis has shifted away from deposits to capturing prime customers wanting credit facilities, raising funds from the market, offering more and more technology-oriented products, and even recruiting and retaining skilled personnel. Perhaps the most significant change is the pursuit of asset led growth.

Top management personnel in most banks had little or no experience about marketing in a competitive environment. They had spent a better part of their career in deposit mobilization and in achieving deposit budgets. There was no consciously planned strategy for achieving a given set of results.

The reform process has awakened the management and staff to the grim realities. The emergence of private sector banks and the way they are forging ahead has made managements sit up and start thinking in right earnest about marketing. Banks will need product laboratories for designing and developing new products.

Attempts were made to attract new customers and to retain existing ones by offering them free remittance facilities or payments within five minutes. After nationalisation, there was considerbale standardization. Uniform service charges and similarity of products became the order of the day. In these circumstances, customer services became the key element in the marketing plan.

In conclusion, financial institutions should adopt marketing approach towards its financial services. If they want to survive and grow in the competitive environment prevailing today.

References

1. *India Today*, February 19, 2001.
2. *The Economic Times*, ***February 11th, 1998.***
3. ***The Hindu***, November 14th 1998.
4. S.M. Jha, "Services Marketing, Himalaya Publishing House, Mumbai, 2000.
5. Harsh Verma, "Marketing of Services," Global Business Press, New Deli, 1993.
6. Vasant Joshi, "Managing Indian Banks the Challenges Ahead", Response Books, New Delhi, 1998.

CRM IN INDIAN BANKS: SOME STRATEGIES

** Dr. P. Malyadri, M.Com., Ph.D. PGDCA.*
*** V.D. Santosh Kumar, M.Com.*

In the Global economic scenario, new trade blocks are emerging and international competition is zooming. It involves replacement of sheltered culture of industry and business by competitive world wide environment and the organizations every where have to reconsider their traditional strategies and methods of operation. In the emerging scenario, the LPG strategy has brought sea changes in the banking sector that have started rocking the bottom lines of many Indian public sector banks. Globalization is transforming the financial services industry significantly by shifting the advantages from the providers of financial service to the users. With the revolution of information technology the traditional role of the banks which used to be that of 'money lending' has assumed broader dimensions. With competition gaining ground, banks are trying to adopt innovative approaches to retain their existing business. One of the recent innovations in the service industry, particularly in the banking sector, in many part of the world is "Customer Relationship Management" (CRM). It is in this context, that the customer service has to be critically analyzed and appropriate strategies drawn up, not only to attract new customers, but also to retain the existing one.

The present paper attempts to examine the major initiatives taken by banks themselves and also to draw up a strategic

---

* Dr. Malyadri is Ph.D. guide in the Dept. of Business Management, Osmania University, Hyderabad. Presently Serving as a Reader in Commerce, Vivekananda Govt. College,, Vidyanagar, Hyderabad -500044.

** Mr. Santosh Kumar is Ph.D. Scholar, Department of Commerce, Osmania University, Hyderabad.

framework for improving the quality of customer service.

CUSTOMER RELATIONSHIP MANAGEMENT (CRM)

Relationship marketing some times is referred to as CRM. CRM is a relationship process which an organization can cultivate with its customer segments in such a way that it could benefit both the customer and the organisations. The growing expectations of the customers, fast changing preference and opportunities available to him as a consumer have made him the king in true sense. Customer satisfaction is a growing concern for the banks who want to grow in this competitive world of today.

The concept of CRM is now gaining wide aceptance and is recognized as a powerful tool for business development and to have an edge over the competitors on account of the universal traits of human behaviour. Organizations has earlier focused on their products as the starting point and then looked around for customers to sell it. But the approach of CRM is different -- it starts with the customer not the totality of customers because each customer is an individual and thus each customer has to dealt individually to find out what they want and design the products as per their need and supply it. In a nut shell, CRM is about growing enduring relationships with profitable customers.

In financial services, Nationalized as well as new generation private banks and foreign banks have introduced customer friendly products and services like.

* Account statements
* ATM (Automated Teller Machines)
* Any where Banking
* Credit Card/Debit Cards/Smart Cards
* Corporate Banking Terminals
* EFT (Electronic Funds Transfer)
* ECS (Electronic Clearing Systems)
* Electronic Data Interchange

* Home Banking
* Internet Bank
* INFINET (Indian Financial Network)
* Integrated Payment and Settlement systems (IPSS)
* Internet Banking
* Mobile Banking
* MICR Cheques
* Online Banking
* Point of sale terminal
* Real Time gross Settlement (RTGS)
* SPNS (Shared Payment Network System)
* Tele-Banking
* Universal Banking
* 24 hours Banking
* 24 hours Toll-free Customer Call centres

ROLE OF PRODUCTS AND SERVICES

By virtue of the Banks operating in the financial service industry, the customer comes in to contact with them for use of various services and products. Products or services are vital link between the customers and the banks. It also needs to be kept in view that each products has a life cycle which means that products will have to be updated on an going basis to keep them suitable as per customer's changing needs. A good product can not be expected to remain in demand for ever as customer' requirements keep on changing wih the change in economic, social and political changes.

The follwing steps and measures were taken by the RBI to redress the grievance of cusomers for the better quality of service.

* Setting up of customer service committees
* Observing customers meet day
* Setting up of customer service centres
* Observance of "Customer Day"
* Setting up of several expert connittees
* Implementing Banking ombudsman scheme.

TOWARDS A STRATEGY

Now the Banks have to face the challenge of modernization and upgradation as well as tailoring quality to fulfil customers expectations. They exhibit uneven strentghs, efficiency, resources, problem dimensions and problem-solving capabilities. With a view to combat competition and to become more effective in the matters of Customer Service, Bankers would do well to draw up strategic frame work addressing the key issues concerning the quality aspects thereof. These have been enumerated below.

E-CRM is fast emerging as an effective CRM strategy. It originated from call centres and found its natural habitat on the world wide web (WWW). An effective E-CRM model makes a judicious use through E-mail, chatting, call centres etc., computer technology integration (CTI) is another emerging facility of reaching out to far-flung customers at low cost. It can also be used to address the customer grievances by offering quick remedies to minor problems.

The banks must be able to collect, store and access all the information it will need on each customer. it should be followed by appointment of highly motivated relationship Manager (RM) who will identify each customer according to current and potential value. RM must develop long range and annual customer relationship plans. The annual relationship plans should state objecives strategies, specific actions and the required resources.

Upgradation of human resources is of utmost importance. it is always the man behind the project on whom the success of any project depends. With greater role being played by technology in this process, it is imperative that the skills of the employees be upgraded to meet the future challenges.

Information Kiosks may be installed which can be accessed by customers for getting account details, by keying in his account number and a password. it would also be possible for the customer to take a print-out of his transactions from the kiosks. Customers would be able to access information regarding various products offerings of the bank, opening of various types of accounts. This would reduce the burden on the staff, as the customers will be in a position to obtain information on their own.

Loyalty and customer satisfaction, are the two aspects strongly linked to CRM programme. Ensuring customer loyalty and satisfaction is basically the philosophy of training and taking good care of employees, who in turn will take good care of the customers. Besides loyalty and satisfaction, communication is a vital aspect of any CRM programme.

Taking advantage of computerization and technological upgradation, banks need to develop a comprehensive customer information system at branches so as to know the customers like age, qualifications, income level, tastes and preferences etc., should be created which will help in providing continuous feed back for anticipating customer needs.

Quality circle should be formed at the branches with more that say 10-12 staff and they should be persuaded to take up at least one project in each month quarter with a view to improve customer service, general efficiency or productivity of the branches. These should be properly recognized appreciated by zonal office depending upon the quality of output and this should be done sooner than later so that the concerned employees feel elated and encouraged.

The publicity campaign undertaken by the joint publicity committee has almost become a routine exercise and is not proving effective with the customer both in scope and scale. As a customer identifies himself with a particular bank and not with a sector of banks. It is necessary to allow the public sector banks flexibility to persue as imaginative publicity policy related to their bank level needs so as to reach their various prospective customers with the service products attractively and effectively designed. The publicity campaign targetted for the bank customers/public in general can be undertaken by the Indian banks association.

The efforts being made by the bank management cannot yield positive results unless the total involvement of the staff, down the line is forthcoming. In view of the competition and threats being faced by the banks the attitude of the staff will have to undergo a drastic change and their reorientation towards the needs and expectations of the customers will have to be brought about so that they display more care and concern for the customers.

Measurement of customer satisfaction through construction of consumer satisfaction index (CSI) would be a novel idea in the context of the imperative for improvement in customer services. The idea of CSI is to evolve a mechanism for a scientific assessment of the performance of public sector banks in serving their clients.

Conclusion

With the changing scenario in the banking industry the concept of universal banking has already started emerging. In the changing phase the customer has become the key focus area of all sectors in the banking industry. The banks which provide value-added services and satisfaction to customers shall bound to become winners. With the tough competition retaining market share still call for adoption of CRM. The main focus should be on measuring profitability of each customer and not the products. There should be gradual shift to relationship marketing by introducing this new approach in select branches and the same can be expanded latter. As times get together banks will have to focus on retaining their key customers. Customers are becoming increasingly more demanding and are looking for better and more convenient services. In such a scenario public sector banks have to play a proactive role anticipating changes in customers demands and equip themselves to face the private banks and the global challenges.

References

Anderson, Alan R and Arthur Best "Consumers complain - Does business respond", Harward Business Review, July-Aug 19787 pp.93-101.

CZEPIEL, John a Larry J Roserberg and Adebayo Akerele, "Perspectives on consumer satisfaction" proceedings, Fall Conference, American marketing Association, 1974.

Gilmore and Pine, "Customer satisfaction is no longer enough", central bank of India Economic Bulletin, Aug 2001.

Latha Kuttappan "Customer Oriented" Business India, November 6-19, 1995, p.100.

MALYADRI P., "Commercial Banks in the customer service: A Study" Banking Finance, June 1988, Vol. 1, pp. 10-12.

Rangarajan C. "Banking in the High-tech Environment" State Bank of Hyderabad, Planning News Letter, March 2000, Vol. No. 95, Pp. 2-6.

Raj Kapila "On going developments in Banking anf Financial Sector" AF Book News, Vol. IX No.5, Feb. 2001, pp.3-5.

Sahoo B. "Banking Technology Vision", IBA Bulletin June, 1999, Vol. XXI, No. pp. 5-9.

Uma Kapila "Financial Sector Reforms" AF Book News, Vol IX, No.5, 2001, pp.5-7.

Yogeshwar Kumar "Electronic Banking" IBA Bulletin March 2000, Vol. XX No. 5, pp. 10-13.

MERCHANT BANKING AND ITS ROLE IN ECONOMIC DEVELOPMENT

Dr. P Niranjan Reddy
Dr. J Prakash Reddy

The Concept

A Merchant Banker has been defined under the Securities Exchange Board of India (SEBI) rules 1992 as "any person who is engaged in the business of issues management either by making arrangements regardin selling, buying or subscribing to the securities as manager, consultant, adviser or rendering corporate advisory service in relation to such issue management".

Merchant Banking refers to an organization that underwrites corporate securities and advices such clients on issues like corporate mergers etc involved in the ownership of commercial ventures. This organization may be a bank or corporate body or properietary concern.

In fact there is no universally accepted definition for "Merchant Banker". It assumes different functions in different countries. As a result, there are varied definitions for merchant Banking, merchant Banker. Merchant Banking is defined as "an institution covering a wide range of activities such as management of customary services, portfolio management, credit syndication, accepting credit, counselling, insurance etc.

Network of Services rendered by Merchant Bankers

A careful reading of various definitions provided above will enlighten us on the wide spectrum of activities carried on by mer-

Lecturers in Business Administration, Rayalaseem Institute of Information and Management Sciences, Tirupati.

chant Bankers. For example 1. Corporate counselling 2. Project counseling 3. Capital restructuring 4. Portfolio Management (individuals, companies, within the country and also those on NRI's 5. Venture Capital 6. Project financing Financial engineering which in its turn includes: (a) Venture capital (b) Public issues Management (c) Loan syndication (d) Financing of working capital (e) Mobilizing fixed deposits (f) Lease financing (g) acceptance credit and some other miscellaneous services. Merchant Bankers are engaged thus in multi farious activities. they also arrange foreign currency loans offshore leasing, indigenous leasing, public issue management of NRI's and finding company promoters.

All these activities of Merchant Bankers can be broadly divided under two heads are as follows:

(a) Non fund based Activities

- Capital issue management
- Private placement of services
- Loan/Credit/Fund syndication
- Corporate counselling;
- Project counselling
- NRI counselling
- Trusteeship management
- Portfolio management
- Management of mergers and amalgamations
- Management of Buy-in and Buy-outs
- Financial Engineering/Capital restructuring
- Reorganization
- Lease-Broking
- Equipment procurement finance liaison etc.

(B) Fund-based activities such as:

- Underwriting of equity/preference shares, bonds and debentures in new capital issues
- Dealing in money market instruments like placement of commercial papers, certificates of deposits

- Under taking equipment leasing
- Venture capital
- Dealing in secondary market operations.
- Inter-corporate placement of Funds.

Growth of Merchant Banking

Merchant Banking in India has been assuming a very crucial role of late particularly in the post liberalization era. The reasons are obvious. The great strides that took place in the banking sector, since the economic reforms introduced in 1991 gave great fillip to the Merchant Banking movement in India. It must be admitted honestly that some of the commercial bank and developing banking institutions in our country have been rendering Merchant Banking services prior to 1991 also. But as stated earlier several commercial banks in our country took up initiate actively of setting up Merchant Banking divisions in their organisations. Some of the leading commercial banks and development banks have gone ahead with establishing separate subsidiaries were carrying on Merchant Banking activities. Every thing went on well for some time in this process of swift growth of Merchant banking in our countryy, But with the passage of time, merchant Banking activity of the country have been subjected to a multitude of severe rules and regulations. For example several guidelines for Merchant Banking have been laid down by SEBI (Merchant Banker regulations 1992). SEBI has issued revised guidelines in December 1990 Classifying the activities of Merchant Bankers In September 1997 again SEBI brought about several major changes in SEBI (Merchant Banker regulation 1992.) Up to 1970 there were only two foreign bankers which performed merchant Banking activities in India. Later on the State Bank of India and ICICI also launched upon Merchant Banking activites in 1972 and 1973 respectively. Now threre are hundreds of Merchant Banking institutions in the country. Apart from the Indian Merchant Banking institutions, several international reputed Merchant Bankers, e.g. Merrill Lynch, Goldman Sachs, Jardie Fleming etc. have entered the scene now the crux of the problem is along with the proliferation of Merchant Banking institutions in our country. There is also a lot of fierce and some times unhealthy competiton among them this has attracted attention of not only the Government of India, the RBI but also a number of experts in the field of finance management in our country.

As stated earlier, the Merchant Bankers are confronted with complex problems. For example (1) some of the guidelines issued by the SEBI have in fact restricted their activity too. (2) According to the regulations issued by the SEBI every merchant Banker has a minimum net worth of Rs. 1 crore. This is a very harsh stipulation for small Merchant Bankers, however much they are professionalised and specialized. (3) Some of the companies even while issuing shares and debentures are creating problems to Merchant Bankers by way of non cooperation in timely allotment of securities and refund of application money. In all these cases it is Merchant Bankers that are taken to task. (4) Merchant Bankers are still operating issue house as is evident from the scramble to manage the issues floated by established forms in corporate sector (5) Private placing of shares and debentures of companies have difficult task due to the lack of agency which can identify viable products (6) It is not mere death of finance that restrict investment but also, the lack of knowledge to utilize the available funds in most profitable manner. (7) It is reported that there are some companies which have surplus funds that remain idle and hence unproductive. On the other hand it is reported that financial strain of the some companies is so intense then it process a threat to their very existence (8) It is further reported that in the field of exports Indian Merchant Bankers were slow and take little initiative. Merchant Bankers which are not operating under the umbrella of their parent banks are not in a position to participate in such programmes.

Suggestions

A few suggestions are given below to overcome some of the problems experienced by Merchant Bankers in our country and to strengthen their functioning and place them on a more economically viable footing. 1. Merchant Bankers are required to abide by a code of conduct. Every Merchant Bank should observe high standards of integrity and fairness in his dealing with his clients and with other

Merchant Bankers. 2. They are also required to take adequate steps for allotment of security and refund of application money without delay and not indulge in price rigging and manipulation. 3. In the sphere of capital formation the skill of Merchant Bankers has to assume the pivotal role in the interest of the development of economy. 4. India needs a large number of competent and experienced Merchant Bankers having a team of knowledgeable experts in view of spirit of service. These institutions should essentially have legal and technical officials in formulating viable financial to guide and assist the concerned plans. 5. Now there is a greater need on the part of the Merchant Banker to bring awareness of their services through effective publicity. Our banks should also explore the possibility of establishing information bureaus at various industrial and commercial centres so that the prospective customers will come to know and avail their services. 6. Merchant Bankers have to assume wider responsibility for saving industrial units from going sick and guiding industries to be set up in industrially backward areas to minimize regional imbalances in industrial development of our country. 7. Merchant Bankers have wide opportunities before them. The economic developmetns of our country during planning era have broad based these opportunities. Merchant Bankers have to tap these wide opportunities. For this purpose they have to originate, motivate, innovate and implement new devices and techniques in management of capital issues and mobilization of capital resources etc. 8. Merchant Bankers can also play a leading role in rapid development of rural areas through mobilizing savings in larger measure in these areas and make all conceivable efforts e.g. rural industries, encouraging rural entrepreneurship, set up more and more business and industrial units in rural sector. 9. Merchant Bankers can also play a leading role in providing better services for portfolio management for small investors through taking resources to mutual funds in a substantial manner. 10. Merchant Bankers have to take greater initiative in establishing secondary market for commercial papers; rediscounting of bills; strengthening their expertise in the field of international merchant banking, utilize the latest technologies available internationally, and encourage foreign investors to take adequate interest in profitable investments in India.

References

1. J.C. Varma's "Manual of Merchant Banking.
2. Merchant Banking - Study material- ICFAI.
3. E. Gorden, K. Natarajan "Financial Markets and Services" Himalaya Publishing House.

SECTION -VII

SERVICE ECONOMY UNDER THE IMPACT OF INFORMATION TECHNOLOGY

OVERVIEW

This section deals with revolutionary sector of the service economy with a pervasive influence - Information Technology (IT). The papers looks at what could be called a knowledge based economy according to Prof. CSGK and Chandrasekhar with heralding of spriitual age. The implications for the developing countries with a pervasive role of IT industry making us to prepare ourselves facing these challenges. The second paper by Krishnaveni focuses on IT enabled services with a range of services that include call centres, online education, medical transcription, legal data bases, insurance claim processing and payroll processing etc. India is becoming a favourable destination to locate many global companies operations as cost effective alternative in the process creating more off share employment opportunity even for more low level IT trained manpower. Krishnaveni suggests a major filip to Indian IT revenues. India appears to be on right path. The third paper by Katyayini & Sudhir looks at the possibility of reengineering the education which enables continuous learning a reality in the internet age. R.S. Ramaprasad and Dr. T.S. in their paper looks at the expanding role of IT industry with the possibility to rural sectors. In particular the ways and means to increase the village prosperity by setting up Farmer IT service centres especially in the context of WTO agreement on Agriculture this assumes significance. Finally this sections ends with a paper on IT application with regard to reduction of long waiting time for pilgrims in the que for darshan of Lord Venkateswara. Dr. Reddy & Rao explains the benefits, costs, limitations, alternatives such as finger print based identification, pupil based identification to Sudarshan.

IT SERVICES GROWTH AND CHALLENGES

** Chandra Sekhar Gotlagunta*
*** Prof. C.S.G. Krishnamacharyulu*

Indian services sector is finding a boom with the ongoing globalisation, emergence of knowledge era and revolution in information technology. Certainly, the future belongs to services and predominantly to the IT enabled services. In this paper an attempt is made to look in to the future that paves way for the dominance of IT enabled services.

Knowledge Based Global Economy

It is universally acclaimed that the knowledge era has begun and information has become a critical resource in living and working environments. The IT revolution, appropriately has furnished the base for information dissemination removing all barriers i.e., physical, social, cultural, political and economic. Simultaneous to the IT revolution is globalisation. By 2050, it is predicted a knowledge based global economy will usher in. The main characteristics of such economy are:

- Limitless, convenient, cheap information.
- Rise of a middle class of 5-10 billion people.
- Integrated markets operating online.
- Every industry and institution transformed.
- 5-7 global corporations per sector.
- Competing regional governments.
- Small companies with niche market.

---

* Research scholar, School of Business Management, S.V. University, Tirupati, A.P. India.

** Professor, School of Business Management, S.V. University, Tirupati, A.P., India.

Corportate Democracy

Naturally, new management, in corporate sector requires being more efficient and democratic. The economic imperatives of knowledge society make management focus on flowering of enterprise and with an approach already advocated by OD specialists. The compelling forces are:

- Markets are needed to manage complexity.
- Educated people want freedom.
- Principle of differentiation.

The emergent organisations are corporate communities which are extensions of democratic institutions. Their features are;

- Cooperation is economically efficient.
- Community creates meaning and purpose.
- Principle of integration.

The future of the work in the society will be:

- Knowledge work
- Idea creation
- Design work
- Project Management
- Multiple jobs
- Lifelong education
- 46% self employed.

Beyond Knowledge - The Spritual Age

Information will trigger off a new set of values and pursuits, already known but ignored in the ambitious drive for prosperity. Knowledge will rise transcendent issues and 'Spiritual Age' driven by technologies of consciousness will blossom by 2010 + 5 years. One of the portenders is Sai Movement worldwide.

Implications for Developing Countries

See A 1, 2,3,4,5.

Role of IT Industry

Given the kind of scenario, it is easy to predict a major as well as crucial role for IT services. The indicators to this are:

- Significant growth rate of IT industry.
- Globalisation of service with WTO agreements.
- Growing IT education.
- The spread of IT into rural sectors.
- Improving Quality of life

The Next round of talks for WTO agreement will be focused on services. As a result, the service sector will find a new boost a 2000-2001. The share of services in the countries? GDP was 54.2% up from the 51.5% recorded in 1998-99. It will further expand the entry of multinational. The variety of services they offer to the Indian consumer will be wide. Among the services IT services will be the growth driver.

The compound annual growth rate recorded by in the last five years (1995-2000) is more than 42.4%, which is almost double the growth rate of IT industries in many of the developed countries?

Prominently in the world, India has got reputation in the field of IT. IT companies like Infosys, Wipro, and Satyam, TCS etc., made significant contributions. The worldwide demand for IT personnel has created a mushroom growth of IT institutions spreading even into less literate rural sectors of Indian economy. Different state governments also now adopted E-governance philosophy and are emphasising on connectivity of village both physically and electronically. Many villages in Indian have internet facilities that enable the people in getting occupation related information.

IT has become the watch word for economic prosperity and social integration. It has improved the incomes, consumption, savings and investment activity of the people and showing the way for better quality of life.

With these indications it can be said that IT enabled services will expand in scope, range and quality. Undoubtedly, in the future the largest industry in the world will be IT enabled services.

The Challenges

How to tap the global knowledge base? B1
How to create and adopt knowledge? B2
How to disseminate knowlede? B3
How to management the innovation system? B4

A1

IMPLICATIONS FOR DEVELOPING COUNTRIES

- Risk of Knowledge Divide with Developed countries and within countries
- Need to develop strategies to use existing and new knowledge to
  - Improve performance in traditional sectors
  - Exploit opportunities for leapfrogging
  - Develop competitive new sectors

Need to

- Learn from other countries
- Develop strategies for own situation and current context.

A 2

STRATEGY OF USING KNOWLEDGE FOR DEVELOPMENT

Strategy not just about high tech or Information and Communication tech.

Is about making effective use of knowledge across economy and society

Requires better interaction between policies, institutions, technology, people, and government

Is about getting knowledge to mothers, farmers, workers, enterprises and government to improve lives.

A 3

ENSURING A DYNAMIC INFORMATION INFRASTRUCTURE

A dynamic information infrastructure is critical to take advantage of the knowledge and information revolution

Not just telephone infrastructure, but Internet and the use of ICT throughout economy.

Not just the hardware, but the content, applications, and skills to use effectively.

A 4

USE OF INFORMATION INFRASTRUCTURE

- Communications
- Electronic Commerce
- Electronic Governance
- Delivery of Social Services (Education, Health)
- Other applications

Software

Skills to use

A 5
KNOWLEDGE SCORECARD (STANDARD)
China

(10.70) Average Annual GDP growth (%)	10	(0.72) Human Development Index
(0.52 (In) Internet hosts per 10,000 people		(38.00) Gross Capital Formation
(2.50) (in) Computers per 1,000 persons		(2.00) Tarrif and nontarrif barriers
(5.15) (In) Telephone per 1000 (mainlines + mobile		(-0.04) Rule of Law
(6.00) Tertiary enrolment		(-0.29) Control of corruption
(70.00) Secondary Enrolment		(4.09) FDI as % of GDP
(83.50) Adult literacy rate (% age 15 and above)		(0.66) Total expenditure for R&D as % of GNi

(17.00) High-Tech exports as % of manuf. exports.

India

(6.00) Average Annual GDP growth (%)	10	(0.57) Human Development Index
(0.28) (In) Internet hosts per 10,000 people		(23.00) Growss capital formation
(1.19) (in) Computers per 1,000 persons		(2.00) Tariff and nontariff barriers
(3.57) (In) Telephone per 1000 (mainlines + mobile)		(0.16) Rule of Law
(7.00) Tertiary enrollment		(-0.31) Control of Corruption
(49.00) Secondary Enrollment		(0.39) FDI as % of GDP
(56.50) Adult literacy rate (% ae 15 and above)		(0.73) Total expenditure for R& D as % of GNI

(6.00) High-Tech exports as % of manuaf. exports.

B 1
TAPPING INTO THE GLOBAL KNOWLEDGE BASE

Trade, Foreign Direct Investment, Technology Licensing

Joint Research/Business/Cooperation

Technical Assistance, Foreign Study, Overseas Nationals, Hiring foreigners

Technical journals, databases, internet.

B 2

CREATING AND ADAPTING KNOWLEDGE

R & D expenditures as share of GDP

Public vs. Private share of R&D expenditures

Nature of R&D Efforts: basic vs. applied vs. development

Interaction among firms, R&D institutes and universities.

B 3

DISSEMINATING KNOWLEDE

Growth of more efficient enterprises

Sales (technical services, equipment, inputs)

Government agricultural and industrial extension services, demonstration projects.

Media, Technical Journals, Internet Links between universities, research institutes, and firms, people.

B 4

MANAGING THE INNOVATION SYSTEM

Link domestic to fast global knowledge system

- **Encourage Joint public and private research with foreign countries/firms**

- **Promote strategic alliances, Joint Ventures, purchase of foreign technology assets.**

Improve efficiency/relevance of existing R&D government programs; encourage private effort

Clearly justify rationale for public intervention

Facilitate interaction among firms, universities, and R&D institutions.

IT ENABLED SERVICES INDUSTRY-- AN OVERVIEW

H. Krishnaveni

Introduction

The world is in the middle era of globalization the first and second eras introduced cross-border trade and manufacturing as the invisible hand of the market, eliminating geographic and other barriers. The same force, armed this time with tremendous advances in technology, has ushered in the current era, the virtual age that allows services to be provided from e-enabled locations, across national borders. This promises to revolutionise service operations by radically reducing costs and improving service standards. Companies that fail to capture the opportunities unleashed by this phenonemnon risk losing their competivie advantage.

IT enabled services are businesses process and services performed or provided from a location different to that of their users or beneficiaries and are delivered over telecom networks and the Internet.

The complete gamut of IT enabled services incldue on-line information and help support through call centres; relationship management, back office data processing, and providing useful information to executive; assisting specialized professional community by providing services through IT services. The services also include following spectrum of broad segments; call centre, medical transcription, legal databses, insurance, claim process, pay roll processing etc.

IT enabled services in India

The McKinsey Quarterly reads, "Multinational companies already understand India's advantages as a platform for software development. But increased bandwidth and universal networking standards are now giving them an opportunity to move many parts of their business systems. By 2008, global remote-service operations may undertake activities accounting for half a trillion dollars around the world and representing every element of the value chain: upstream activities such as research and design, manufacturing-related activities such as procurement and logistics, front-end activities such as marketing and sales, and staff functions such as accounting, information technology, and human-resources management. Such operations could generate cost and other savings of about US $ 400 billion, to be shared by the users and the providers as profits. Seizing the opportunity, one global financial services company has already achieved annual savings of mroe than US $ 250 million -- according to its management, only a fraction of the total savings potential. "This view is shared by rapidly increasing number of Fortune 500 companies.

IT enabled services found its place in India after major companies across the globe started looking for alternative and cost effective destinations to work on back-office operations. The result was British Airways, Lufthansa, American Express and GE Capital, setting up large units to look after their back office activity in India from managing call centres to looking after their payrolls. These companies have started shifting their back-offices to India where these services can be taken care with little expenditure. These services are set to give a major fillip to Indian IT revenues.

Now we have reached yet another stage by making non-engineers participate in the IT-revolution through IT-enabled services. According to industry experts -- India has started on the right path and in the right direction in the field of IT enabled services.

The IT enabled Services Industry Performance at a Glance Survey by NASSCOM

IT Enabled	1999-2000 Employed	Revenue (Rs.Crore)	2000-2001 Employed	Revenue (Rs.Crore)
Customer interaction services include call centres	8,600	400	16,000	850
Accounting/Data Entry/Data conversion including finances accountancy/HR services	15,000	950	19,000	1,350
Transcription/Translation services	5,000	120	6,000	160
Content Development animation/engg. & Design/GIS	15,000	820	27,000	1,600
Other services include remote education data search, market research, network, consultancy and management	1,400	110	2,000	140
Total	45,000	2,400	70,000	4,100

Spectrum of IT enabled Services

- Call centres
- Medical Transcription
- Back office operations, Revenue accounting and other ancillary operation.
- Insurance claims processing.
- Legal databases.
- Online education
- Data digitization/GIS
- Payroll & HR services

Among others, the spectrum of IT enabled services applications already evident in India include following broad segments.

CALL CENTRES

* Call centres combine the use of highly effective and empowered company representatives with a service framework that relies heavily on state-of-the-art communications and information technologies.

* A call centre is sometimes defined as a telephone based shared service centre for specific customer activities and are used for number of customer related functions like marketing, selling, information dispensing, advice, technical support etc.

* Area where call centres used:

  - Telebanking in financial sector.
  - Telemarketing in product offering.
  - Television and home shopping.
  - International enterprises in foreign markets.
  - Each and every sector where customer service is called for.
  - It allows a wider customer base to do business with.
  - It allows customers easy access to experts.
  - It offers economical means of reaching diverse and widely distributed customer groups.
  - It allows company to avoid the overheads of brick and mortar branches.

Type of Call Centres

1. Captive in-house

2. Outsourced bureau.

I. Captive call centres used are for various vertical segments like insurance, investments, securities, retail banking, other financials, telecommunciations, technology, utilities, manufacturing, travel and tourism, transport, entertainment, health care, govt. education etc.

II. Outsourcing bureau have experience in running call centres, help in dealing complex labour market, use latest technology types;

(i) Set-up outsourcing

(ii) Transitional outsourcing.

(iii) Overflow outsourcing.

(iv) Longterm outsourcing.

Potential Customers

Industries: Airlines, banks, insurance, financial services, boutiques, telecome services, IT product services.

Market size:

According to a survey there are more than 100,000 call centres and this is expected to grow to 300,000 by 2002 employing approximately 18 million people.

As per survey conducted by NASSCOM, customer interaction services including call-centres in India employed about 10,000 people as on 30th July, 2000 generating an annual revenue Rs. 450 crore. It is estimated that during 2008, this segment will create employment for 2,70,000 people generating revenues of Rs.20,000 crores.

Call Centre Technology Suppliers

I. Hardware : Aspect, Clarify, Brightware, Cisco Convergys, Corepoint, Siemens, Service Soft, Eshare, Lucent, Nortel, Quintus, Rock Well.

II. Software: Sitel Corporation, Sun, Telequent, Answersoft, Genesys Labs, IBM/Lotus etc.

Summary: Call centres have clearly emerged as one of the most favoured of all IT enabled services. On one hand this is due to success and prominence achived by call centres already operating in India. On other hand global call centres have proven to be amongst most stable revenue growth centres amongst all related services.

Further encouragement through proactive encouragement by government of India to promote this industry agurs well for India emerging as a preferred choice for setting up call centres in India.

ONLINE EDUCATION

- The online education market is booming the world over and is currently considered a hotly growing sector.

- Studies have shown that nearly 92% of large organizations will implement network - (internet, intranet) training in 2000.

- 41% of global majors have placed atleast one on-line course for employees.

- Atleast 516 service offerings are available in market for on-line and technology mediated learning.

- According to Peter Drucker, the growth in education spending won't be in traditional colleges and universities but instead would be web-enabled continuing adult education.

- Surveys have also indicated that 85% of schools will have some form of on-line learning by 2002.

Indian scenario

- The computer training market in India is as extremely vibrant one and maintains a close nexus with the software sector.

- The training segment of the Indian-IT industry had a good year during - 1999-2000.

- Growth took place both at student education as well as profession corporate IT courses.

- According to industry estimates about Rs. 1750 crore worth of revenue was generated by training segment representing growth of 34% over previous year.

- All industry segments including government go for large scale computerization leading to demand for skilled manpower.

- Training services therefore are emerging as a major growth opportunity for segment of education companies.

On-Line Education in India

- The online education market in India is showing potential and is expected to be a significant revenue earner for the industry in the years to come.
- Steps are being taken by various state governments in India to incorporate net based training into their IT agendas.
- An example are the AP & MP governments who have initiated pilot programs involving education dissemination through the television, with student responses coming back over the internet.

- Yet another trend has been foreign university tying up with Indian training institutions.

- In recent months a number of computer institutes have tied up with Indian universities to jointly offer net-based training.

- The tie-up of IGNOU with Satyam Infotech is a case in point.

Summary

- The on-line education market in India is poised to take off. The advantages of training over the internet far out spaces the conventional means of disseminating computer education.

- It is an opportunity that needs to be exploited for complete benefit.

DATA DIGITISATION

Digitisation is the process by which physical or mannual records such as text, images, video and audio are converted into digital forms. This is of paramount importance when projects need directions based on already established facilities and the implementing agency needs to find the scope for expansion.

Digitised data offers the following benefits

- Long term preservation of documents

- Orderly archiving of documents

- Easy and customized access to information

- Early information dissemination through images and text, CD-ROMS, Internet, intranet and extranets.

- **Data digitisation offers a very good market place due to relatively lower costs and technical skills are available.**

- **Many overseas companies like Bechtel have set up engineering design centres in India.**

MEDICAL TRANSCRIPTION

Medical transcription is the process through which one accurately and swiftly transcribes medical records directed by: doctors and other health care professionals. It is the method of translating the dictation (that forms the basis of providing health care) into a format suitable for inclusion in a medical record (hard copy or electronic).

In countries like the USA, A doctor's time is at high premium. The current practice is for doctors to simply record their findings through a dicta phone or some such device. These sound tracks are then sent through datacom lines to companies that employ "medical transcriptionists" who hear these recordings, transcribe them into reports and send them back electronically through datacom lines. Information and communication technologies are used to send voice recording on satellite line to far-off, low cost locations where these recordings are transcribed into reports that are again sent back to the hospitals or clinics digitally through the same lines and printed as reports locally. Turn around time is less than two hours.

In India nearly 5 companies are providing medical transcription services. They are:

1. Eyered Infotech - New Delhi
2. Acme's MT Centre - Rajkot
3. Microsphere Infotech - Chandigarh
4. Viswakarma Global solutions - Chennai
5. Eagle Enterprise - Chennai.

Data Processing

Data processing is a category of IT enabled services pertaining to caputre, digitisation and processing of data emanating from various sources. traditional data processing services comprise of punching data from manually filled forms, images or publications; preparing database and integrating them. With advent of multimedia and internet sources have widened to include manually printed documents, images, sounds and video.

Process

The data may be scanned or physically sent and transmitted to vendor's facility. Many companies enter it manually (from image or paper) or through computer assisted data capture, using OCR (Optical - Character recognition) ICR (Intelligent character recognition), mark sense, MICR and barcode information is checked through validation routines.

Range of Services

Document preparation, data entry, image capturing, image keying, OCR & ICR processing.

Back Office Operations, Revenue Accounting, Other Ancillary Operations

Industries such as banks, Airlines require large scale data entry and revenue accounting work to be done. For revenue accounting and other Back Office accounting operations, paper documents/raw data are sent to remote locations, which are used for data entry and necessary reconciliations. Using high-speed datacom links for their back office and data processing operations, these banks, airlines and other organizations with extensive data turnover and customer interface, are able to save costs and valuable resources. The prime concern of these companies is 100 per cent availability of data and uptime of facility. This can be ensured through high-speed datacom links from India to the parent country. Over the last few years, there has been a steadily growing trend to outsource these services to major I.T. service providers, with contracts running into decades. The prime criteria for such projects are quality of organizational processs, availability of abundant manpower and ability to dedicate resources to client's needs. India stands to gain from such a trends, as the Indian software industry has been able to make a mark and also has access to huge pool of skilled as well as semiskilled professionals with relative cost advantage.

Insurance claim processing

Insurance companies have two basic activities that internal efforts, i.e. creating and setting up an insurance policy and then processing the large volume of insurance claims and accounting for the insurance claims. Apart from processing, there is a large amount of logistics involved in this activity. But the guidelines to the process are well established and hence can be easily performed remotely. In this business also, there is an element of help desk, providing annual apraisal update service by maintaining an updated database of all property records, creation of low cost property value estimates and providing for claims reporting centres round the clock.

Legal data Bases

There is a constant need for lawyers who counsel cases to go through relevant laws, rulings and precedents in order to build up their case. This is usually done by very junior lawyers in legal firms. However, in the U.S. and other developed countries, even junior lawyers, services are highly priced. One of the ways to get around this hurdle is to have a readily accessible source of well managed and intelligent information technology. The job comprises working closely with the firm to create a database of their existing records, index on the basis of various useful and common understood criterion, keeping track of new documents being created and incorporating them into a database as per well established parameters. Lawens can them simple us their computers to draw up a history of like cases and draw a clear plan of action. Once again, the rules, are clear and only average qualifications and ability one required.

Payroll/HR Services: HR services is another area that has immense potential in the field of IT enable services. HR services components include.

1. Recruitment, screening
2. Administration and relocation services
3. Payroll processing
4. Compensation administration
5. Benefit planning
6. Administration and
7. Regulating compliance

References

1. S. Venkat Kumar, Strategic Management - IT enable services Industry.

INTEGRATED E-EDUCATION SYSTEM

Dr. J. Katyayani (B.Tech MBA,Ph.D.)*

&

B. Sudhir (B.Tech.MBA Ph.D)**

The industries now-a-days are implementing IT enabled Knowledge Tone frame works in their organizations. This is creating demand for continuous learning about new e-business methodologies. Many IT enabled services are also emerging now in this internet age. This emphasizes the creation of integrated e-education System to meet the new education standard propositions. The learning community also demanding new value added education services from the institutions the value added education service is nothing but the system which is continuously imrproving learning methods, content and processes as shown in Fig.1. It is useful to consider three levels of integration which must be supported by the IT infrastructure for creating integrated e-education system. The three levels of integration are the high performance team. The integrated e-education system and the extended virtual institution.

I. The High Performance Team

The new paradigm support the redefinition of eduction process around the enabling capabilities of workgroup computing. Workgroup computing now includes a wide range of tools building on presence of powerful personal computers (clients), work group servers and associated networks. Today's "power user" has facilitated with core technologies and technology services which are as shown in fig.2.

---

* Assistant Professor, Dept.of Computer Science and Engineering SVEC, A. Rangempet.

** Assistant Professor, School of Business Management, SVU, Tirupati.

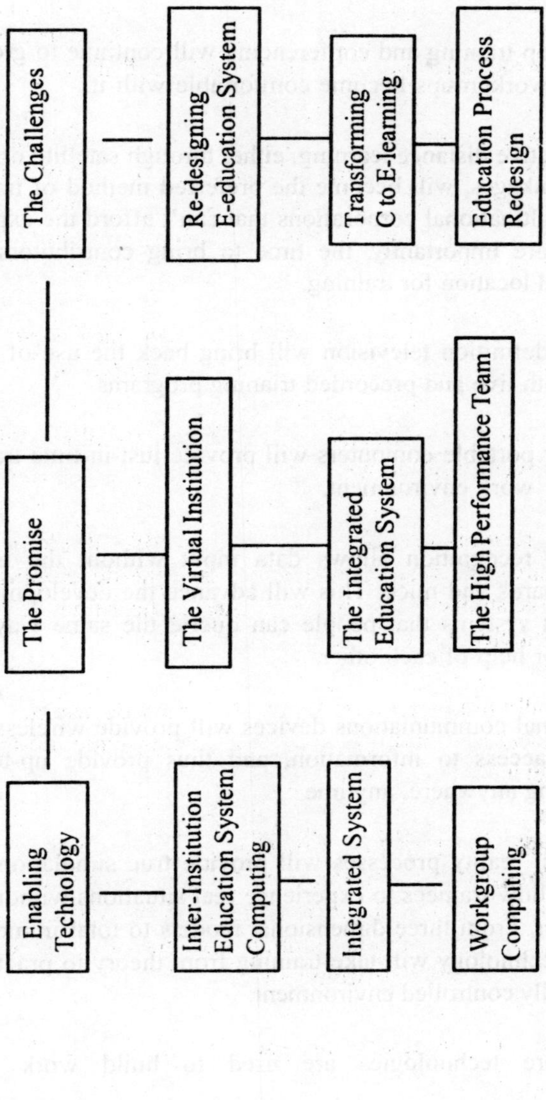

Fig. 1 Multilevel Opportunities for Integrated Education System

The Technology Services

- Web-based training (WBT) through internal and external networks will become a standard as problems with bandwidth and speed are solved.
- Desktop training and conferencing will continue to grow as more workgroups become comfortable with it.
- Interactive distance learning, either through satellite or land-line linkages, will become the preferred method of training for multinational corporations that can't afford the expense, or, more importantly, the time to bring contributors to a central location for training.
- High-definition television will bring back the use of video for both live and precorded trianing programs.
- Easily portable computers will provide just-in-time training in any work environment.
- Voice recognition allows data input without the use of keyboards and mice. This will advance the development of expert systems that people can querie the same way they ask for help of each other.
- Personal communiations devices will provide wireless real-time access to information, and thus provide up-to-date training anywhere, anytime.
- Virtual reality processes will provide true simulations that will allow trainees to experience real situations without real danger. From three-dimensional models to total immersion, this technology will take training from theory to practice in a totally controlled environment.

These core technologies are used to build work group

environments like e-learning, e-assessment, e-courses, e-quality, etc. The workgroup teams are not based on a single institution, but more often will consists of individual multiple desciplines from different departments of the education system working at different locations. Teams are dynamic, they come together to address a particular need, and finish, disband this means that workgroup computing standards and support services cannot be set by individual institutions. They must be chosen and set as education standards while taking onto account technology trends and learning commuity acceptance standards.

E-education Solutions
Technology E-facilitator
Services I
Core Technologies WBT E-learning
Networking Tools
Multimedia Tools WRA E-courses
Java, Javascript
Data Warehousing Data Mining E-classrooms
RDBMS Packages

Knowledge Management

E-assessment

Calc Centres

E-quality

Fig. 2: Integrated E-Education System

II. Integrated e-Education System

The second level of opportunity addresses the need to integrate across the functions of the present education system. Hence process modelling is essential for creating a common understanding of the desired improvments in the system. The various education process models that are emerging now includes e-learning, e-courses, e-quality. This integration transforms present class room learning (c-learning) into electronic learning (e-learning).

E-learning

E-learning covers a wide set of applications and processes, such as web-based learning, computer-based learning, virtual classrooms, and digital collaboration. It includes the delivery of content via internet, intranet/extranet (LAN/WAN), audio and videotape, satellite broadcast, interactive TV, and CD-ROM.

There are a number of services institutes may need to implement an e-learning strategy effectively, including.

- ❖ Learning management system (LMS). Freqently referred to as the backbone of e-learning, an LMS is enterprise-wide software that integrates with the education system to track course requirements, web-based training and classroom delivered courses, and online course enrollments. Its user interface allows learners to review, register, and launch online courses.

- ❖ Off-the-shelf courseware, web-based courses are delivered over the internet or prints, pre and postassessments, job ainds, glossaries, simulations, continuing education credits, and continuing education filing and license support services.

- ❖ Synchronous, collaborative learning tools. While synchronous learning can occur using such simple tools as chat and teleconferencing, a new generation of tools bundles online chat, video and audio conferencing, application sharing, and more,

- ❖ Advisory or information services. Information services can be subject specific, or they can provide general education information. These include news services, e-newsletters, discussion forums, and more.

- Coaching and mentoring services. These services often are aimed at an IT audience, helping students to pass certification examinations. However, online coaching services for general subjects are emerging, such as Coaching.com.

- Knowledge management tools. These tools are internal department-wise tools that collect, store, and distribute information within institution.

- Competency management tools. These tools are used to identify skills and knowledge available within the institution and can exist as stand-alone tools or as components of LMS.

- Library software. These tools can manage circulation, print knowledge of various subject areas, import and export data, and allow you to publish a catalog to the Internet or an intranet.

Sorting through the functionality of e-learning tools is a complex process. Adding to the confusion is determining the needs of the education system and how a tool can support those needs.

E-courses

I In designing of e-commerce the questions to be considered are

- Is the curriculum structure logical and complete?

- Are the courses user-friendly and easy to navigate?

- Are the courses engaging and interactive?

- Do courses use effective instructional design?
- Do courses meet your learning objectives?
- If needed, can the courses be customized? What are cost and maintenance implications?
- How often is the course content updated?
- What is the review process for course development?

E-assessment

Online testing often offers untapped potential for instructional designers building e-courses assessments are foundation of effective instructional practices and return on investment studies. The power of tests and asessments will become exponentially more important with the advent of content management systems and learning management systems, once those applications become standard, course developers can take advantage of assessments as a means of driving advanced learning practices, such as branching and personalisation.

In addition to offering a variety of instructional practices, data from testing can be used to conduct item analysis and strengthen courses. Indeed, often it's test questions that drive the following instructional practices.

Postests assess a learner's mastery of content at the course completion. Test data is to determine wheather the learner mastered the principles, and a comparative review of scores can determine course effectiveness.

Pretests assess learner's readyness for instruction and can exempt learners from studying material they already know.

Remediation test items can pinpoint knowledge that the learner lacks and branch to additional matter.

Adaptation questions get a feel for to the learner's strengths and weaknesses. Personalisation can be used in combination with adaptation questions to create programs that offer individual instruction.

Other assessment tests are online tests with true and false, fill-in-the-blank and matching questions and testing-building software options which will have features like timing, scoring, testbanks and randomisation, reviewing and submitting answers.

E-quality

Quality of the e-courses can be assessed by using the following criteria.

Accuracy

Authority

Currency

Objectivity

Coverage

Consistency of Information

Appropriateness of Format

Software/Hardware/Multimedia requirements

III.The extended virtual institution

The Third Level of integration extends education institutions vertually so the new e-education process model is extended to consider the changes in the educational requirement as demanded by e-organisations. The goal is to get the educational needs addressed in most efficient and effective manner by designing vertual institutions. These three levels of opportunity are not independent. To the contrary they are synergistic.

Road map to e-education Frame Work:-

1. Identify the goals of e-education project.
2. Determine what type of services need to be provided.
3. Determine the Technology services to be used.
4. Build the suitable model while balancing local and global community needs.
5. Check the validity of the model.
6. Deploy the model.
7. Monitor the model.
8. Measure ROI of the project.

Conclusion

The above model is attempting to describe need for reeingineering the education system process and proposes a design of e-education portals.

References

1. Christine L Duckworth, An Instructors guide to livé E-learning, Learning circuit Dec. 2000.
2. Kevin Kruse, Web rules, Learning Circuits Feb. 2000.

FARMER IT SERVICE CENTRES FOR VILLAGE PROSPERITY

Dr. R Sivarama Prasad
Dr. T Srinivas

Introduction

Village dynamics are best known to the local village managements through the newly formed management structure at village level would enhance the capabilities of managing the produce to the International Market by using the E-Commerce applications at the Gram Panchayat.

Seed, quality fertilizer pesticides, precautions and increasing the yield harvesting with precautions, packing and forwarding at the international standards could be monitered right at the village level without middlemen.

Agriculture is the 'life blood of the country.' India boasted of 100 million farmers engaged in agricultural activity over an area of 143 million hectares. The country which had all the agro climate zones in the world and 46 out of 60 soil types, provided employment to 650 million in the agricultural sector, while every US$6 foreign exchange came from agriculture, over the past decade this sector has been relatively ignored in the most economic discussions; conentration was made on reforms in Trade, Finance and Industry. In the same period WTO agreement came into effect and removal of QR on about 1,452 items has almost turned Indian farming communities to the stage of pauperization. The P.V. Narasimhara Rao Govt. signed the WTO without involving or consulting any of likely victims in India. A handful of bureauerats

* Management Faculty, Department of Computer Science and Engineering, Nagarjuna University - 522510.

and secretaries have sealed the fate of India. Since 1995 the successive Governments and policy makers wasted time and resources only through goal less discussions. After Doha conference, which was conclude very recently (in November 2001) the Govt. of India got some assurance regarding to agriculture outputs and related from the West and developed countries, eventhough the problem of Indian farming communities not disappeared. How is India going to overcome this situation which was raised by globalization? Answer is mobilizing and motivating the Indian farming communities towards supply chain management through the Information Technology. Now a way forward by outlining some solutions. These are:

- Focusing on better farming to improve farm productivity even within the current land holding pattern and other constraints.

- To create farmer IT service centres in every village with the help of local farmers and corporate bodies.

- Creating a structure to facility growth of a vibrant food processing Industry in village level.

- Motivating the farming community towards Information Technology in combination with Bio Technology and motivate the Indian farmers for using E-Commerce application facilities for better remuneration prices.

FARMER IT SERVICE CENTRE AT VILLAGE LEVEL

Low-cost access to information as well as highly interactive distance learning. The "Information Village" concept developed and implemented by M.S. Swaminathan, Research Foundation (MSSRF) in a Pondichery Village is a path-breaking experiment to demostrate the potential of information revolution. On the same pattern "Warna wired village" concept is successfully implemented in Kolhapur district of Maharastra State. This is the ideal example of use of internet on co-operative basis. With the help of this centres a farmer is able to get good information about weather, seed, fertilizer, and pesticides.

DIAGRAM

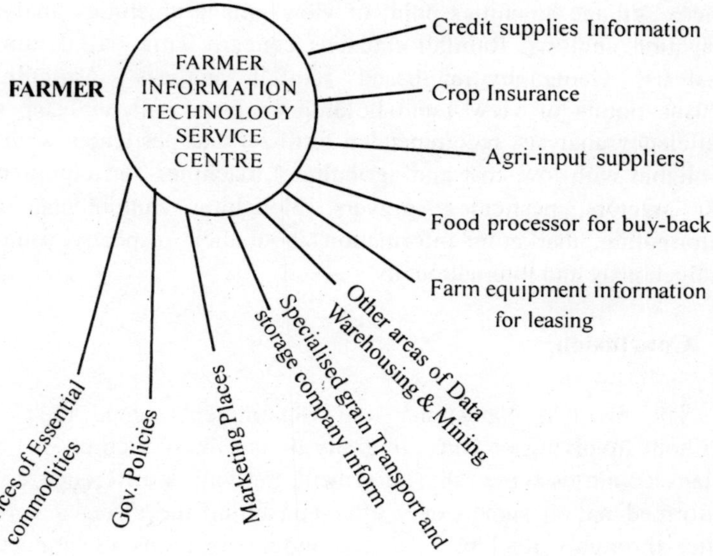

The Govt. of India recently framed Food Industry process policy, keeping it in the mind we should motivate the farmers towards starting food process companies regarding their respective outputs with the help of NABARD and Agricorporates. APEDA already have been giving information and also giving financial aid to the farmers as well as enthusiastic entrpreneurs, this must be construct at village level. Employment opportunities also generated maximum through the starting food process industry at village level.

USING WEB-ENABLED DATA WAREHOUSING SERVICES

Like GISTNIC (General Information Service Terminal of

National Informatics Centre) was handled by NIC web-enabled data warehouses should provided basic information regarding to the requirement of farming community. Essential commodities, fertilizer wholesale prices and retail prices pesticides prices, updated information about trends in price change, commodity prices like Rice, Vegetables, Sugar, Oil, Cereals, Red chilles and other output of forming community, Forecasta essential commodity prices. Village amenities point of view village amenities analysis, irrigation analysis. Rainfall statistics concern Time-based rainfall analysis, Geography/time-based rainfall analysis. Agricultural census points of view Land holding analysis, soil analysis, soil deficiency analysis, recommended fertilizer and pesticides where it available with low cost and agricultural machines and equipments like tractors, pesticides sprayers, ploughing equipments, seed information, marketing information about their respective outputs indigenously and Internationally.

Conclusion

The Sri P.V. Narasimha Rao Government signed the WTO without involving or consulting any of the likely victims in India. Many countries signed this agreement, but with a difference. Every informed nation signed only after consulting the affected people, after throughly reading it, understanding its terms its impact on them. Most western nations actually involved their businessmen, farmers, trade unions, bankers and professionals even to draft the provisions of this agreement. Now from Government's point of view there is no alternative except developing agriculture sector that is only possible through mobilizing and motivating Indian farming communities towards Farmer IT service centres in village level, automatically the Indian farming community certainly face the troubles which were arised for the cause of WTO agreement.

Suggestion

Andhra Pradesh Government always ahead regarding the use of New Technologies. The objective of 73 amendment of Indian Constitution was to develop the village Panchayats Financially sound and give good amenties that is only possible to develop the village farming communities in respect of their profession, keep it in the mind the Government of Andhra Pradesh already created 21943 village secretariats, on experimental basis Government or Private Entrepreneurs should provide former IT service centres along with the secretariats we should expect positive results and also effectively faced WTO adverse impact on agriculture sector of India.

Reference

Magazines and different seminars, newspapers which discussed this issue.

BETTER WAYS FOR 'SUDARSHAN'

Dr. M.S. Reddy
Associate Professor
School of Business Management
S.V. University
Tirupati

The Tirumala Tirupati Devasthanam (TTD) in its endeavour to reduce the long waiting time of pilgrims in the queue for darshan 'Sudarshan'. The Sudarshan scheme has launched to scheme of functioning is similar to any computerised reservation system.

It works as follows: A local area network (LAN) was established with counters at Tirupati and Tirumala. When a pilgrim at TTD pilgrim recetion centres approaches one of these counters he/she will be a particular tried a plastic strip to the wrist with time to join the queue to have the lord's darshan. That time will be printed along with a bar code on this plastic strip which is tied and sealed to pilgrim's wrist, so that band will be read at the queue for darshan, for authentication. With this arrangement the pilgrim is free between the arrival and darshan times, required of waiting in the que. The survey conducted by a team of S.V. University faculty confirmed the reduced waiting times and the associated satisfaction of pilgrims due to the sudarshan scheme.

System Benefits: The real benefit of the above system is reduced waiting time of the pilgrims. If the TTD proposal bears fruit, the system will be extended to many other towns and cities. Then the pilgrims can have the darshan time specified even before leaving for Tirumala.

System Costs: LAN consisting of computers, bar code readers, and printers is being maintained by a private agency. TTD was paying around Rs. 2.60 per each wrist band, which was reduced to Rs. 1.30 recently. Though the scheme is technically feasible, it is becoming a costly affair to the TTD. During the first year of introduction around 50 lakh people had used this facility costing TTD more than Rs. 1 crore. When all devotees use that utility it is expected to cost Rs. 2 crore per annum to TTD.

System Manipulation: The system is being misused by some travel agencies, by colluding with people working in 'Sudarshan' counters. They get the Sudarshan strips ready well before the arrival of pilgrims, to save time. These strips printed in advance will be tied to the pilgrims wrists, who are coming through the travel agents having special arrangement with people manning 'Sudarshan' counters. Thus some people have been jumping the queue.

Other Limitations: In addition to the enormous recurring cost, the scheme is generating high volume of plastic waste through the discarded wrist bands, which is polluting the environment heavily. In the light of these drawbacks of the existing system, the need of searching for other feasible alternatives emanates.

System Alternatives: The limitations of the existing scheme are arising due to the use of a plastic wrist band as the non transferable identification mark, and time indicator. The alternative schemes can be designed based on either finger print or pupil of the pilgrim.

The process of using finger prints and eyeballs to verify a person's identity is known as biometrics technology. Microsoft has decided to incorporate that technology in its operting software i.e. windows, from this summer. Microsoft's decision is expected to make biometrics as practical and universal standard for identity solutions.

Finger print based identification: Identification based on finger prints is time tested and technically feasible. If this method is adopted the pilgrim will be issued paper token indicating the darshan time and a bar code. When the pilgrim approaches the queue for Lord's darshan the bar code on the paper token will be read by bar code reader to retrieve the finger print stored at the time of issuing the paper token to verify the identity of the pilgrim. If the finger prints match, the pilgrim will be allowed into the queue.

Pupil Based Identification: Similar to finger print the eye balls of humans are also unique for each person. Identification based on pupil is increasingly becoming popular, and the devices to read and store the images of various parts of eye are available. This method is similar to the previous one in all respects, except the basis of the identification. It can also be used as a preliminary health checkup to millions of devotees visiting the holy shrine every year (see box 1.) Based on the preliminary health checkup the pilgrims can be alerted for further necessary investigations.

The pupil can be a window for doctors to deduce our state of health, including possible addiction to drugs and susceptibility to life-threatening diseases. The size of the pupils is determined by a range of factors, including the health of the retinoa and optic nerve exposure to light, disease and even the state of mind. The pupil is controlled by two muscles, one causing it to constict, and the other to dilate. In normal circumstances, these muscle activity is regulated by the release of neuro transmitters in the brian, which start the chain of events that results in a change in the pupils.

The pupilo meter, designed by British researchers, consists of a personal computer, pupilfit software, and a camera with two lenses and special optics that give a split field of view.

According to Don Taylor, who developed pupillometry, "The advantage of pupillometry over many other techniques is that it is both objective and non-invasive. It makes available a range of diseases like glaucoma, sleep disorders, cancers, and opiate addiction".

Source: The Sunday Review Feb 27, 2000 page 6.

Box No.1

Conclusion

TTD may adopt the combination of the above two methods for the convenience of pilgrims. Then TTD can save huge sums of recurring expenditure and avoid the manipulation to jump the in the state and country through internet, unlike the existing system. At the same time it can cater to public health checkup needs and temple security as well.

SECTION-VIII

SERVICE ECONOMY AND INFRASTRUCTURAL SYSTEMS

OVERVIEW

The last secton deals with most important sectors of the service economy such as Hospitality, Transport, Power and Communication sectors with one paper each in the crucial sectors of the service economy. First paper in this deals with hospitality industry. Indian Hotel Industry made rapid advancement by better training the hotel service staff which is a lynch pin for survival and growth according to Sivakumar & PT Srinivasan in the highly competitive and volatile business environment. A model for training hotel staff to deliver service quality called "Serqual" explained. The second paper by Subhas and Sandya recognises the importance of transport and communication systems. Transport through rail, road, coastal shipping and air as the various modes of transport. Railways as public utility services are premier modes of transport for freight and passengers as a country's life line. During 146 years of rail history contributing enormously to the economic development of the country as speedy, convenient economical and attractive means. A case against for total privatisation for profit maximisation is the suggestion? Mr. Madhavaiah examines the development of telecommuniations in India as the biggest driver of the new economic growth and profit from its evolution to present e-revoltuion. The paper registers post liberalisation economy with partial privitasation of telecom services many changes observed sectorally, technologically, policy, service and market wise still there is a gap in provision to only few than to all. Saravana Kumar focusses on the most crucial infrastructure service of the economy. According to the author the survival, growth of the economy to a large extent depends on the availablility of economical, reliable and high quality power. The challenges of power sector include continued poor performance of SEBS, issues of subsidies, investment private sector participation, corruption and inefficiency etc.

A "SERVQUAL" MODEL APPROACH FOR TRAINING HOTEL STAFF TO DELIVER SERVICE QUALITY*

C. Padmanaba Sivakumar
and
*Dr. P.T. Srinivasan**

Hotel Industry is one of the fastest growing sectors of the Indian Economy. Indian Hotel Industry has to make strong strides on the path towards "Service Quality" by better giving training to the hotel service staff.

Service Quality is the lynchpin for survival and growth for Hotel Industry in this highly competitive and volatile bsiness environment. Hence, there is a growing need to train the service staff of Star Hotel to deliver quality service. The area that has been focussed in this paper deals with the service quality evaluation by hotel customers or guests, and the need to train the service staff of the hotel using "Servqual Model".

Key words: Service Quality: "Servqual Model" training, Service Staff, Hotel Industry.

Introduction

The service sector is one of the single largest sectors in India contributing steadily towards the growth of Indian Economy, other than agricultural and industrial sectors. This growing services sector has proved to be India's most dynamic sector with its gradual increase in its growth and expansion in recent years.

---

* C Padmanaba Sivakumar is doctoral research scholar and Dr. P.T. Srinivasan is Professor in the Department of Management Studies, University of Madras, Chennai.

The Service sector's contribution to the GDP of India has remarkably grown from 45.62% in 1993-94 to 51.16% in 1998-99. In line with the global trend, the services sector in India has been growing rapidly and in the year 2000-2001 the GDP recorded was 54.2%.[1] A comparison of service sectors contribution to the GDP of India from 1993-94 to 1998-99 is indicated in the following Table 1.

Table 1: Service Sector's Contribution to the GDP (in Rs. Crores) of India

	1998-99	1997-98	1996-97	1995-96	1994-95	1993-94
Services	569005 (51.16)	537642 (51.24)	498572 (49.91)	463988 (50.08)	423200 (49.15)	108974 (45.62)
of which Trade, Hotels and Restaurants	213422 (13.02)	164355 (15.68)	155954 (15.61)	143848 (15.53)	127532 (14.81)	31057 (13.00
of which Hotels and Restaurants	14452 (0.90)	9235 (0.88)	8649 (0.87)	7771 (0.84)	5986 (0.70)	2975 (0.83)

Source: Studies by Reserve Bank of India. Figures in brackets indicate percentage share of different sectors and sub sectors. Figures for 1994-95 onwards are on a changed base (1993-94 = 100) as they show huge increases compared to the preceding period.

www.onestp india.com/ indiaeconomicsurvey.com

This gradual increase in the services sectors contribution to the GDP of India with a consistent performance, and a overall contribution to the growth and development of Indian economy over the past few decades has instilled confidence, to give this sector due importance by the Government, emerging enterpreneurs and academics.

Globalization has thrown open the gates of Indian Economy, developing numerous new opportunities and unleashing fresh challnges for the services sector industries like banks, hotels, hospitals and tourism, etc.

The contribution of Hotel Industry to the Service Sector is 0.88% in the year 1997-98. (Table 1) For the past few decades their contribution to the services sector assumes much greater significance in the light of various economic hairpin bends.

In services sector, particularly the Hotel Industry or hospitality service has a major role to play along with Tourism Industry in earning foreign exchange besides offering employment opportunities for many people in India.

Table 2: Labour Force by Occupation (1995 estimates)

Agriculture	67%
Industry	15%
Services	18%

Source: www.cia geos/cia/publications/factbook/geos/in.htm

LITERATURE SURVEY

To get a holistic picture of service quality in Hotel Industry, it becomes necessary to very briefly define the term "Hotel" and other concepts related to "Service" and "Quality".

Pragati Mohanty (1992) explains how this word "Hotel" industry would have originated. According to her the term "Hotel" is of ancient origin. But its utility of offering accommodation and food services in hotels for travellers is from modern times. A more detailed and most commonly accepted definition comes from William Benton in Encyclopaedia Britannica (1964) that the word "Hotel" was derived from an old French word "Ostel", meaning an inn servant. The other version is that, the Latin word "Hospitum", meaning the hall in medieval monasteries where guests were given hospitality became in French, "Hospice", then "Hostel" and eventually "hotel". Also, the word "Hospitality" is derived from the French root "hospice" a medieval "house of rest" for all kinds of toruists and travellers. The term "Hospitality" means "receiving and entertaining guests, visitors or strangers with liberality and goodwill.

The Hospitality Industry in modern times has undergone a sea of dynamic change, in terms of services and facilities offered. Sudhir Andhrews (1994) echoes this principle and explains vividly. Acording to him a hotel may be defined as "A place where a bonafide traveller can receive food and shelter, provided he is in a position to pay for it and is in a fit condition to be received". Hence, a hotel must provide food and beverage and lodging to travellers on payment and has, in turn, the right to refuse, if the traveller is drunk, disorderly, unkempt or not in a position to pay for the services.

The term "Service" was defined by various management associations and management gurus differently, however this paper adopts the most commonly accepted definition of "Service" given by Stanton (1981) and is as follows.

"Services are those separately identifiable, essentially intangible activities which provide want satisfaction, and that are not necessarily tied to the sale of a product or another service. To produce a service may or may not require the use of tangible goods".

SERVICES QUALITY AS A LINCHPIN FOR ORGANISATION'S SURVIVAL

In recent years Star Hotels throughout the world have realised that the best way to retain a guest or customer is by delivering service with quality. The concept of service quality assumed much greater significance when every effort by the service provider, to creat a loyal customer failed to bear fruit.

Globalization and expansion of service business has led to a situation, where the expectations of the hotel customers are very high and they evaluate the service quality of the hotel with that of the competitors. Customers, who are exposed to various kinds of mass media, get to know about the services of their other competitors in the market and intend to try out their services too (Balachandran, 1999) by visiting their hotels.

SCOPE OF THE STUDY

It is evident from the preceeding discussion that service quality is the linchpin for the star hotels to survive in this present volatile business environment, with many Star Hotels mushrooming in various corners of the cities in India.

In the present study The "Service staff" are those front line staff who have direct contact or link with the Hotel customers. These service staff can either enhance or mar the customer's experience by their quality of service delivered. A mere classification of hotels under Star category and acquring ISO certification from International Standards Organisation for its quality of products and services, do not guarantee the delivery of quality service by the service staff to hotel customers at all times. But in spite of this solid justification, the hotels tend to assert that they provide quality service in accordance with the customers' expectations.

In Star Hotels the word "Customers" is referred to as "Guests". Therefore, in this paper the words "Guests" and "Customers" are used interchangeably, and it denotes hotel customers.

The hotel guests are the direct consumers of the hotel services. How they perceive the functional quality (the actual performance of service) and the technical quality (core services like hotel rooms, quality of food and beverages etc.) and also the type of training that should be given to the service staff to correct deficiency in delivering service quality are discussed in this paper.

Schary and Larsen 1970 view that the customers' perceptions of quality, is more important then the service providers' perception of service quality and delivery. This demands an understanding of what attributes did the customer take into account and by what parameters the customer judges the service quality.

Thus learning customers' experiences of service quality would provide good insights to know and where the service quality deficiency factor occurs and how the hotel service staff training should be so designed to transform the service deficiency into service effeciency with quality service being delivered to the hotel guests by the staff at all times.

OBJECTIVES OF THE STUDY

The purpose of the present study[2] is to find out the deficiency in service quality and to suggest a suitable training method for the service staff of a Three Star Hotel where the service staff are given conventional training.

For this study, a three star category hotel[3] in Channai was selected because it is centrally located in a metropolitan city with a confluence of many cross-sections of people with diverse expectations.

In this study, other star hotels and specific factors like training the Managers. Supervisors, etc., have been kept out of scope. The focus here is more on training the Hotel Staff who have more contacts with the guests.

Specifically this study is undertaken with the following objectives.

- To analyse the Service Quality of each outlet in the hotel from hotel guests point of view.

- To explore the hotel guests perceptions of the various service quality characteristics like politeness, timely services, etc., exhibited by the hotel staff.

- To suggest a suitable training method for developing the efficiency and effectiveness of hotel staff in delivering quality service to hotel guests.

THE METHOD OF INQUIRY

The hotel guests were provided with a structured questionnaire. The questionnaire was designed to make a guest evaluate the service quality of the hotel in general and a specific outlet in particular where he or she just visited.

The purpose was to generate service quality evaluations by the hotel guests from specific service outlets. Five service outlets in the hotel were chosen for this purpose: They were Restaurant, Banquet, Bar, Room Service and Hotel room (Accommodation Division). Then the hotel guests were asked to rate the hotel services based on the quality of services delivered by the service staff in the hotel.

For the purpose of this study a total of 250 hotel guests were given questionnaries. In a sample of 250, a total of 193 questionnaires were returned in usable form (77.2%).

The method of sampling used was convenience sampling as this study was exploratory in nature.

In this study, Service Quality variables (such as Tangibles, Reliability, Responsiveness, Assurance and Empathy) taken from "Servqual Model" are used to interpet the results of research findings on evaluation of service quality.

RESEARCH FINDINGS

The study on Hotel guests' evaluation of service quality reveal various areas of service delivery where the service staff have faltered to delivery quality service, which suggests a serious lack of training of service staff.

The major findings in the five service outlets in the hotel are as follows.

TANGIBLE ELEMENTS

Tangibles are defined as the appearance of physical facilities, equipment, personnel and communication materials. Tangibles are often used by service companies to enhance their image and provide continuity and signal quality to customers. (Zeithaml and Bitner, 2000).

On the whole 49.6% of the guests who availed of the services of restaurant, banquet, room service and accomodation in rooms means score expressed dissatisfaction about the tangible elements of the service quality in the hotel (viz., quality of food and beverage served is poor..., slightly soiled cutleries, crockeries were used in services...., too dim lighting in restaurant ...., etc.) which is illustrated in Figure 1.

Tangible elements are the key aspects to reflect the quality of the hotel. Deficiency in providing good quality food and beverage to hotel guests, offering clean, hygienic cutleries, crockeries and tableware are the important core aspects of service, which the hotel management cannot ignore. The percentage of 49.6% is higher for any Star Hotel and it suggests that nearly half of the hotel guests utilising those services will have second thoughts and a serious thinking of utilising the services of this hotel in near future.

Fig.1: Deficiency Factors in Service Tangible Elements

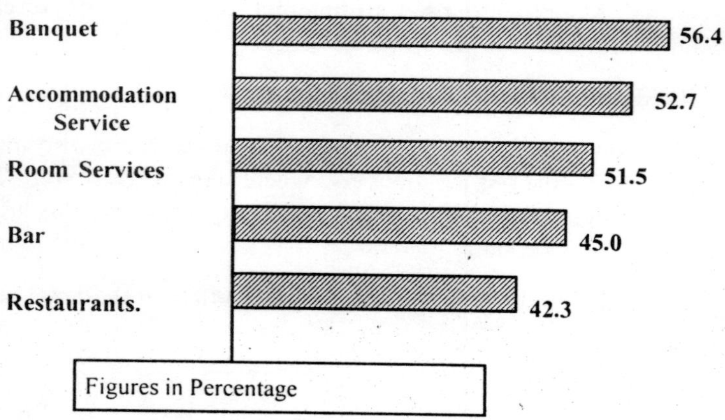

SERVICE QUALITY DIMENSION:

RELIABILITY AND RESPONSIVENESS

Zeithaml and Bitner (2000) define Reliability as the "ability to perform the promised service dependably and accurately". According to them it is considered as the most important determinant of perceptions of service quality. All firms need to be aware of customer expectations of reliability. Firms that do not provide the core service that cusotmers think they are buying fail their customers in the most direct way".

They also define "responsiveness" as "the willingness to help customers and to provide prompt service".

It is to be pondered over here as to what is the performance of the hotel taken in this study in terms of realibility and responsiveness. A glance at the figure 2 reveals that 61.9% of the room guests who ordered food and beverage through Room Service were disatisfied with the service quality delivered by room service staff. It is seen that a substantial number of guests complained that their food and beverage orders took a long time to reach them, with a significant percentage of the guests complaining that it took more than thirty minutes for the items ordered reach them (coffee ordered came very later ...., Breakfast took so much time to reach etc.). This is rather a failure on delivering quality service.

Further, 86% of room guests who ordered food and beverage through room service are businessmen who are too busy to visit the coffee shop or restaurant to have their breakfast, lunch or dinner in a relaxed manner. In order to save time, they order food and beverage through room service and in the meantime they pre-occupy themsleves with their work. Failure or deficiency in delivering food and beverage within a reasonable time reflects poor co-ordination between the service staff and the kitchen department.

Surprisingly, only an average of 14.7% the means caves of there services outlet viz restaurent, banquet and bar of the guests who visited these outlets complained about this factor of lack of prompt and timely service. This is probably becaue the kitchen is close to the restaurant and banquet area, and in the bar the inebriated guests seldom complain about the prompt and timely service.

Fig. 2: Deficiency Factor in Service Realiability and Responsiveness

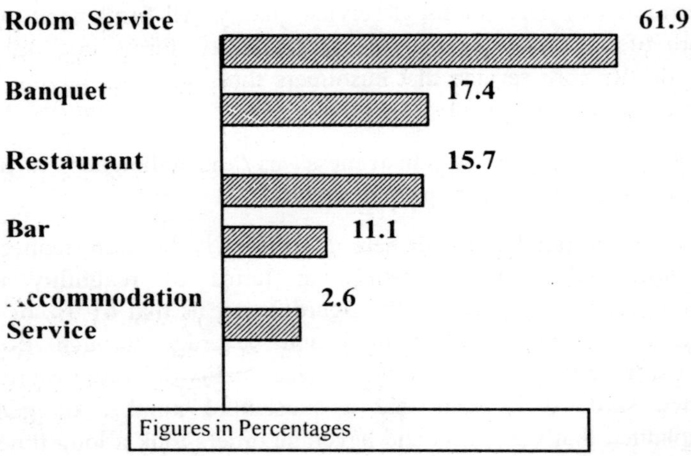

ASSURANCE

Assurance is defined as the "employeese knowledge and courtesy, and the ability of the firm and its employees to infuse trust and confidence". In the early stages of relationships, the customer may use tangible evidence to assess the assurance dimension (Zeithaml and Bitner, 2000).

The visible evidence factor like hotel's quality certification, any quality awards won by the hotel, if they are displayed within the premises or used on their advertisements, may build confidence in the hotel guests about the hotels' service quality.

A quick look at the chart (Figure 3) will receal that the Assurance factor with regard to the "Courtesy" shown to the hotel guests is not really encouraging.

Fig.3: Deficiency Factor in Service Assurance

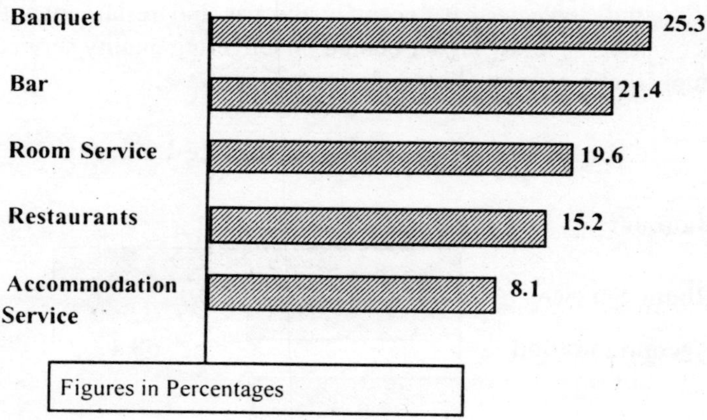

An average of 17.9% means scares of all the service outlets of the hotel guests, patronising all the service outlets expressed their dissatisfaction with regard to the courtesy and politeness shown to them (indifferent attitude in giving reply ...., hotel staff not having sufficient knowledge to explain about the facilities.... etc.)

The chief difference between an ordinary hotel and a Star Hotel is the customer relationship, in terms of extra-ordinary courtesy and politeness shown to the guests in Star Hotels. If this atrribute lags far behind, then it projects the image and reputation of the hotel in poor light. This is a deficiency of serious nature and, if remains unchecked, will ruin the reputation, future prospects, and the overall service quality level of the hotel.

EMPATHY

Empathy is defined as the "Caring, individualized attention the firm provides to its customers". The essence of empathy is conveying, through personalised or customised service, that customers are unique and special (Zeithaml and Bitner 2000).

In star hotels, the service staff are trained to offer service in such a way that the guests feels that they are special to the hotel.

This study reveals that except in the bar and restaurant, other service outlets severely lag far behind in delivering quality service in an emphathetic manner (Figure 4).

Fig.4: Deficiency Factor in Service Empathy

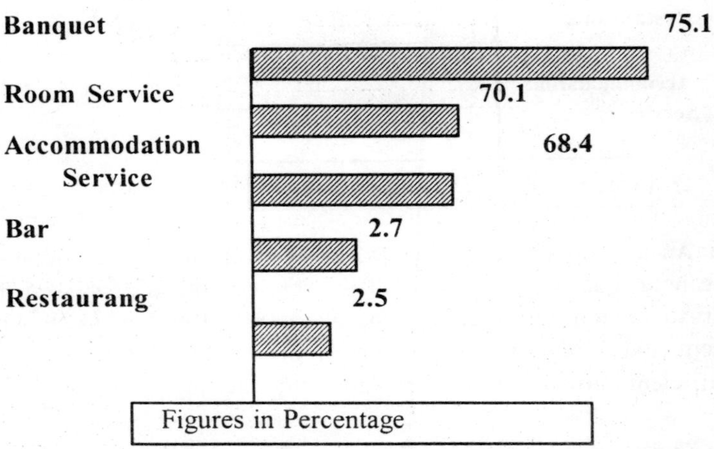

It is evident that an overall average of 71.2% mean score of Banquet, room service and accommodation services of the guests from Banquet, room service and accommodation service felt that there is a definite deficiency in delivering individualised service to them.

On the contrary it is interventing to note that only 2.6% mean score of bar and restaurant services of the bar and restaurant guests expressed concern about this problem. This may be due to the reason that 83.1% of the guests are regular guests to the hotel, and are due to their possible affinity with the bar and restaurant staff over a period of time they had been provided with personalized service by the hotel staff.

DISCUSSION

When there is a service failure or deficiency of service delivery, the customers response is often predictable; the customer either chooses to complain to the manager of the departemnt concerned or opts to deflect to another service provider by showing his silent protest. The hotel guest whenever possible, exercises his option to switch over to the best service provider, wherever available unless he or she is not constrained by TINA (There is No Alternative) effect.

One may not have much choice about infrastructure services like roads, telephones, warehousing or retailing, but there is plenty of choice available for the customer to choose the kind of hotel services (Balachandran, 1999).

This study on service quality in a star hotel clearly reveals that there is a serious deficiency in delivering service quality, when the findings are interpreted using the "Servqual Model". Thus all the aspects of service quality which are characterised into five broad dimensions in "SERVQUAL" Model are severely lacking when the hotel staff delivery service to the hotel guests.

The deficiencies that are revealed in the service quality through using "SERVQUAL" Model can be efficiently and effectively transformed by trianing the hotel staff in the lines of the same "SERVQUAL" Model by using the ten broad generic characteristics.

Every hotel guest comes with a series of expectations in mind, (i.e.) to derive satisfaction from the services offered. But when there is a deficiency in delivering quality service by the service staff, this results in guests' dissatisfaction with the hotel service quality.

The expectations of the hotel guests are distinct, diverse and varied in nature depending on the individual upbringing, peer group influence and exposure to mass media. The Hotel Staff can understand the guests' expectations to a very great extent by undergoing training based on the principles of the "SERVQUAL" Model developed by Parasuraman, Zeithaml, and Berry (1980). The "SERVQUAL" Model they developed was a survey research instrument designed to measure the customers satisfaction with different aspects of service quality.

These five broad dimensions of 'SERVQUAL' namely Tangibles, Relability, Responsiveness, Assurance and Empathy when defined encompasses the 10 Generic Dimensions used by customers to evaluate service quality of any service firm. This is taken as a premise to design a comprehensive training module based on "SERVQUAL" Model to train the service staff

In the study the "SERVQUAL" Model with 10 characteristics used by the customers to evaluate service quality is suggested as a tool, named as "SERVQUAL Model Training" to train the hotel staff towards achieving service quality.

The training method based on "SERVQUAL" Model is illustrated.

"SERVQUAL" MODEL TRAINING APPROACH FOR HOTEL STAFF

Service Dimension	Definition	Type of Skills/Training to be imparted in to the Service Staff by giving "SERVQUAL" Model training.
Access	Easily accessible and approachable	Service Staff positioning himself/ herself in a convenient place for customers to approach.
Compe-titiveness	Possession of nece-cessary skills to perform the service	Job Skill orientation Training to enhance their technical competence
Courtesy	Service Staff exhibiting consideration and respect towards customers	Soft skills Training

Communi-cation	Educating and informing customers in plain language and listening to them	Service Staff avoiding jargons, possessing knowledge of different languages both written and oral. Multi-lingual Proficiency Training (MLPT) to be given to the Hotel Staff.
Credibility	Trustworthiness, honesty and caring attitude of theHotel Staff	Training the Hotel Staff to make eye contact with the hotel guests, having confident approach and appearance by the Hotel staff.
Reliability	Consistency in Service Staff performance, delivery of promises and doing things right first time and every time	Encouraging the Service Staff to strictly follow the guidelines laid by the Service Organization to deliver efficient and effective service. Aspiring for zero defects in service delivery.
Responsi-veness	Timely deliverance of Service, taking pleasure in providing service and displaying willingness to please the hotel guests.	Training the Service Staff in efficnent and effective time management and speedy delivery of service.
Security	Physical and psycho-logical freedom from risk, and doubt.	Training the hotel staff to show much concern about the safety and security, welfare and well being of the Guests. Making the guest to fcel safe and secure in the hotel. And also clearing the doubts and apprehensions of the hotel guests.
Understan-ding	Listening and under-hotel guests' problems, delivering, personalized service and promptly recognising the regular guests.	Training the service staff to anticipate the guests' needs and deliver service the right time and at right place. Also, training the service staff not to wait for the hotel guests to approach them the guest to approach them first. Instead, hotel staff should be on their toes, to first greet the hotel guest and approach them.

TANGIBLE	Facilites and equipment in hotel must be well maintained and personal appearance of the staff should be decent and impressive	Service Staff should be trianed to maintain the aesthetic apprearnce of service area (where the guests visti). Training the staff to always maintain good personal grooming pleasing manners and neat appearance while on duty.

Conclusion

Service Quality is the emerging new mantra for survival and growth of the Hotel Industry. Globalization, Liberalization and Privatization ahve led to a situation of very intense competition, which along with the accelerated growth of Information Technology has further made today's knowledge customer more knowledgable about the latest development, choice of service offerings, pricing and positioning strategy of the various competitors in the market place, and above all a thorough knowledge of the service quality delivered by various star hotels.

If the hotel staff are trained on the basis of "SERVQUAL" Model, along with the conventional training methods, any star hotel regardless of star category will not only survive, but can also tremendously grow in the current business environment.

The present study has proposed a theoretical framework which is yet to be tested empirically. In future, star hotels of various star categories can attempt to implement this proposed "SERVQUAL" model training to supplement or restructure their existing training methods.

In this present globally competitive environment hotels can give training to their staff on the basis of "SERVQUAL" Model, in an experimental basis, which is poised to deliver results instantaneously or in the long run, depending on the time taken by teh hotel staff to learn the new skills developed through "SERVQUAL" Model Training.

Above all this "SERVQUAL" Model trianing has a holistic approach to comprehend and anticipate the expectations of the hotel guests and to deliver service accordingly. Therefore, training hotel staff using "SERVQUAL" Model will yield desired and definite result in the services delivered by the Hotel Staff which would be truly world class.

Notes

1. Statistics are obtained from www.onestopindia.com/ indiaeconomicsurvey.htm
   www.cia.geos/cia/publications/factbook/geos/in.htm
   www.economist-com, countrybriefingsindia.htm
   www.fieo.com
   www.rediff.com.mney/2001/feb/index.htm
2. The first author conducted the survey for his Masters degree in Business Administration, Dissertation from Jaya Engineering Collge, Chennai, during 2000.
3. Owing to the sensitive nature of the research findings in this study, the name of the hotel is not mentioned in this paper.

Reference

Ashok Chandra Prasad H. (1996), *Exim Dynamic and Service and WTO and Indian Perspective,* Commonwealth Publishers, New Delhi, p.9.

Balachandran S. (199), *Customer-Driven Services Management,* Response Books, (A division of Sage Publications), New Delhi.

Christopher Lovelock (2001), *Service Marketing People Technology, Strategy,* (Fourth Edition), Pearson Education Asia, first Indian Reprint.

Christopher, M. Schary, P. and Skjott - Larsen T (1970), *Customer Service and Distribution Strategy,* Associated Business Press, London.

Donald W. Cowell (1984), *The Marketing of Service,* Heinemann, London.

Harsh V. Verma (2001), Service Failure and Recovery in Selected Industries, Journal of Management Research, Volume 1, Number 2, January-April 2001, University of Delhi, Delhi (p.69-78).

Karunesh Saxena, Nawal Kishor (winter 1996), *"Quality in Tourism Industry: A key to customer satisfaction"*, Abhigyan, (a quarterly Journal of FORE and FORE school of Management),, pp.58-59.

Parasuraman, A. Valerie A. Zeithaml, and Leonard L. Berry (1988), *"Servqual: A Multiple Item Scale for Measure Consmer Perception of Service Quality"*, Journal of Retailing 64 (1988), pp. 12-40.

Roland T. Rust, Antony J. Zahorik, Timthy L. Keiningham (1999), *Service Marketing,* Addison-Wesley Longman Inc., Singapore.

Sanjeev Bhat (1988), *"New Services evolution Process", in Management of the Frontiers,* Indian Institute of Management, Ahmedabad, pp.202-205.

Staton W.J. (1981), "Fundamentals of Marketing", McGraw Hill, New York, p.441.

Sudhir Andrews (1994), *Hotel Front Office Training Manual,* Tata McGraw Hill Publishers, New Delhi.

Valarie A. Zeithaml, A Parasuraman, and Leonard L Berry (1990), "*Delivering Quality Service: Balancing Customers Perceptions and Expectiations",* New York, the Free Press.

Valarie A Zeithaml and Mary to Bitner (2000), Services Mastering: Integrating Customer Focus across the firm. Tata Mcgraw Hill Publishing Company Ltd., New Delhi.

William Benton 91964), Encyclopaedia Britannica, Volume II, London p.746.

ABSTRACT

INDIAN RAIL ON RIGHT TRACK: IS A SIGNAL OF PRIVATIZATION NECESSARY?

Sandhya R Anvekar
and
M.S. Subhash

A country's economic growth and prosperity is indicated by the availability of infrastructural facilities. The major component of infrastructure is transport and communication systems. The transport system of a country includes different modes of transport like rail, road, coastal shipping and air.

Railways as public utility services are premier mode of transport for freight and passengers. They are considered as life-line of a country. Started in Europe after the Industrial Revolution, today they constitute the most important system of transport in many of the countries of world. They are very useful in carrying bulky and heavy goods like raw-materials, foodgrains, minerals and manufactured goods over long distances.

In India, railways are one of the principal modes of transport. During the last 146 years of rail history, they have made significant development. They have emerged as speedy, convenient, economical and atrractive means of transport. They have contributed enormously to the economic development of our country.

* Management Faculty, Institute of Business Management, KLE Society, Bangalore -560010.

** Director and Chairman, Board of Studies, KIMS, Karnataka University, Dharwad-580003.

The present paper evaluates the performance of Indian Railways and poses whether there is a case for privatization of railway serices in India amidst globalization. It tries to assess whether it is feasible on the part of the Public Authority to give a signal of privatization at Indian Railways to run on the track of profit maximization rather than service maximization.

INDIAN RAIL ON RIGHT TRACK--IS A SIGNAL OF PRIVATIZATION NECESSARY?

The service industry or tertiary sector is an important part of the economic system. In most of the developed countries around 50% of the total employment is sought in service sector and it contributes almost half of the G.D.P.[1] In developing economies too, the service industry is an index of the economic development and prosperity.

Service industry covers wide range of services like transportation- its distributions and storage, banking and insurance, real estate, communication and information services, public utilities of government and defence, health care, recreational and hospitality services, education and other non-profit organizations.

The service sector mainly depends on 'people' in general and the 'customer' in particular since they are the key factors in the marketing of services. When public utilities are concerned especially when discharged by a public autority, the quantum, quality and efficiency of services directly reflect on masses of society. The evaluation and assessment of performance widely come from the general public who are 'customers' for these services in huge quantum.

Transportation is a significant segment of service sector which denotes the physical movement of men and materials from one location to the other. Services like rail, road, air are the carriers

---

1. Gopalaswamy T.P. Rural Marketing: Environment, Peoples and Strategies Wheeler Publishing, New Delhi, 1997.

which provide the transportation services. Transportation system has a reflection on three components of society.

Transportation directly affects the individuals, the business operations and the economic development. To the individual, it facilitates the travel, changes life-styles, makes mobility a reality and adds to personality development. When applied to business, it directs flows of materials, purchases, production and distribution processes.[2] In the economy, as an integral part of the national production and distribution systems, an adequate transportation network is necessary to provide a means of servicing domestic and international markets. This is of primary importance in the early stages of economic development because it promotes an accumulation of capital, which allows the economy to progress from the subsistent level at which most production is consumed locally.[3] Further due to the steady urbanization of the economy, transportation has become vital. The increasing demand for transport system necessitates the provision of high capacity mass rapid transit system and the functioning of the city depends on the efficiency of this system.[4]

Railways are premier mode of transport for freight and passengers. They are considered as lifelines of a country. Started in Europe after the Industrial Revolution, today they constitute most important system of transport in most of the countries of world. They are very useful in carrying bulky and heavy goods like raw-materials, foodgrains, minerals and manufactured goods over long distances.

India has been endowed with extensive plains, long geographical distances and huge population. In such a nation, railway have

---

2. Contemporary Transportation - Donald Wood and James Johnson, Macmillan Publishing Co., New York, 1989.
3. Transportation: The domestic system - Robert C. Lieb Reston Publishing Co Inc. 1978.
4. Transportation system studies: Analysis and Policy Edt. S L Dhingra & S.G. Orpe - R.K. Jha "An approach to the preparation of Commuter Railway improvement and Investment plan for ....." Tata Mcgraw Hill Publishing Co., New Delhi, 1988.

tremendous potential to carry bulky freight and passengers to long distances. Today they have emerged as speedy, convenient, economical and attractive means of transport.

INDIAN RAILWAYS: A BRIEF PROFILE

In India, railways are one of the principal modes of transport. The railway services in India started on 16th April 1856, when the first train carrying 400 people with 14 carriages ran on the tracks from Bombay to Thane. It covered a distance of 34 km. in 75 minutes. Thereafter Indian Railways have made significant development. It has contributed enormously to the economic development of our country.

During the last 146 years of Railway history, Indian Railways have grown into an impressive network of 62,809 route kms with 6896 stations and carries 12 million passengers per day with more than a Million Tonne freight traffic daily. The network has been on broad, meter and narrow guages and has 108413 route kms. Further the Indian railways today employ around 1578.4 thousand regular emloyees which indicates that it has largest number of workers for any public service sector undertakings in our country.[5]

Indian railway network is dived into 16 zones. These are subdivided into divisions with a total of 62809 route kms. The broad guage, which is of 1676 mm. covers 44,216 route kms with 62184 running track ms with a total of 85429 track kms. The meter guage is of 1000 mm with a total track kms. of 19158 and has 15178 route kms. and 15875 running track kms. The narrow guages, which varies from 610 to 762 mm. has a total of 3826 track kms., 3415 route kms and 3452 track kms.

During the year 1999-00, the Indian Railways collected revenues worth 33125 crores with an expenditure of Rs.30910 Crores with a surplus of 7.47% over expenditure.

5. Indian Railways, Year Book 1998-99, Govt.of India, Ministry of Railways, New Delhi.

The electrification was introduced in 1925 for the first time in Indian Railways and at present 5 major trunk routes connecting Mumbai, Kolkatta, New Delhi and Chennai are fully electrified. The PRS (Passenger Reservation System) was first tested in Secunderabad in October 1997 and resulted in 441 locations having computerised reservation facility. Around 14225 railway telephone lines are connected to Digital Electronic Exchange.

KNOW THE INDIAN RAIL FACTS

Indian Railways network is the largest public sector undertakings in the country and occupies top position in Asia and is the secod largest in the world managed by a single public authority. Indian Railways has been continuously growing and has been contributing enormously to the socio-economic development of our country.

The general working of Indian Railways has been tremendously improving and indirectly is a lifeline of our services sector. The following table cites some important facts about Indian Railways before us.[6]

VOLUME OF PASSENGERS AND FREIGHT CARRIED

Annexure 1

The route kilometres of railways open for traffic has increased from 62458 km. in 1991-92 to 62759 km. during 1999-00. The gross earnings including all earnings from passenger traffic, goods, traffic, parcels, luggage and other miscellaneous sources of revenues has shot up from Rs. 13848 crores in 1991-92 to Rs.33125 crores in 1999-00. While the working expenses have been incurred Rs.12391 crores during the same period to Rs.30910 crores clearly showing a net earings of Rs.2215 crores which stand about 7.4% of total earnings over expenditure.

6. Statistical Abstract, Govt. of India, 2000.

ANNEXURE 1

Table 7.1 Railway Statistics - Summary

Item	Unit	1991-92	1993-94	1994-95	1995-96	1996-97	1997-98	1998-99	1999-00
1	2	3	4	5	6	7	8	9	10
Route open for traffic at the end of year	**(km.)**	62458	62462	62660	62915	62725	62495	62809	62759
Broad gauge		35109	37824	39612	40620	41971	43083	44216	44383
Metre gauge		23283	20653	19210	18501	17044	15804	15178	15013
Narrow gauge		4066	3985	3838	3794	3710	3608	3415	3363
Capital-at-Charge at the end of year	(Rs.Crore)	18875	22438	23583	24264	25635	27627	29803	32392
Gross earning	(Rs.Crore)	13848	18259	20077	22494	24352	28566	29824	33125
Working expenses		12391	15142	16591	18548	20997	25971	27838	30910
Net earning	(Rs.Crore)	1457	3116	3486	3947	3355	2595	1986	2215
Percentage of working expenses of gross earning	(Rs.Crore)	89.48	82.93	82.64	82.45	86.22	90.92	93.34	93.31
Percentage of net earning to total Capital-at-Charge (1)		8.21	14.9	15.99	17.71	14.29	10.25	7.25	7.47
No.of passengers carried	**000**	4048618	3708044	3914895	4017518	4153170	438378	4411471	4584917
A.C. Ist class		522	530	613	761	731	723	773	889
A.C. Sleeper		4615	5920	6560	8098	8279	8451	9459	12300
A.C. 3 Tier		-	-	535	1541	2636	3777	4686	8421

Table 1b: Railway Statistics-Summary

Item	Unit	1991-92	1993-94	1994-95	1995-96	1996-97	1997-98	1998-99	1999-00
1	2	3	4	5	6	7	8	9	10
Ist Class Mail/Express		-	-	-	-	3593	3568	2744	2589
Ordinary (3)		161446	133332	142114	169048	177074	183791	186308	190540
A.C. Chair Car		1328	3090	4243	6208	6547	6972	6985	8027
Sleeper class Mail/ Express		-	-	-	-	100838	105987	120791	146306
Ordinary (3)		-	82483	93549	101212	4968	5015	3264	3555
2nd Class Mail/Exp.		-	-	-	-	297786	334885	337353	296033
Ordinary (3)		3880707	3482689	3667281	3730650	3550718	3695209	3739108	3916257
Passenger kilometres	Million	314564	296245	319365	341999	357013	379897	403884	430666
Average rate charged per passenger per kilometre	(Paisa)								
A.C. Ist Class		102.8	138.2	171.7	181	189.1	203.6	221.7	215.7
A.C. Sleeper		61.8	82	80.5	88.9	99.8	108.6	111.8	103.9
A.C. 3 Tier		-	-	48.3	50.7	55.7	61.1	66.9	75.8
Ist Class Mail/Express		-	-	-	-	73	75.2	78.9	78.7
Ordinary (3)		30.3	41.9	41.1	42.2	26.2	25.9	26.2	26.3
A.C. Chair Car		28.8	40	40.6	42	45.6	49.8	52.5	59.9
Sleeper class Mail/		-	22.4	22.3	22.1	23.4	24.9	27.1	26.3
Express (2) Ordinary (3)		-	-	-	-	14.6	17.1	17.4	16.6
2nd Class Mail/Express		-	-	-	-	19.2	20	21.2	21.7
Ordinary (3)		10.5	13	12.8	13.2	10.3	11.3	12	12.2

Table 1 c: Railway Statistics- Summary

Item	*Unit*	*1991-92*	*1993-94*	*1994-95*	*1995-96*	*1996-97*	*1997-98*	*1998-99*	*1999-00*
1	*2*	*3*	*4*	*5*	*6*	*7*	*8*	*9*	*10*
Total Goods Carried (4)	**000** Tonne	360042	377469	318547	405499	423398	4454450	441579	478184
Net tonnes kilometres 4	crore km.	25689	25713	25297	27352	27999	28677	28427	30804
Average rate charged per tonne kilometres	paisa	37.1	48.6	53.8	55.4	58.9	68.9	69.9	71.3

(1) Percentage has been worked out after excluding Capital-at-Charge of MTPs and Circular Railways.
(2) Sleeper class was introduced w.e.f. 1.4.1993.
(3) The figures for ist class/Sleeper class/2nd class ordinary include those of Mail/Express for the year of 1995 and prior to it.
(4) Includes non-revenue traffic also.

Source: Statistical Abstract, India 2000

The train kilometres run by trains carrying passengers or goods or both as well as the kilometres run by empty trains also indicate a pace of development.The passenger kilometres have increased from 314564 million km. to 430666 million km. during the last decade.

The total goods transported also have increased from 360042 thousand tonnes to 478184 thousand tonnes during the same period.

REVENUE ACCOUNT OF INDIAN RAILWAYS

In case of revenues in respect of which government is financially responsible, is showing a sign of surplus since last decade. The table below presents revenues earned by the Indian Railways including state railways gross recipts, subsidised companies, miscellaeous receipts.

Annexure 2

Table 2: Revenue Account of the Railways in Respect of Wich Government is Financially Responsible

Year	*Revenue Account*		*Gain (+) or loss (-)*
	Revenue	*Expenditure*	*to State*
1990-91	1245155.16	1227588.18	(-) 17566.98
1993-94	1836329.72	1655722.03	(+) 180607.69
1994-95	2052911.24	1672100.51	(+) 380810.73
1995-96	2281384.27	1994320.98	(+) 287063.29
1996-97	2480131.12	2268425.50	(+) 211705.62
1997-98	2913423.52	2759900.81	(+) 153522.71
1998-99	3023395.44	2983487.29	(+) 39908.15
1999-0	3385567.59	3300978.78	(+) 84588.81

Source: Ministry of Railwayss (Railway Board)

Notes: 1. Items included under "Revenue" are State Railways, gross traffic, receipts, subsidided compansion to (Government Share) surplus prfilts etc. and Railway misellance.

2. Items included under"Expenditure" are State Rialwyas' working expenses, subsidy paid to companies miscellaneous expenditure, dividend on loan capital and payment to General Revenues in lieu of tax on passenger fate and dictnt.

ANNEXURE 2

The expenditure include state railways working expenses, subsidy paid divident on loan capital and payment to general revenues in lieu of tax of passenger fare.

The gain to the State is Rs. 84588.81 lakhs during 1999-2000.

Further the table below presents the capital-at-charge, earnings and expenditure positions separately of government and non-government railways.

ANNEXURE 3

There has been 6.84% of net earnings to total capital-at-charge during 1999-2000.

In short, the gross traffic receipts of the Indian Railways increased from Rs.29619 crores in 1998-99 to Rs.32939 crores in 1999-00, representing a growth of 11.2%. Over the same period, its working expenses (including appropriations to the depreciation reserve fund and pension fund) increased from Rs.27834 crores to Rs. 30844 crores reflecting an increase of 10.8%. Higher growth of gross traffic receipts has increased Railways' net traffic receipts to Rs. 2095 crores is 1999-00 as against Rs.1785 crores of 1998-99. The net Railway revenue comprising net traffic receipts and net miscellaneous receipts amounted to Rs.2736 crores in 1999-00. Consequently, the ratio of net revenue to capital-at-charge (including the investment from capital fund of Railways) has improved to 6.9% in 1999-00 as against 5.8% in 1998-99. After discharging the dividend liability of Rs.1890 crores towards general revenues, the Railways generated an excess of Rs.846 crores in 1999-00 towards investment. However, in order to meet the full requirement under plan expenditure, the Railways had to draw down Rs.1107 crores from the balances under various funds like the depreciation reserve fund and the pension fund.[7]

---

7. Economic Survey 2000-01, Govt.of India, Ministry of Finance, New Delhi.

7. Economic Survey 2000-2001, Govt.of India, Ministry of Finance, New Delhi.

Annexure 3

Table 3: Capital at Charge Earnings and Expenses of Railways

Year	*Total Capital at-charge (1) Rs.lakh*	*Gross earnings Rs.lakh*	*Working expenses Rs.lakh*	*Net earning Rs.lakh*	*% age of wor king expan-ses to gross earning*	*% Age of net earning to total Capital at charge (2)*
1990-91	1711851	1213351	1115940	97411	91.97	6.04
1991-92	2243825	1825862	1514214	311648	82.93	14.93
1994-95	2358304	2007677	1659108	348569	86.64	16.02
1995-96 (3)	2426406	2249499	1854755	394694	82.45	17.74
'996-97 (3)	2563540	2435207	2099709	335498	86.22	13.08
1997-98 (3)	2762715	2856618	2597139	259479	90.92	9.39
1998-99 (3)	2980326	2982486	2783810	198676	93.34	6.67
1999-00 (3)	3239167	3312471	3090992	221479	93.31	6.84

1. Relates to open lines and on lines wholly or partly under construction (including ferries and suspense)
2. Percentage is on Capital-at Charge including Capital-in-Charge of MTPs and Circular Railway project.
3. Capital-at-Charge includes Rs.201621 Lakhs, Rs.216073 Lakhs, Rs.230687 Lakh, Rs.249042 Lakhs and Rs.273639 Lakhs pertaining to MTPs and Circular Railway projects for the year 1995-96, 1996-97, 1997-98, 1998-99, and 1999-2000 respectively.

PUBLIC SECTOR UNDERTAKINGS UNDER INDIAN RAILWAYS

"The performance of the Public Sector Undertakings has been satisfactory during the year 2000-01. IRCON International Ltd. had a turnover of Rs.811 crores and earned a net profit of Rs.66 crores. it paid a dividend of Rs.14,85 crores. RITES Rail India Technical and Economic Services achieved highest ever turnover of Rs.181 crores and paid a dividend of Rs.2 crores. CONCOR

Container Corporation of India Ltd. had a turnover of Rs.1075 crores earning a profit of Rs.217 crores and paid Rs.43.54 crores as dividend. Its turnover increased by 29% in 2000-01 as compared to the previous year and the dividend increased by 33% IRFC Indian Railway Fiannce Corporation earned a net profit of Rs.238 crores. It mobilised a total of Rs.2950 crores from the market in 2001-01 to supplement the plan resources of Indian Railways. It paid a divident of Rs.64.96 crores. All these four PSUs have been graded as 'excellent'.[8]

PRIVATIZATION IS THIS SIGNAL NECESSARY FOR INDIAN RAILWAYS?

Britain and Germany have had experiences of privatizing the railways and suffered huge losses post-privatization. Indian Railways have been making continous profits since more than a decade. it will not be feasible on part of the Central Government to privatize the system. The Government as proposed earlier can privatize only the non-core areas like production units, workshops, hospitals and railway school. More is needed to emphasise in this direction.

8. Excerpts from the speech of Railway Minister, Railway Budget Feb. 26th 2002.

SERVICE SECTOR REVOLUTION AND EMERGING TRENDS IN TELECOM SERVICES IN INDIA

Mr. C. Madhavaiah, Ms. K. Lavanyalatha***

Service sector is, globally, fast emerging sector apart from other manufacturing sectors. This sector symbolizes the third Revolution in our modern history after first one being agriculture and second industrial revolution. Today, services sector is the biggest driver of the new economic growth and profit earner in the new millennium for the world as well as for India. This paper examines the development of tele communications in India from its evolution to present e-revolution.

Telecommunications are associated in the minds of most with plain old Telephone Services (POTS). But as a result of rapid changes in the technology in the fields of micro-electronics, software, satelllite communication and fibre optics, telecom in modern world means much more than POTS. Actually, Alexander Graham Bell invented telephones only in 1870. But three decades earlier, in 1840, Samuel F.B. Morse and Alfred Vail had already produced the electric telegraph. The 20th century has witnessed the development of wireless communication from simple wireless telegraph to radio and now even to television and that too with intercontinental satellites. In view of all these, the term telecommunication sector in today's world encompasses the service of communication over distance by electrical, electronic and optical devices as well as the reauisite physical infrastructure for this purpose.

---

* MBA IV Semester, School of Business Management, S.V. University, Tirupati.

** Research Scholar, School of Business Management, S.V. Univeristy, Tirupati.

The Growth Driver

Telecommunication services have these days expanded much beyond mere POTS. We live in the age of wired video text or view data and even of video-conferencing and Voice over Internet Protocol (Vol.P.). The OECP Committee for Information, Computer and Communication Policy (ICCP) in 1989, looked upon telephone network based services (VANS) as those that combine the production, manipulation, storage, and/or distribution of information with the use of telecommunication facilities and software functions. Telecommunication services can hence be split into two parts. Firstly, there are basic services provided by POTS, which allow for the making of local, national and international calls and secondly, there are also value-added services (VAS). These include enhanced horizontal services like voice messaging, electronic mail, facsimile (fax), etc. and also vertical services specific to particular industries or situations involving data processing procedures, graphics etc. and requiring interaction between the service provider and the user, besides the telecom carrier, an example of this being the computerized reservation system.

Telecommunications was looked upon in the early 60's as a superfluous status symbol of the affluent few. The last four decades have, however, witnessed a sea change in such a view. It is being increasingly recognized that telecommunication services help considerably in the efficient production and distribution of goods in any economy. As a result of this and also due to the enabling of speedier and more efficient discharge of social services and of Government administration, it is universally agreed that telecommunications lead to a definite improvement in the quality of human life. Telecommunication is hence looked upon as an essential infrastructure for economic development.

A good deal of evidence can easily be produced to substantiate such a view. In the 90's, the developing countries with around three-quarters of the world population had only around one-ninth of the main telecommunication lines of the world. India with around

$ 300 GNP per capita, possessed one of the lowest number of main lines per 100 persons (0.5), USA had a GNP per capita 600 times higher, but the number of main lines per 100 persons was as much as 120 times higher compared to India. Even a small European nation like Sweden had main lines per 100 persons, 151 times as high as India, which is not surprising because it had a per capita GNP 51 times that of India. As for India, the International Telecom Union of Geneva has estimated that each additional telephone in India will add Rs. 1,12,000 to India's GNP.

Three additional factors have made the development of the telecommunications sector the sine qua non for economic growth not only for developing economies, but also for the industrially well advanced countries.

- **Globalization:** The considerable globalization of capital flows, trade, manufacturing and other activities the worldover, makes it imperative for any country to have less costly and better and more varied communication facilities to participate in the globalization process while maintaining and increasing its competitive edge.

- **Telecom Technology:** Rapid changes in microelectronics, software and optics have made the adoption of these technologies an essential pre-requisite for the growth of any economy.

- **Information Revolution:** The information sector has assumed not only greater relative importance in the industrial structure of all economies, in terms of % share in GDP and in total employment, but it has also come to be looked upon as a basic input like labour and capital.

The Indian Scenario

The Indian telecom sector is a key growth sector in the context of the existing infrastructure in India. Telecom can be described as the infrastructure of all infrastructures as it provides and attends to all the information needs of other infrastructure sectors. India did not lag behind the developed nations of the world as regards the introduction of telecommunications. Being a British Colony, both telegraph and telephones were introduced into India almost contemporaneously with the United Kingdom.

Electric telegraph made its appearance in India as early as in 1851. Telephone followed a littie later and came to India in the year 1882. First telephone line between Calcutta and Diamond Harbor was opened for traffic in 1851. By 1900, telegraph and telephone had started serving Indian Railways. Telephone serices were introduced in Calcutta in 1881-82, barely six years after invention of telephone. First automatic exchange was commissioned at Shimla in 1913-14 with a capacity of 700 lines. Over a period of 150 years since its inception in the country, telecommunications have indeed grown by leaps and bounds to occupy an important position in the Indian economy today. We have at present 3,32,10,000 fixed telephone lines operating in India, bringing in a revenue of Rs.22,000 crores per annum. Capital assets of the sector come to around Rs. 94,000 crores and about 4.5. lakhs of workers are engaged in the telecommunication sector in India.

There have been achievements to be proud of on a number of aspects of telecom development in India over time. For instance, since our independence in 1947, telephone lines have increased more than 140 fold from 80,000 to 3,32,10,000. The number of villages and towns having telegraphs went up from 500 to around 8000. Exchanges have gone up from 400 to over 24,870. Our country has been able to provide national and international direct dialing to almost all countries of the world, to more than 90% of our subscribers. Our international telephone circuits increased almost 12 fold from 1000 to 11,600 just 10 years from 1986 to 1995. To crown it all, our achievements extend also to manufacturing of equipment. We have, in fact, indigenously designed and competiti.ely produced switches of more than 26 million-line capacity.

Apart from all these developments, all is not well with telecom development in India, particularly if we consider our progress with that of many other coutnries. It is apparent that, there are not enough telephones in India. There being just, 3,32,10,00 phones for a population of around 100 crore people. In fact, telephone density, defined as main line availability for 100 persons, was a low as 2 in India as compared to China 4.5 per 100 and world average of 10 per 100 in 90's. Cellular penetration is also low at 0.1% compared to China (1.1%) and Malaysia (2%). But in terms of network India has the sixth largest telephone network in the world, with 32 million fixed lines (Table 1).

Table 1: Telephone Network in the World

Country	*No.of Fixed Lines*
USA	180
China	135
Japan	70
Germany	47
France	35
India	32
Russia	31
Italy	26
Brazil	22

Emerging Structure of the Telecom Sector: Structural Changes

Telegraphs have, since inception been run in India by the government as a Departmental Undertaking. In India where however, initially in the private sector this is being true even of international telephone connections. But problems mostly of coordination, necessitated the confining of telephones also in government hands and the government declined to renew the licenses granted in this regard to the private sector. Telecommunications in India continued to be governed till recently by the Indian Telegraph Act of 1885, which gave the government the exclusive right to establish and operate telecom. Thus telephone companies were nationalized in India in 1943. This coupled with the

Indian Telegraph Rules of 1951 and the Industrial Policy Resolution of 1956 resulted in telecom being the exclusive domain of the public sector from at least the 60's to the 80's. The Department of Posts and Telegraphs was given the ultimate and exclusive responsibility of policy making, network establishment, manufacturing of equipment and regulation which included price fixing, licensing, grievance settlement, interconnections etc., during this period.

The increasing importance of telecommunications nationally and internationally for India over time, made it apparent that the entire gamut of issues connected with telecom cannot be handled any longer by a department dealing with posts and Telegraph together. In 1978, Telecom Consultants India was setup to discharge the responsibility of providing telecom services in foreign countries. The Center for the Development of Telematics (C-Dot) was established in 1984, to promote research and development of indigenous technology in the field of telecom. The year 1985 saw the creation of separate Department of Telecommunications (Dot). Till 1986 it was only telecom service provider in India. it played a role beyond service provider by acting as a policy maker, planner, deveoper as well as an implementation body. A separate Telecom Board, later named, Telecom Commission was also setup mainly to decide matters of policy, but this again composed mainly of the officers of DoT. The fact that telephones in big cities are too difficult to be run as mere Departmental Undertakings, necessitated the setting up of the Mahanagar Telephone Nigam Ltd. (MTNL) on 28th February, 1986 to look after telephones in Bombay and Delhi. MTNL control 21% of India's telecom network with over 3.6 million telephone lines in its 2 metros. The 1986 (Ist April) also witnessed the setting up of the Videsh Sanchar Nigam Ltd., (VSNL) to take care of India's overseas communications. Department of Telecommunications with Department of Telecom Services (DTS) and the Department of Telecom Operations (DTO) was corporatised in 1st October 2000 and a new body called Bharat Sanchar Nigam Ltd. (BSNL) was formulated. Now BSNL is a Rs. 22,000 crore state owned service provider which is India's largest fixed line operator with 33,21 million lines (Market Share 87%) and with 3.26 lakh route km. of Optical Fibre Cable (OFC).

Driven by national and global imperatives, India initiated telecom reform process since mid 80's albeit at slow phase. Since early 90's after liberalization of Indian economy this process as accelerated. Reforms have included separation of Postal and Telecom Departments, Liberalizing the equipment market, and at present investment of private operators in both basic and Value-added Services (VAS), along with competitive service provision. Although the reform process started in the absence of any regulatory framework, increasing pressure on the government to redress the situations resulted in the enactment of Telecom Regulatory Authority India Act 1997, setting up the Telecom Regulatory Authority of India (TRAI). Since the liberalization of Indian economy and partial privatization of telecom service there occurred many changes in the telecom field sectorally, technologically as well as policy wise, service wise and market wise.

Table 2: Trends in Telecommuniation Services in India

TREND	Change	
	From	To
OBJECTIVE	Providing basic telephone services to the needy	Providing world class telecommunication services to all and with in the reach of all, on demand as soon as possible.
	Providing services to accessible areas in the country	Encouraging development of telecommunication facilities in remote, hilly and tribal area of the country
POLICY	Formulating with an aim of improving India's competitiveness in the global market rapid growth the exports and attracting FDI and stimulating domestic investment.	Formulating with an aim to achieve specific objectives and targets with in a definite time frame by effective utilization of existing and new technological developments.
SECTOR	State owned monolithic	Intensive involvement of private operators to provide basic to value added services.

STRUC-TURAL	Nationalization of telecom Companies (1943)	Deregulation of telecom equipment manufacturing (1991)
	Establishing Public Call Offices (PCO)	Setting up of TRAI. (1997) Corporitasation of DOT. And establishment of BSNL. (2000). Converting in to public teleinfo centres having multimedia capability lie ISDN services remote date abase access, government and community information systems etc.
TECHNO-LOGY	Providing services with existing technology. (Morse key, POTS)	Providing quality service by creating a model and efficient telecommunications infra structure taking in to account the convergence of IT, Media, Telecom and consumer electronics.
FUNCTI-ONAL	Having all functions like licensing policy making and the service provision under single umbrella	Separating policy and licensing functions from service provision function to ease the provision of services.
SERVICES	Plain old basic services like telephone telgraph, telex etc.	Value added services like E-mail, voice-mail, WLL, VOIP, Cellular mobile Phone, Radio paging etc.
MARKET	Monopoly in which DoT MTNL, VSNL are major Players in their respective areas.	Monopolistic in which private operators also compete with state owned monoliths in both basic and value added services.

Sectoral Changes

In the era of nationalization of private enterprises, telecom companies were nationalized in 1943. After that, for nearly 42 years there were no any considerable changes in this sector. Drastic changes were occurred in this sector after the liberalization of Indian economy early 1990s. As a first step in this direction telecom equipment manufacturing was completely deregulated in 1991, holding basic telephone serices under public sector, value added services were thrown open to private sector participation in 1992. Basic services were also opened to private participation in 1994 by dividing the country into 21 telecom circles and allowing one private operator for each circle to compete with DOT. A new policy for Internet Service Providers (ISPs) was announced in 1998 allowing independent service providers to enter the sector ending the earlier monopoly of VSNL.

Technological Change

Telecommunications technology can be broadly classified in to three segments: Transmission, Switching and Terminal Technologies. Transmission technologies stands for information between two or more communicating entities that are spatially separated from one another. Switching technologies establish and release connections between two communicating entities. In addition they manage the routing, billing and other administrative functions that are becoming associated with newer intelligent networks. Terminal technologies initiated and receives various types of electronic communication. Key transmission technologies include cables of various types (Coaxial, dry core, jelly filled and optical fibre), radio's (Microwave, cellular, paging) and satellite (Geo stationary, low and medium earth orbit). Cables could be laid on land or submerged. Various switch technologies consists of manual, electro-mechanical and electronic switches. Electronic switches come in analog and digital variety. Size in terms of number of lines and distance further classify these technologies. These technologies a re very useful for all basic services provided by telecom. In due course of time, due to addition of number of value added services to the service portfolio are the ultimate result of technological development in the telecom sector. These developments occurred both in the domestic and overseas services.

Portfolio of Services

Telecom services can basically divided into two categories: basic services and value added services.

- Basic service is mainly voice communication. The subscriber's connection to the telecom netowrk is called direct exchange line (DEL) and people use it for talking. Basic services can be differentiated as per call destination in to domestic and international domestic calls, both local and long distance are routed through cables/wireless fillings. International calls are routed overseas mainly through satellite links.

- Value added services can be provided with most sophisticated equipment and they are over numbered the basic services.

Service Portfolio of Bharat Sanchar Nigam Ltd.,BSNL is as follows

- **Basic telephone services.**

Plain old countrywide telephone service through 52,000 electronic exchanges. Digitalised public switched telephone net work (PSTN) with a host of phone plus value additions.

Internet

Keeping with global network of net work of networked the country wide internet services of BSNL under the brand name Sanchar Net included internet dialer/leased access service for web browsing and e-mail/ applictions.

ISDN

Integrated Service Digital Network service of BSNL utilizes a unique digital network providing high speed and high quality voice date and image transfer over the same line. it can also facilitate both desktop video and high quality video conferences.

Intelligent Network

Intelligent network service (IN service) offers value added services such as

- Free phone services (FPS)
- India telephone card (Free paid Card)
- Account Card Calling (ACC)
- Virtual Private Network (VPN)
- Televoting
- Premium Rate Service (PRM)
- Universal Access Number (UAN)

- **I-Net**
- **Leased lines and data com**

BSNL provides leased lines for voice and data communication for various applications on point to point basis. If offers a choice of high medium and low speed leased date circuits as well as dial up lines. Bandwidth is available on demand most cities. Managed leased line network (MLLN) offers flexibility of providing circuits useful for internet leased lines and international principal leased circuits (IPLC).

GSM Cellular Mobile

BSNL project of GSM Cellular Mobile service envisages a customer base of 4 million and will support application like voice mail, e-mail, short message services (SMS) call broadcast service, international roming, IN services like free paid card premium rate, free phone, universal access number etc.

Wireless in Local Loop

This is communication system that connects customers to the Public Switched Telephone Network (PSTN) using radio frequency signals as substitutive for conventional wireless for all or part of the connection between the subscribers and telephone exchange.

- Countrywide induction of WLL under way for areas than are non feasible for the normal network.

- Helping relieve congestion of connection is the normal cable or wire based network in urban areas.

- Connecting the remote and scattered rural areas.
- Limited mobility with out any air time charge.

Various projects which are under development in BSNL such as GSM Cellular Mobile Telephone Services (CMTS), Sanchar Sagar Project, wireless in local loop (WILL), Voice over IP (VoIP), broad band services- ADSL and High Speed internet, e-commerce and internet dhabas are good indication of revolutionary changes occurring in the field partial privatization of sector is responsible, to maximum extent, to these changes. Also services provided by Videsh Sanchar Nigam Ltd., (VSNL) are as follows.

- International telephone, telex, telegraphs.
- International maritime mobile communication.
- Home cum direct service.
- Data service through packet switch.
    - Electronic mail
    - Electronic data inter change
    - Data base access.
- Internet services
- Managed data network services-CPS
- INTELSAT business leased service leased services
    - Low speed
    - Voice grade
    - High speed data
    - Bureaufax, T-Fax

- Teleconferences services
- Videoconference service
- News broadcast for ministry of External Affairs
- Radio Photo
- Meteorological Broadcasts
- Standard time and frequency broadcast for national physical laboratory
- Press news caste
- International television
- Just recently VSNL has put India in cyber space by offering the Gateway Internet Access services.

Policy changes of and emergency of private sector

The changes relating to policy issues were accelerated only after the liberalization of economy and on 13h May 1994 national telecom policy (NTP 94) was announced by setting objectives and goals to achieve with in a stipulated time period. This was announced keeping in mind the key role telecome place in the growth of economy, and also to solve the licensing imbroglio. This was done to promote private sector participation in the telecom sector. The policy aims to establish a framework that defines the roles of DoT, TRAI, the private sector and the government. Availability of telephone on demand, provision of world class services at reasonable prices ensuring India's emergence as major manufacturing or export base of telecom equipment and universal availability of basic telecom services to all villages are some of the objectives of this policy. It also announced a series of specific targets to be achieved by 1997. As against the NTP 1994 target of provision of one PCO per 500 urban population and coverage of 6 lakh villages. As against DoT has achieved an urban PCO penetration of one PCO per 522 and has been able to provide telephone coverage to only 3.1 lakhs villages, NTP 1994 also recognized that the required resources for achieving these targets would not be available only out of Govt., sources and concluded that private investment and involvement of the private sector was required to bridge the resource gap. The government invited private sector participation in a phased manner from the early 1990s. Initially for value added services such as Paging Services, Cellular mobile Telephone Service (CMTS) and there after for Fixed Telephone Services (FTS).

But because of far -- reaching developments in the field of telecom, information technology, consumer electronics and media industries worlds wide, some of targets envisaged in NTP 1994 were not fulfilled. Developments in various areas have thrown challenges to include further objectives and targets. As a result, new telecom policy 1999 (NTP'99) was announced by specifying targets. After the entry of private players in to the sector many changes occurred in the sector in providing good quality telecommunication services.

Conclusion

The development of any economy depends upon the development of infrastrucure facilites especially telecommunication, which are essential for growth of other infrastructure facilities. The growth of economy should be in proportion with the changes occurred in various areas of telecommunication. India has achieved a unique position in adopting upto date world class technological developments through which services are provided to only few. So good planning with development oriented attitude in formulating objectives and goals is essential which should be monitored by an effective system to provide services to all.

CHALLENGES OF EMERGING INDIAN POWER SECTOR

M.P. Saravana Kumar
S. Illayaraja
Lecturers, Department of Management Studies
SALN School of Management, Palluru

ABSTRACT

Power sector is playing a vital role in the development of an economy. The working of the economy is determined by the Infrastructural facilities like transport and communication, banking insurance, power. The word "Infrastructure" has been redefined to include telecommunications, oil exploration, industrial parks and also IT field for the purpose of fiscal incentives.

Shortcomings in infrastructure is one of the India's biggest problems. And this has been realized by all political parties. So, no matters, which party forms the government, boosting the infrastructure will reamin a National priority.

The New Economic Policy, New Industrial Policy, Fiscal Policy, Export-Import Policy etc. are centred around the infrastrutural development of the nation.

In the present scenario, the survival and growth of Indian industry depends to a large extent, on the availability of economical, reliable and high quality of power. Obviously, there is a close relation between the degree of economic growth, percapita income and percapita consumption of energy. And this paper deals in particular with the **"Power as vital sector of Service sector"**.

Guided by
Dr. S.R. Natarajan
Principal SALN School of Management, Palluru

Contents

INTRODUCTION

"The link between infrastructure and development is not a once for all affair. It is a continuous process; and progress in development has to be preceded, accompanied and followed by progress in infrastructure, if we are to fulfill our declared objectives of a self-accelerating process of economic development."

-- *Dr. V.K.R.V. Rao*

Shortcomings in infrastructure is one of the India's biggest problems. And this has been realized by all political parties. So no matters, which party forms the government, boosting the infrastructure will remain a National Priority.

In the present scenario, the survival and growth of Indian industry depends to a large extent, on the availability of economical, reliable and high quality of power. Obvisouly there is a close relation between the degree of eocnomic growth, percapita income and percapita consumption of energy.

Infrastructure and Economic Development

The development of a country largely depends directly upon the development of agriculture and industry. However the first requires power, credit, transport facilities etc. Also Industrial production depends not only on Equipment's and machinaries, also man power, management, energy, banking and insurance facilities, transport facilities communication facilities.

All these services and facilities collectively constitutes the infrastructure of an economy and the development and the expansion of these facilities are an essential precondition for increasing agricultural and industrial product in country.

Infrastructural facilities often referred as:

(a) Energy, Coal, Electricity, Oil and non-conventional sources.

(b) Transport: Railways, road, shipping and civil aviation.

(c) Communications: Posts and telegraphs, telephones, telecommunications etc.

(d) Banking, finance and insurance

(e) Science and Technology

(f) Social overheads: health and Hygiene and Education

Growth of Power Sector After Independence

High priority was given from the first five year plan to the expansion of these facilities since there is a link between Infrastructural facilities and economic development. As a result of high investment, there has been phenomental increase in these facilities. For example, coal production rose from 32 million tonnes to 316 million tonnes between 1951 and 1999. During the same period power generation rose from 5 billion Kilo watt to 448 billion Kilo Watt.

Its Impact on Economy

Even though the heavy investments by the Government on Infrastructural facilites are easily justifies since they have provided the necessary impetus for rapid agricultural and industrial development, the emphasis was given on the provision of Infrastructural facilities mainly for the urban areas. And due to this, inadequate employment opportunities in rural areas occurs.

Secondly, this is not only on urban biased but also it is in favour of rich. These facilities are enjoyed by the higher income groups who could take full advantages of such facilities as power, transport and communications, health etc. The gigantic maor and medium irrigation works have benefited only the rich farmers.

SOURCES OF ELECTRIC POWER

There are three main sources of generation of electric power namely, thermal, hydel and nuclear power. Hydro electric power is a renewable natural resource. In 1950-51 installed capacity of hydro-power was 560 MW by 1998-99 it had increased to 2,400 MW.

Hydel power has several advantages;

- It is the most economical source of power.

- There is no problem of pollution or disposal of wastes

- Other resources like oil, coal, gas are in short supply.

One drawback in hydel power when compared to thermal power plants, it consumes long gestation period. This point was examined by the Power economy committee which after thorough investigation concluded that in case a hydro project is thoroughly examined. and designed before implementation, the actual period of construction is nearly the same as that of a thermal project. After the tremendous enthusism for hydro electric projects. This was an unwise step, and there was a need to reverse this trend. The power economy (1971) stated that "Under the existing conditions in the country, the hydel schemes constitute the most economic source of electric production".

In spite of these clear advantages claimed for hydro-power, and despite the fact that only one-fifth of hydro power has been harnessed in the country so far, the government, has been relying more on thermal power to relieve the power shortage in India.

POWER SHORTAGE

The power sector has been characterized by shortage of supply vis-a-vis demand. In 1990-91, the country faced peaking shortage of around 16% and energy shortage of about 8%. The position has worsened with peaking shortage of 18% and energy shortage of about 12% at the end of the 8th plan since capacity addition during the 8th plan was much below the target.

TRANSMISSION AND DISTRIBUTION LOSSES

Transmission and Distribution losses in India are very high. Against a normal T & D losses of 8 to 10%. All India figures were alarmingly high in excess of 21% upto 1995-96. It is a matter of concern as well as potential for saving, which may reduce the demand supply gap. A reduction in T&D losses by 1% would result in saving in capacity of about 800W.

Energy Shortage

Year	*Demand (Billion Kwh)*	*Available (Billion Kwh)*	*Shortfall (Billion Kwh)*	*%*
1990-91	267.632	246.560	21.072	7.87
1991-92	288.974	266.432	22.542	7.80
1992-93	305.252	279.824	25.442	8.33
1993-94	323.252	299.454	23.758	7.35
1994-95	352.260	327.281	24.979	7.09
1995-96	389.721	354.045	35.676	11.51
1997-98	313.098	286.190	26.908	8.60

Peaking Shortage

Year	*Demand*	*Available (Billion Kwh)*	*Shortfall (Billion Kws)*	*%*
1990-91	44,005	37,171	6,834	15.53
1991-92	48,005	39,027	9,208	18.79
1992-93	52,805	41,984	10,821	20.49
1993-94	54,875	44,830	10,045	18.31
1994-95	57,530	48,066	9,464	16.45
1995-96	60,981	49,836	11,145	18.28
1997-98	63,056	55,998	7,058	11.20

Installed Capacity (Mw)

Year	**Thermal**	**Hydro**	**Nuclear**	**Total**
March 1992	48,086	19,194	1,785	69,065
March 1993	50,749	19,576	2,005	72,330
March 1994	54,369	20,379	2,005	76,753
March 1995	58,113	20,833	2,225	81,171
March 1996	60,083	20,986	2,225	83,294
March 1997	61,877	21,643	2,225	85,744

NINTH PLAN PRIORITIES AND PROGRAMS

The working Group report on power emphasized on a capacity addition of 57,730 MW during the Ninth Plan. The Planning

Commission, however, estimated.

(a) The installed capacity requirement in the year 2002: 1,331,730 MW.

(b) The installed generation capacity (as on March 1997): 84,910 MW.

(c) Capacity addition required during the Ninth Plan (1997-2002); 46,820 MW.

As against the above estimate, the Planning Commission carefully considered the status of the ongoing sanctioned and new projects in the pipeline and assessed that a capacity addition of the order of about 40,250 MW would be feasible during the Ninth Plan Period. This would consist of.

Central Sector	:	11,910 MW (29.5%)
State Sector	:	10,750 MW (26.7%)
Private Sector	:	17,590 MW (43.7%)

This whole exercise is indeed not practical because (a) the State sector has neither the financial resources nor the managerial capacity to augment capacity by 10,750 MW in the 5 year period and (b) the capacity addition of 17,590 MW by the private sector is an impossibility.

The scope for capacity augmentation in the power sector in the Ninth Plan is indeed bleak. The private sector power policy that was introduced in India in 1992 with so much fanfare has not really taken off- with acrimonious debate on various aspects of the policy continuing till today. The case of Enron's power project in Maharashtra shows clearly that the Indian politicians and the top breaucrats were just interested in making money out of the entry of the private parties into the power sector and were clearly not bothered about the delay in the augmentation of power capacity. Under these conditions, experts assume that not more than 3,500 MW which are actually under construction will materialize during the Ninth Plan period. At the same time, the Central Power Undertakings and SIBs have had very few starts for commissioning any new plants in the Ninth Plan.

The Government of India has formulated the revised mega ower policy to develop mega power projects in both private and public sector supplying power to more than one state. The main objective of this policy is to generate power at the lowest possible cost by utilizing the economics of scale and setting up of mega plants at pitheads, in the hydel or coastal areas so that it can act as catalyst for development in the beneficiary state.

The new mega power policy envisages establishment of a company called Power Trading Corporation with majority equity participation by Power Grid Corporation of India Ltd. (PGCIL), alongwith National Thermal Power Corporation (NTPC), Power Finance Corporation and other Financial Institutions. The PTC would purchase power from the identified private projects and sell it to the identified SEBs.

PRIVATE SECTOR PARTICIPATION

In India, as in all developing countries, power generation and distribution have been a Government monopoly. Since the middle of the Eighties, many developing countries started opening up the generation and distribution of electricity to the private sector, basically because of paucity of financial resources. Besides, the World Bank and other international financial institutions which were approached for funds forced governments of developing countries to bring in private producers into the power sector with a view to introduce competiton. It was in this background that India too fell in line with other developing countries and introduced the New-Fower policy 1992 and invited private investment, both Indian and foreign into the power generation business through the concept of Independent Power Producers (IIPs).

Ever since the Narasimha Rao Government announced its new power policy for private power, this country had witnessed one of the most acrimonious debates on various aspects of the policy. The quantum of return on equity, the counter guarantees to be given by the Government and the project selection process have all been the subject of debate. This has resulted in delay in signing of power purchase agreements (PPAs) guarantees and counter-guarantees, environmental clearness, matching transmission networks and legally enforceable contracts. The utter incompetence of the top bureaucracy in the power sector and the frivolous interference of NGOs have delayed the implementation of new power policy.

Problems in Power Sector

- The critical problem area in the power sector is the poor performance of the State Electricity Boards (SEBs) which generate and distribute power, set power tarrifs and collect revenues from the users.

- Each SEB operates as a state monopoly combining functions relating to generation, transmission and distribution of electricity.

- A serious weakness SEBs have continued to suffer over the last 5 decades is the sub-optimal capacity utilization of their thermal generation units and high transmission and distribution losses. These T&D losses have been around 20 to 22% against the total consumption of power.

- The most serious weakness of SEBs is their inability to arrive at and implement an economic power tarrif.

- Other serious weakness is both agriculture and domestic sectors are highly subsidies and SEBs are incurring heavy losses on their sale of power to agricultural and domestic sectors. Uncovered subsidy amounted to Rs.3230 crores in 1991-92 and rose to Rs.23020 crores in 1999-2000 and it is anticipated to rise to Rs. 28,520 crores in 2001-2002.

- A minimum agricultural power tariff of 50 paisa per unit as accepted the Power Ministers conference as for as 1991 is still to be implemented universally by all SEBs.

If implemented, this would bring an additional revenue of Rs. 2,420 crores to SEBs during 1997-98.

- If SEBs were to earn the stipulated 3 per cent rate of return they would have generated an additional revenue of Rs.12,270 crores in 1996-97 itself.

In Practice, nothing has been done to mobilize additional revenues for SEBs. The net result is that nearly all SEBs have accumulated huge losses and have become almost bankrupt.

Many commissions and committees have studied these problems and have suggested many key changes, all in vain.

Challenges of Power Sector

* Investment in service sector required heavy investment. Such investment required long gestation period to reap the fruit from such investment. Hence private sectors are hesistant to make investments.

* Even though the power, the monopoly of Govt. agencies they are not giving any attractive returns. Most of electricity boards are incurring loss. These losses may be due to overcrowding and the major reason for loss is subsidy and concession given to the weaker sections.

* Free power supply to the small tiller and huts is another reason for the heavy loss in power sector.

* There is a conflict between profit motivated private sector and the power corrupted politicians.

* Supply of the free power to the weaker section is a way of tapping the vote to their parties. Thus the politicians are against the charging high for power consumption.

* Profit motivated private sector don't want to burn their fingers by charging subsidized rates or by providing free power.

* Overcrowding in administration, underutilized and unutilized power generation is adding the fuel to the existing fire.

Conclusion

Service econmy is a multidimensional. It cannot be solved with immediate effect. It should be dealt in different angles and in a phased manner.

Bibliography

* *"Indian economy"* by Ruddar Datt (Forty third revised edition 2001)
* Economic Survey 1999-00.
* Internet {www.google.com (India Infoline)}

INDEX

A

B

C

D

E

F

G

H

I

J

K

L

M

R

S

T

U

V

W

Y